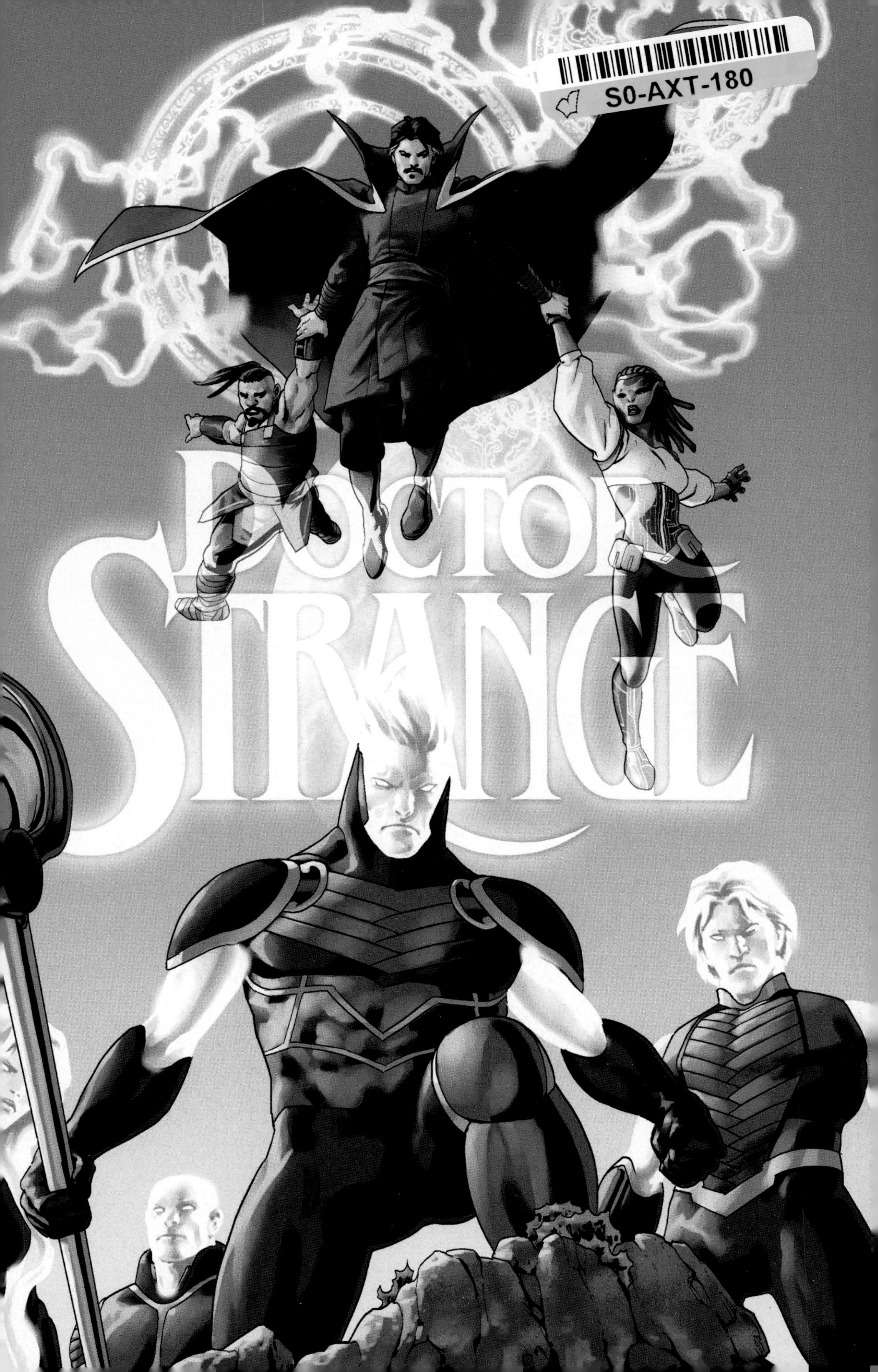
DOCTOR
STRANGE

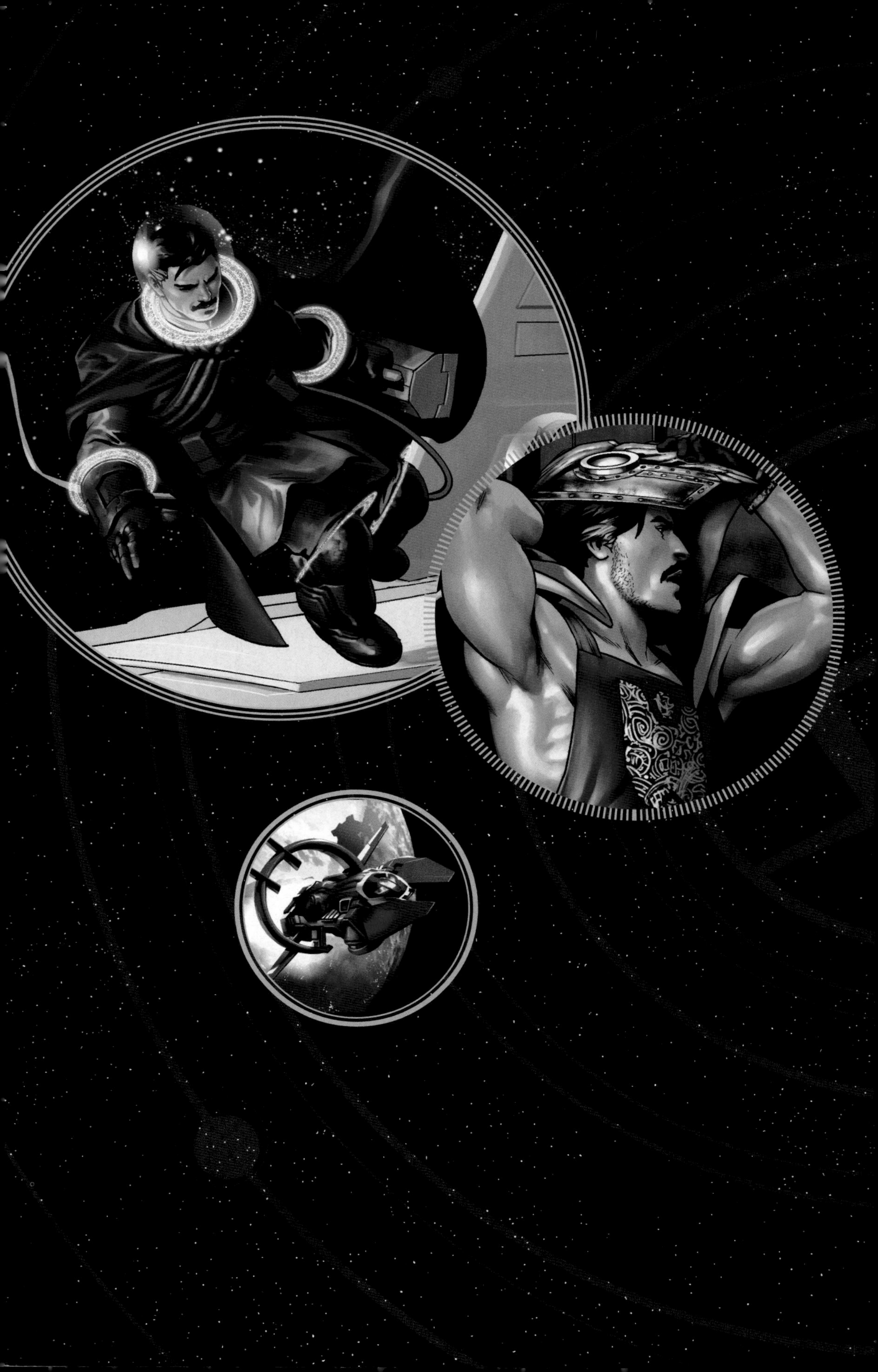

STEPHEN STRANGE WAS A PRE-EMINENT SURGEON UNTIL A CAR ACCIDENT DAMAGED THE NERVES IN HIS HANDS.
HIS EGO DROVE HIM TO SCOUR THE GLOBE FOR A MIRACLE CURE. INSTEAD, HE FOUND A MYSTERIOUS WIZARD
CALLED THE ANCIENT ONE, WHO TAUGHT HIM MAGIC AND THAT THERE ARE THINGS IN THIS WORLD BIGGER
THAN HIMSELF. THESE LESSONS ENABLED STEPHEN TO BECOME THE SORCERER SUPREME, EARTH'S
FIRST DEFENSE AGAINST ALL MANNER OF MAGICAL THREATS. HIS PATIENTS CALL HIM...

AFTER SOME TIME AWAY, DOCTOR STRANGE RETURNED TO THE SANCTUM SANCTORUM IN
GREENWICH VILLAGE, NEW YORK CITY, READY TO FULFILL HIS ROLE AS OUR REALM'S
LEAD DEFENDER AGAINST ALL THREATS OCCULT AND ARCANE.

WRITER
Mark Waid

ARTIST
Jesús Saiz

LETTERER
VC's Cory Petit

COVER ART
Jesús Saiz (#1-4) AND *Javier Garrón* & *Dean White* (#5)

ASSISTANT EDITOR
Kathleen Wisneski

EDITOR
Nick Lowe

──── DOCTOR STRANGE CREATED BY STAN LEE & STEVE DITKO ────

COLLECTION EDITOR: **JENNIFER GRÜNWALD**
ASSISTANT EDITOR: **CAITLIN O'CONNELL**
ASSOCIATE MANAGING EDITOR: **KATERI WOODY**
EDITOR, SPECIAL PROJECTS: **MARK D. BEAZLEY**

VP PRODUCTION & SPECIAL PROJECTS: **JEFF YOUNGQUIST**
SVP PRINT, SALES & MARKETING: **DAVID GABRIEL**
BOOK DESIGNER: **ADAM DEL RE**

EDITOR IN CHIEF: **C.B. CEBULSKI**
CHIEF CREATIVE OFFICER: **JOE QUESADA**
PRESIDENT: **DAN BUCKLEY**
EXECUTIVE PRODUCER: **ALAN FINE**

DOCTOR STRANGE BY MARK WAID VOL. 1: ACROSS THE UNIVERSE. Contains material originally published in magazine form as DOCTOR STRANGE #1-5. First printing 2018. ISBN 978-1-302-91233-8. Published by MARVEL WORLDWIDE, INC., a subsidiary of MARVEL ENTERTAINMENT, LLC. OFFICE OF PUBLICATION: 135 West 50th Street, New York, NY 10020. Copyright © 2018 MARVEL No similarity between any of the names, characters, persons, and/or institutions in this magazine with those of any living or dead person or institution is intended, and any such similarity which may exist is purely coincidental. **Printed in the U.S.A.** DAN BUCKLEY, President, Marvel Entertainment; JOHN NEE, Publisher; JOE QUESADA, Chief Creative Officer; TOM BREVOORT, SVP of Publishing; DAVID BOGART, SVP of Business Affairs & Operations, Publishing & Partnership; DAVID GABRIEL, SVP of Sales & Marketing, Publishing; JEFF YOUNGQUIST, VP of Production & Special Projects; DAN CARR, Executive Director of Publishing Technology; ALEX MORALES, Director of Publishing Operations; DAN EDINGTON, Managing Editor; SUSAN CRESPI, Production Manager; STAN LEE, Chairman Emeritus. For information regarding advertising in Marvel Comics or on Marvel.com, please contact Vit DeBellis, Custom Solutions & Integrated Advertising Manager, at vdebellis@marvel.com. For Marvel subscription inquiries, please call 888-511-5480. **Manufactured between 10/12/2018 and 11/13/2018 by LSC COMMUNICATIONS INC., KENDALLVILLE, IN, USA.**

10 9 8 7 6 5 4 3 2 1

1

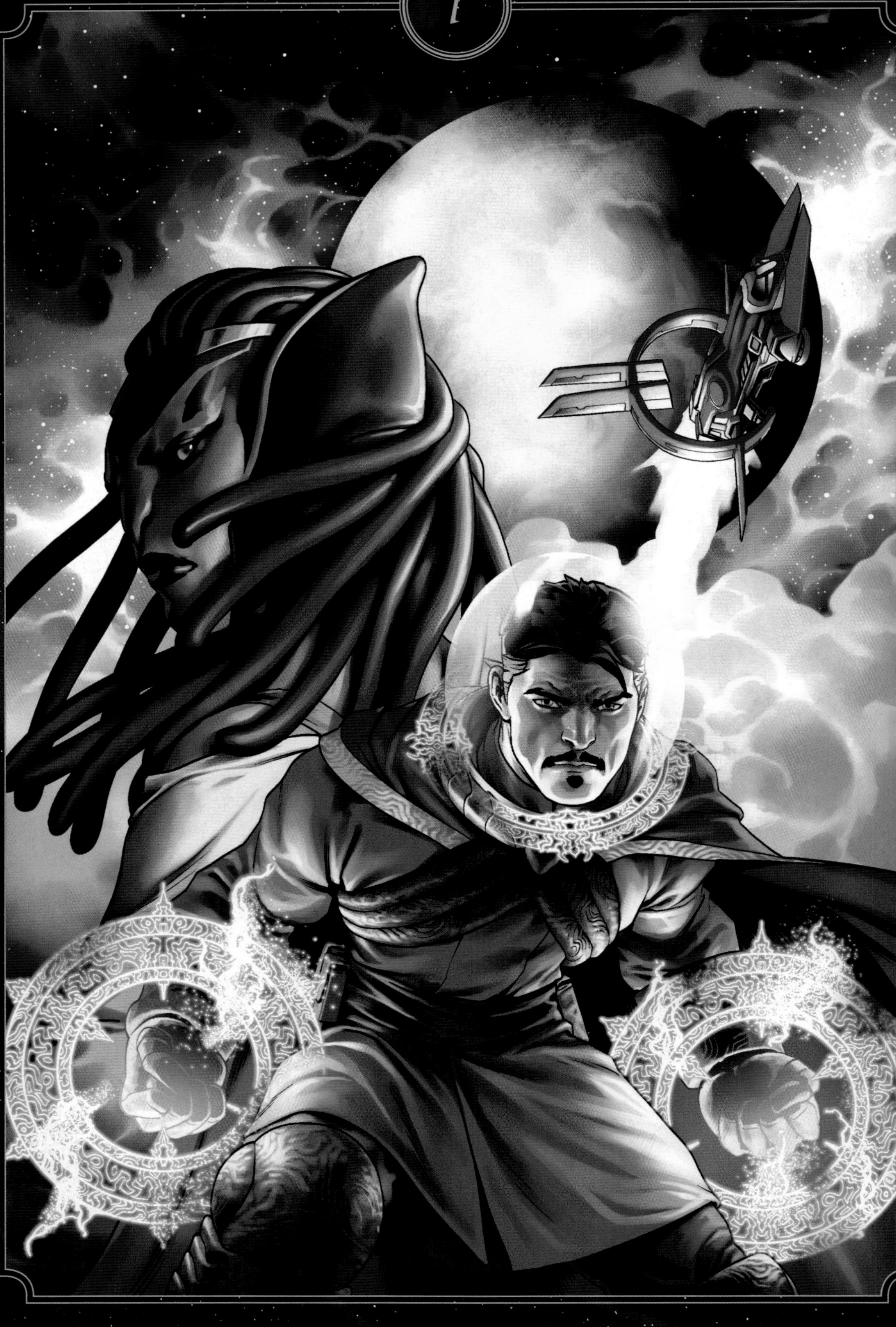

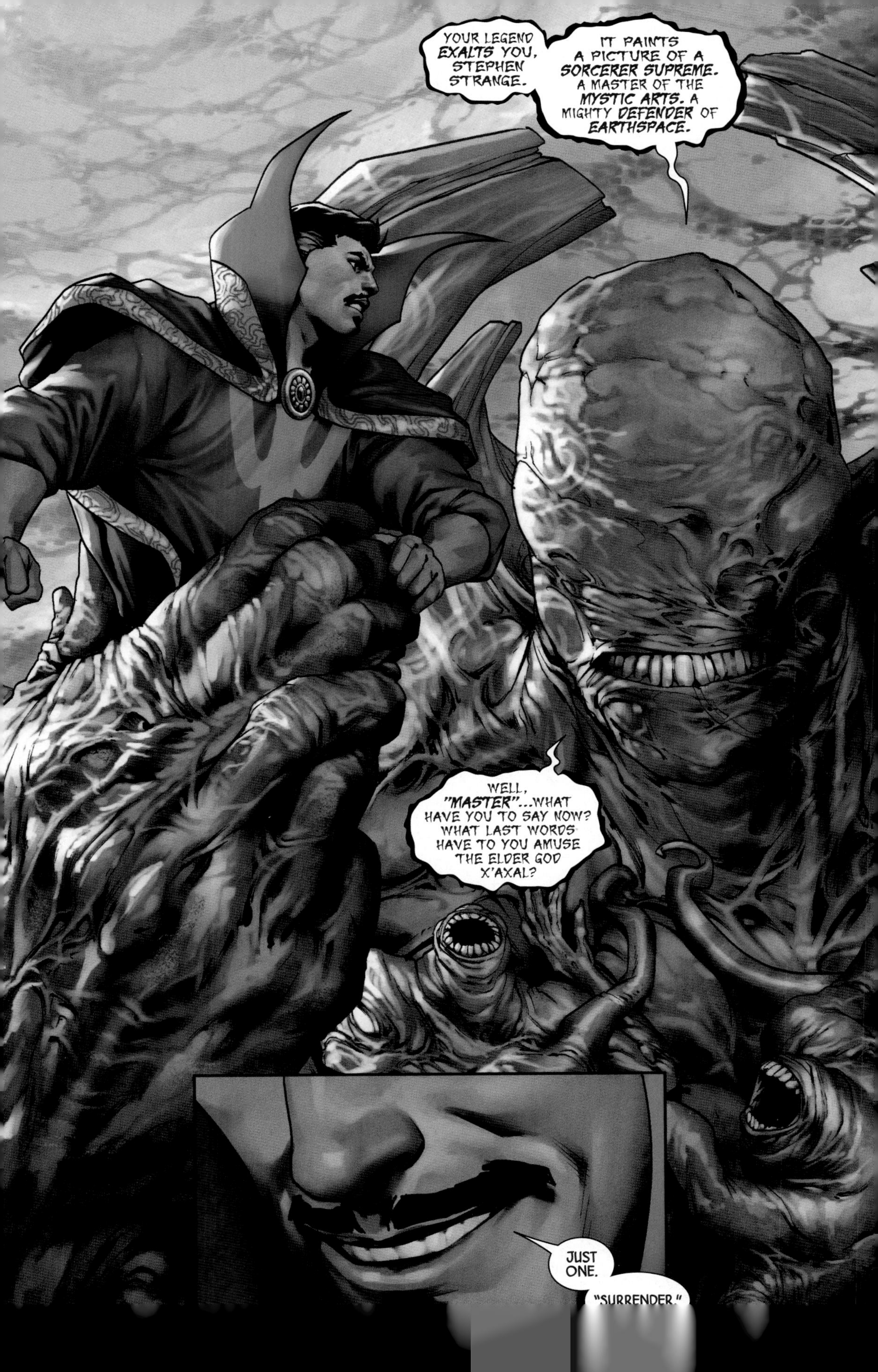
YOUR LEGEND EXALTS YOU, STEPHEN STRANGE.
IT PAINTS A PICTURE OF A SORCERER SUPREME. A MASTER OF THE MYSTIC ARTS. A MIGHTY DEFENDER OF EARTHSPACE.
WELL, "MASTER"...WHAT HAVE YOU TO SAY NOW? WHAT LAST WORDS HAVE TO YOU AMUSE THE ELDER GOD X'AXAL?
JUST ONE.
"SURRENDER."

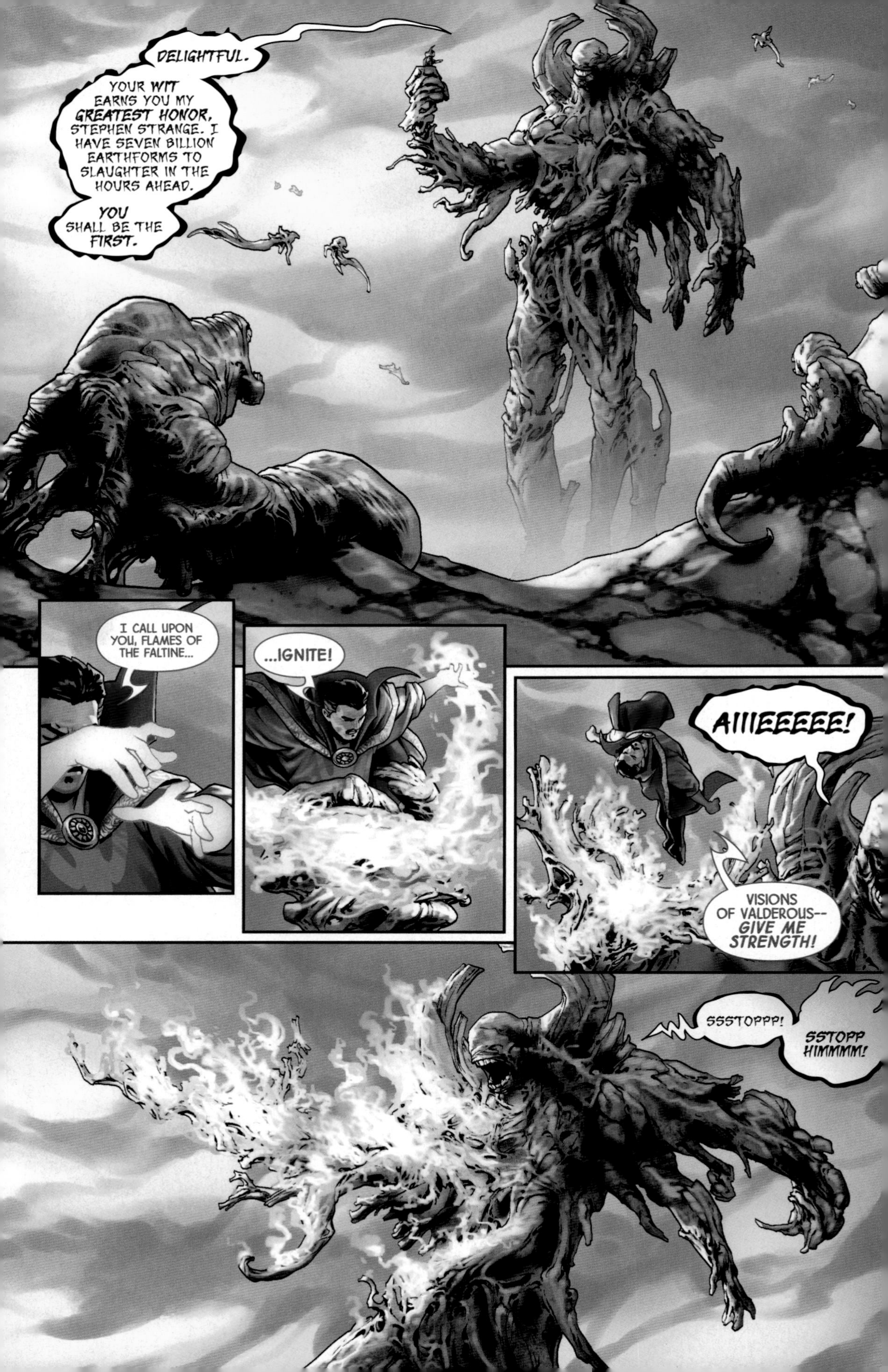
DELIGHTFUL.
YOUR WIT EARNS YOU MY GREATEST HONOR, STEPHEN STRANGE. I HAVE SEVEN BILLION EARTHFORMS TO SLAUGHTER IN THE HOURS AHEAD.
YOU SHALL BE THE FIRST.
I CALL UPON YOU, FLAMES OF THE FALTINE...
...IGNITE!
AIIIEEEEEE!
VISIONS OF VALDEROUS-- GIVE ME STRENGTH!
SSSTOPPP!
SSTOPP HIMMMM!

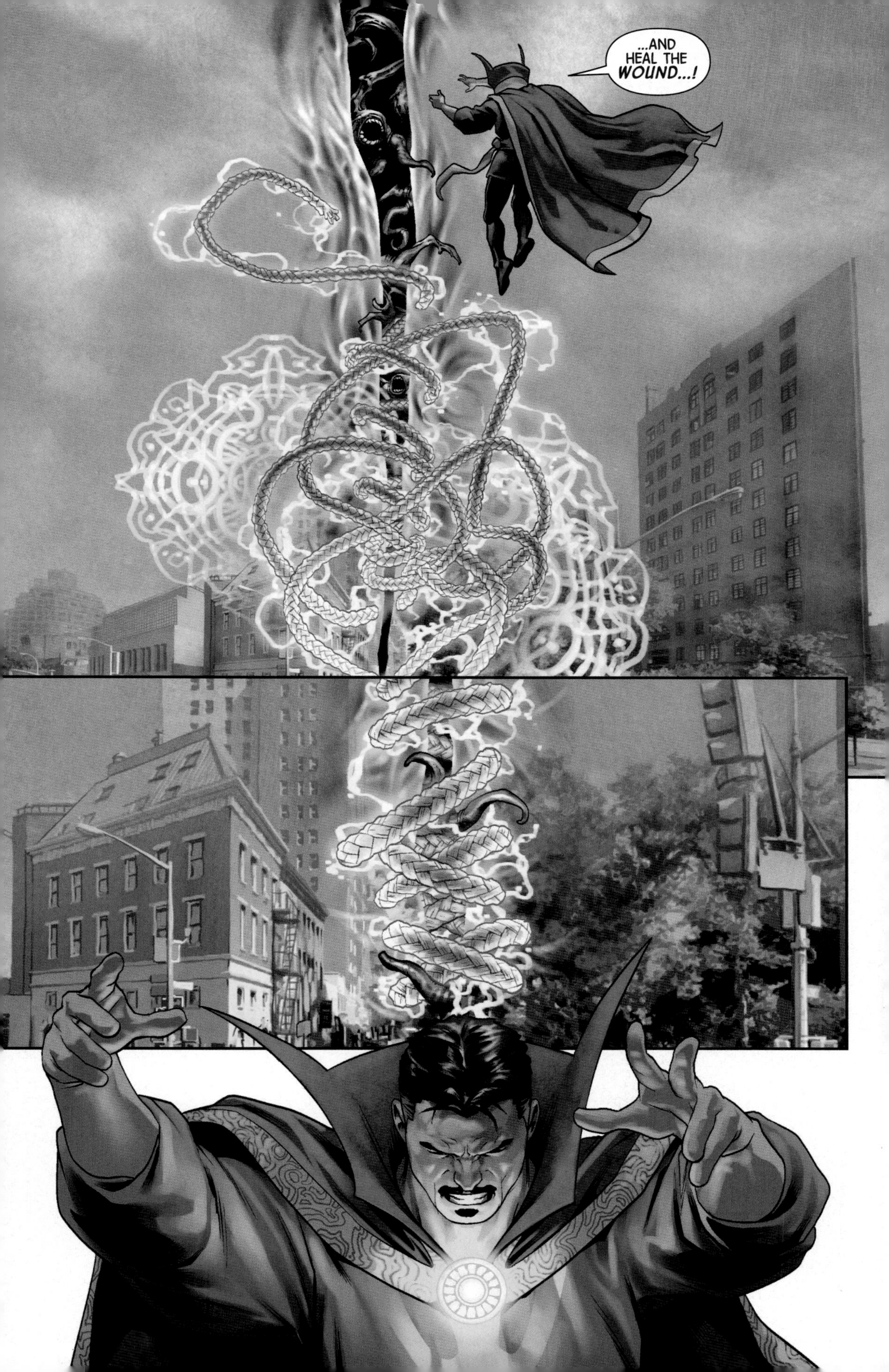
...AND HEAL THE WOUND...!

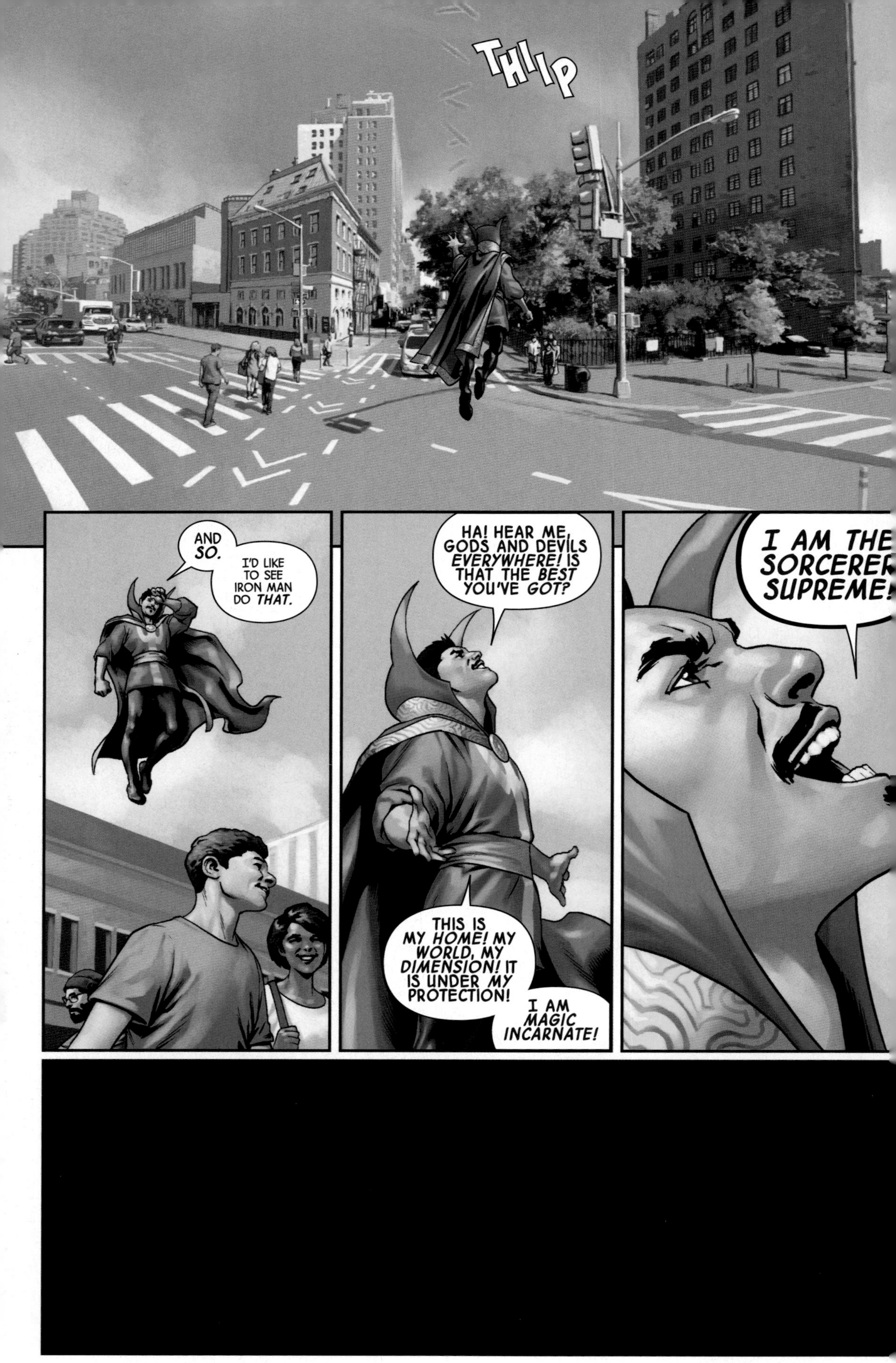
THIIP
AND SO.
I'D LIKE TO SEE IRON MAN DO THAT.
HA! HEAR ME, GODS AND DEVILS EVERYWHERE! IS THAT THE BEST YOU'VE GOT?
THIS IS MY HOME! MY WORLD, MY DIMENSION! IT IS UNDER MY PROTECTION!
I AM MAGIC INCARNATE!
I AM THE SORCERER SUPREME!

SEVEN YEARS LATER

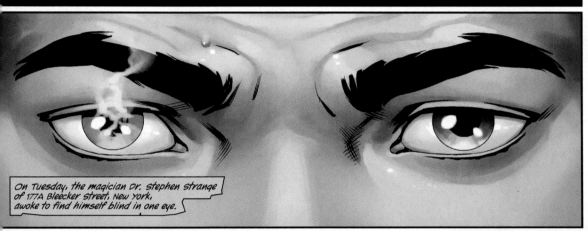

On Tuesday, the magician Dr. Stephen Strange of 177A Bleecker Street, New York, awoke to find himself blind in one eye.

Not blind as you and I would think of ourselves. Rather, sightless to a reality behind that obvious to mortals:

A view of existence that beholds the magic behind all living things.

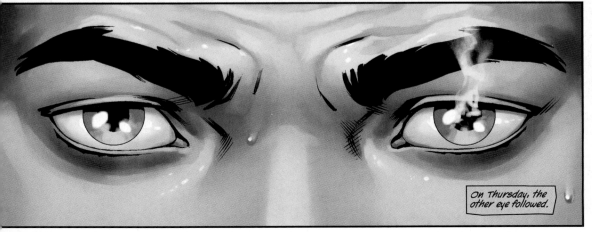

On Thursday, the other eye followed.

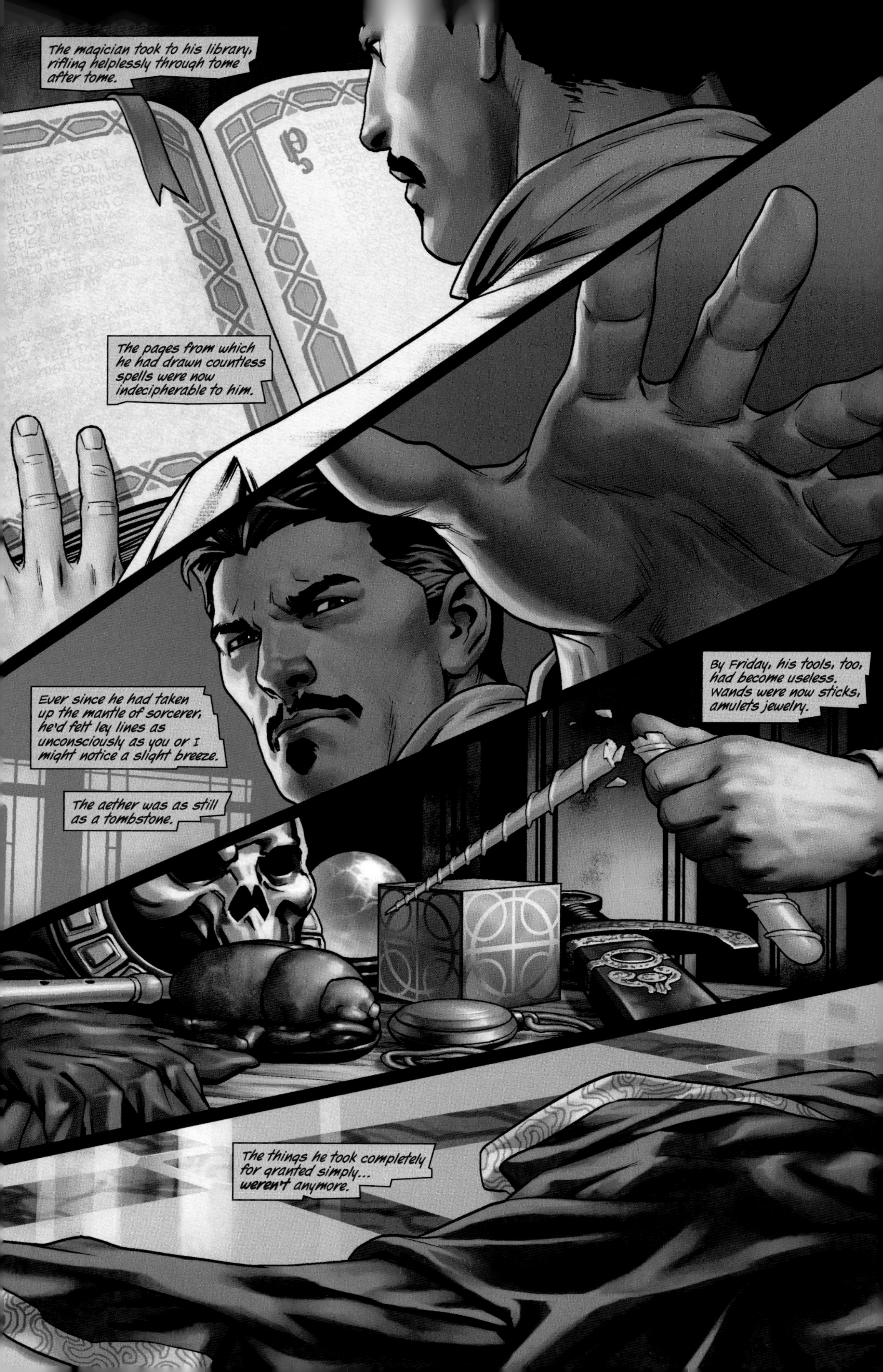
The magician took to his library, rifling helplessly through tome after tome.
The pages from which he had drawn countless spells were now indecipherable to him.
Ever since he had taken up the mantle of sorcerer, he'd felt ley lines as unconsciously as you or I might notice a slight breeze.
The aether was as still as a tombstone.
By Friday, his tools, too, had become useless. Wands were now sticks, amulets jewelry.
The things he took completely for granted simply... weren't anymore.

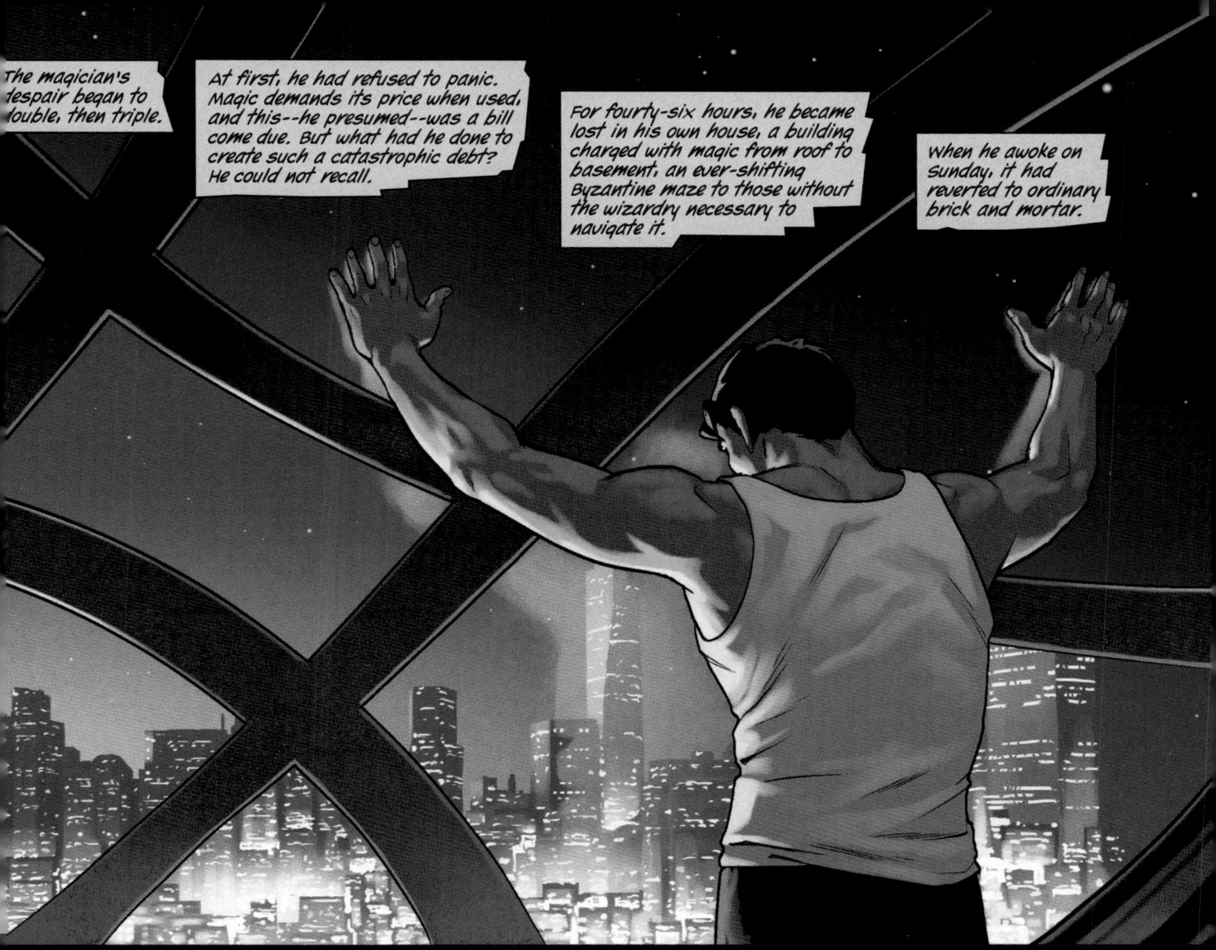
The magician's despair began to double, then triple.
At first, he had refused to panic. Magic demands its price when used, and this--he presumed--was a bill come due. But what had he done to create such a catastrophic debt? He could not recall.
For fourty-six hours, he became lost in his own house, a building charged with magic from roof to basement, an ever-shifting Byzantine maze to those without the wizardry necessary to navigate it.
When he awoke on Sunday, it had reverted to ordinary brick and mortar.

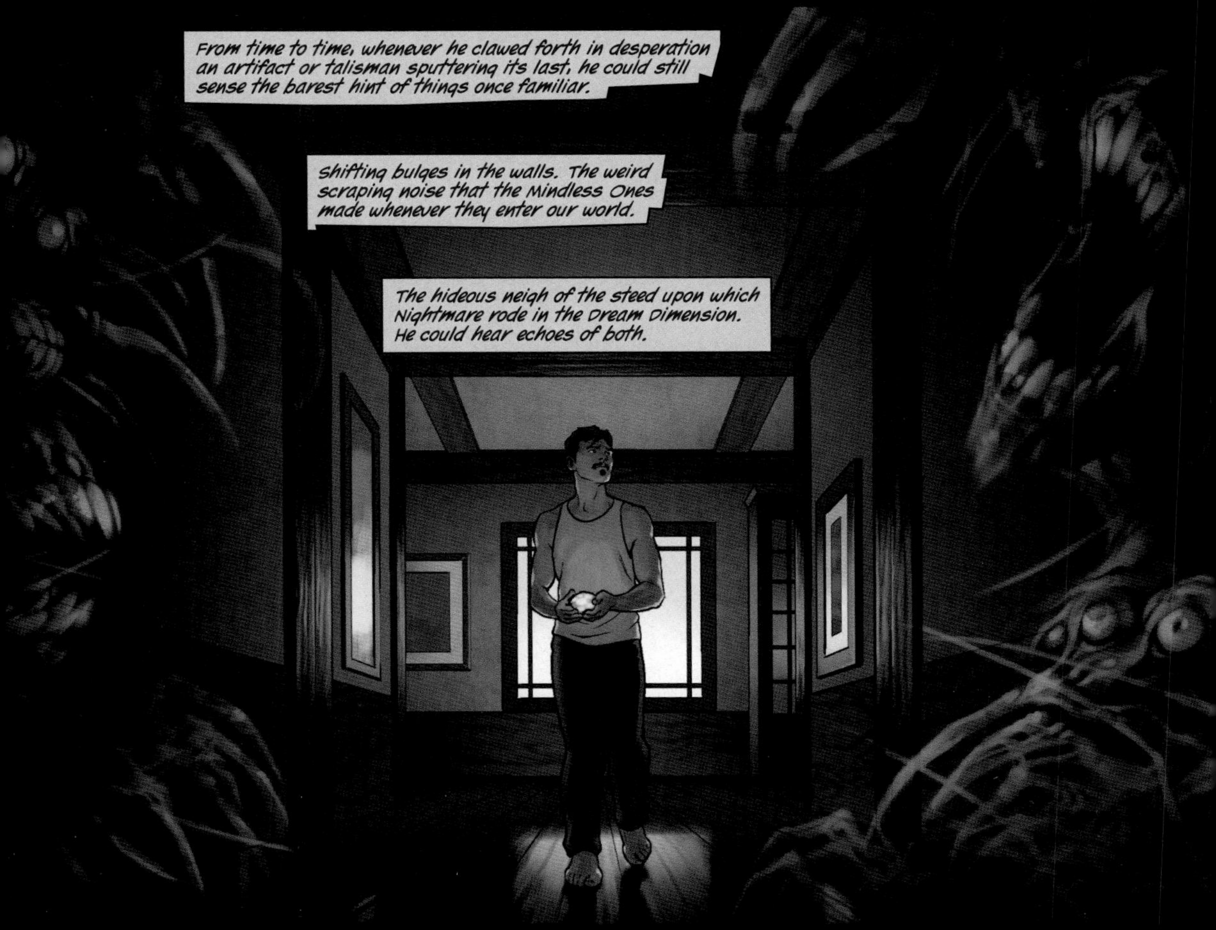
From time to time, whenever he clawed forth in desperation an artifact or talisman sputtering its last, he could still sense the barest hint of things once familiar.
Shifting bulges in the walls. The weird scraping noise that the Mindless Ones made whenever they enter our world.
The hideous neigh of the steed upon which Nightmare rode in the Dream Dimension. He could hear echoes of both.

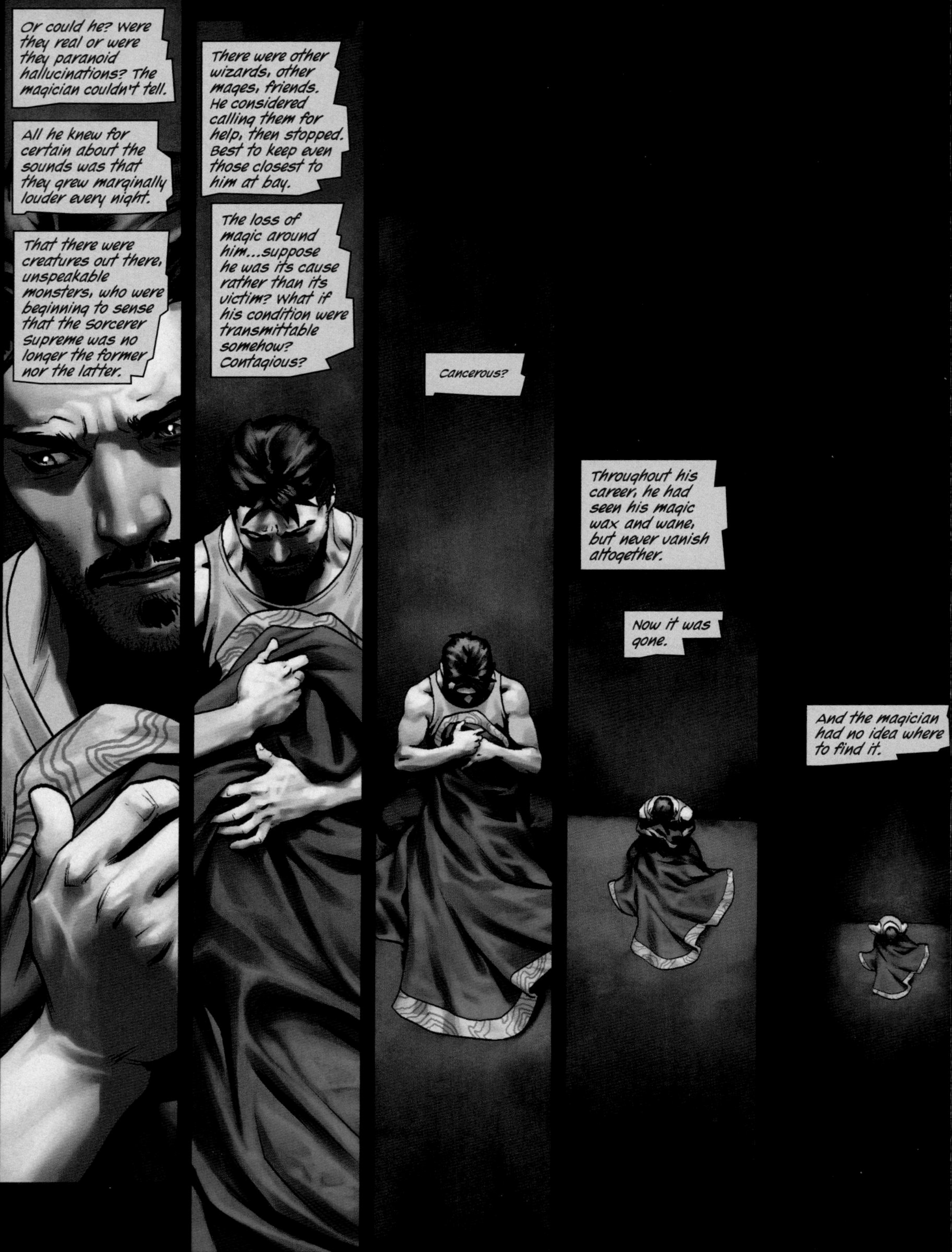

Or could he? Were they real or were they paranoid hallucinations? The magician couldn't tell.
All he knew for certain about the sounds was that they grew marginally louder every night.
That there were creatures out there, unspeakable monsters, who were beginning to sense that the Sorcerer Supreme was no longer the former nor the latter.
There were other wizards, other mages, friends. He considered calling them for help, then stopped. Best to keep even those closest to him at bay.
The loss of magic around him...suppose he was its cause rather than its victim? What if his condition were transmittable somehow? Contagious?
Cancerous?
Throughout his career, he had seen his magic wax and wane, but never vanish altogether.
Now it was gone.
And the magician had no idea where to find it.

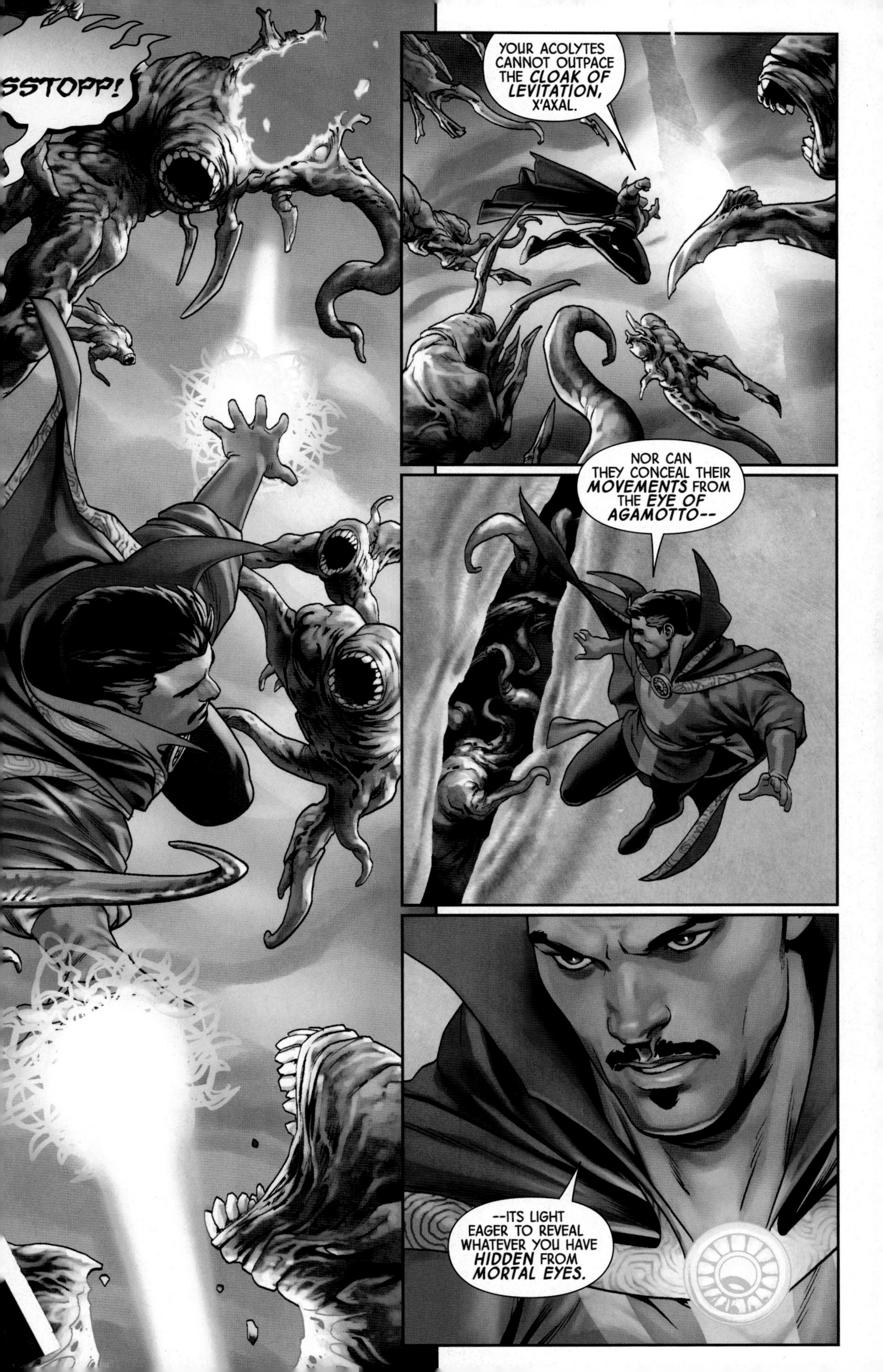
SSTOPP!
YOUR ACOLYTES CANNOT OUTPACE THE CLOAK OF LEVITATION, X'AXAL.
NOR CAN THEY CONCEAL THEIR MOVEMENTS FROM THE EYE OF AGAMOTTO--
--ITS LIGHT EAGER TO REVEAL WHATEVER YOU HAVE HIDDEN FROM MORTAL EYES.

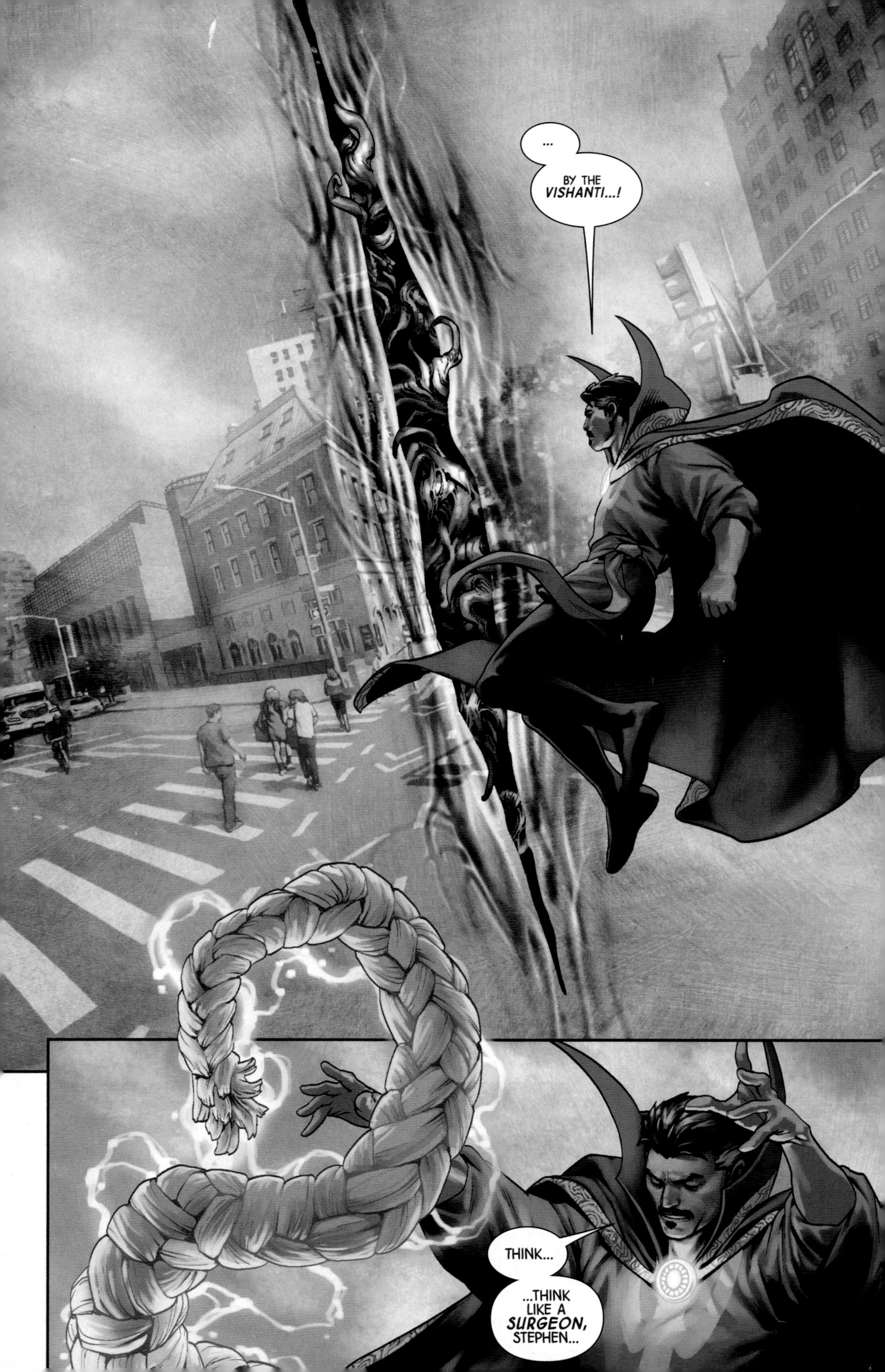
...
BY THE VISHANTI...!
THINK...
...THINK LIKE A SURGEON, STEPHEN...

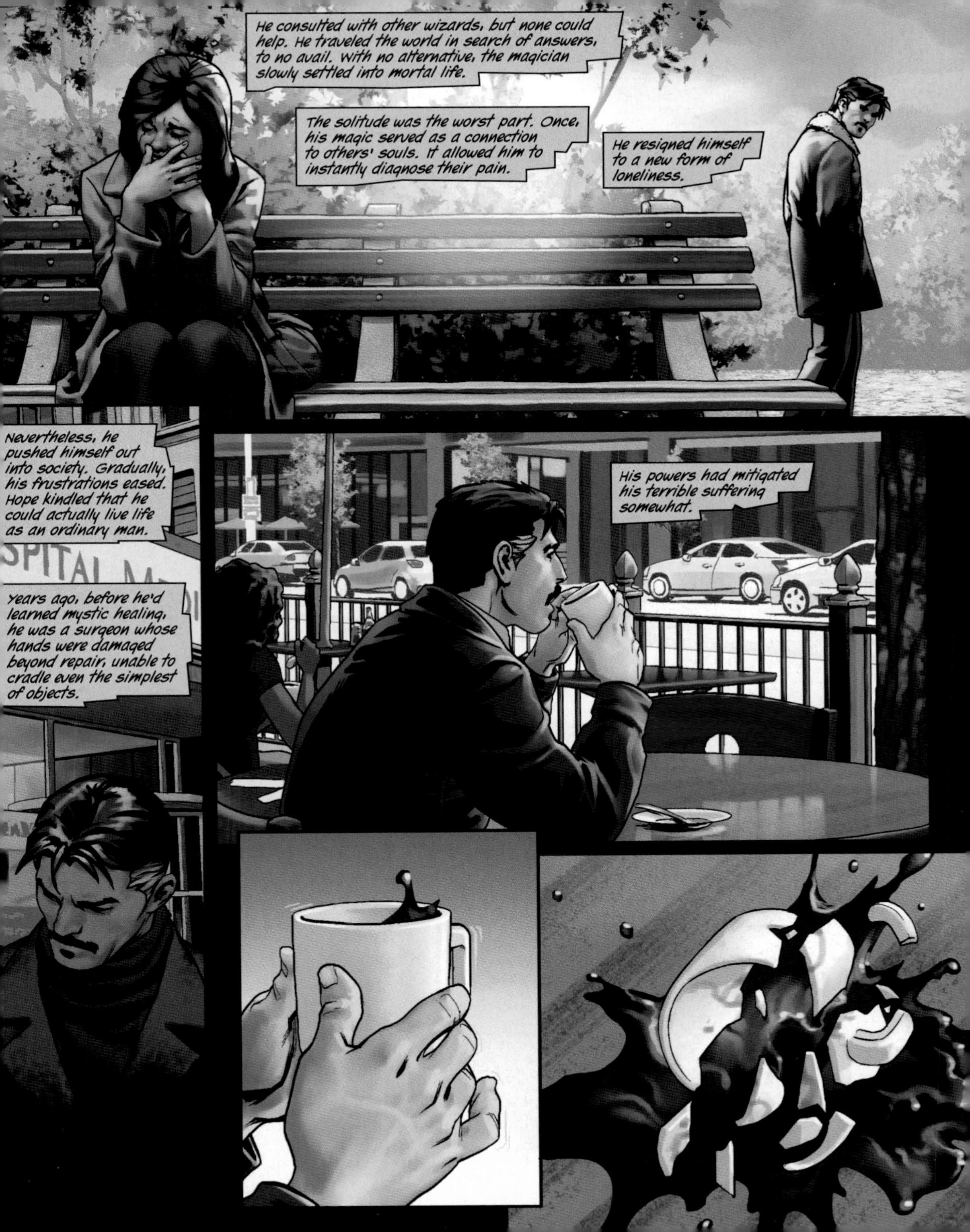
He consulted with other wizards, but none could help. He traveled the world in search of answers, to no avail. With no alternative, the magician slowly settled into mortal life.
The solitude was the worst part. Once, his magic served as a connection to others' souls. It allowed him to instantly diagnose their pain.
He resigned himself to a new form of loneliness.
Nevertheless, he pushed himself out into society. Gradually, his frustrations eased. Hope kindled that he could actually live life as an ordinary man.
SPITAL M
Years ago, before he'd learned mystic healing, he was a surgeon whose hands were damaged beyond repair, unable to cradle even the simplest of objects.
His powers had mitigated his terrible suffering somewhat.

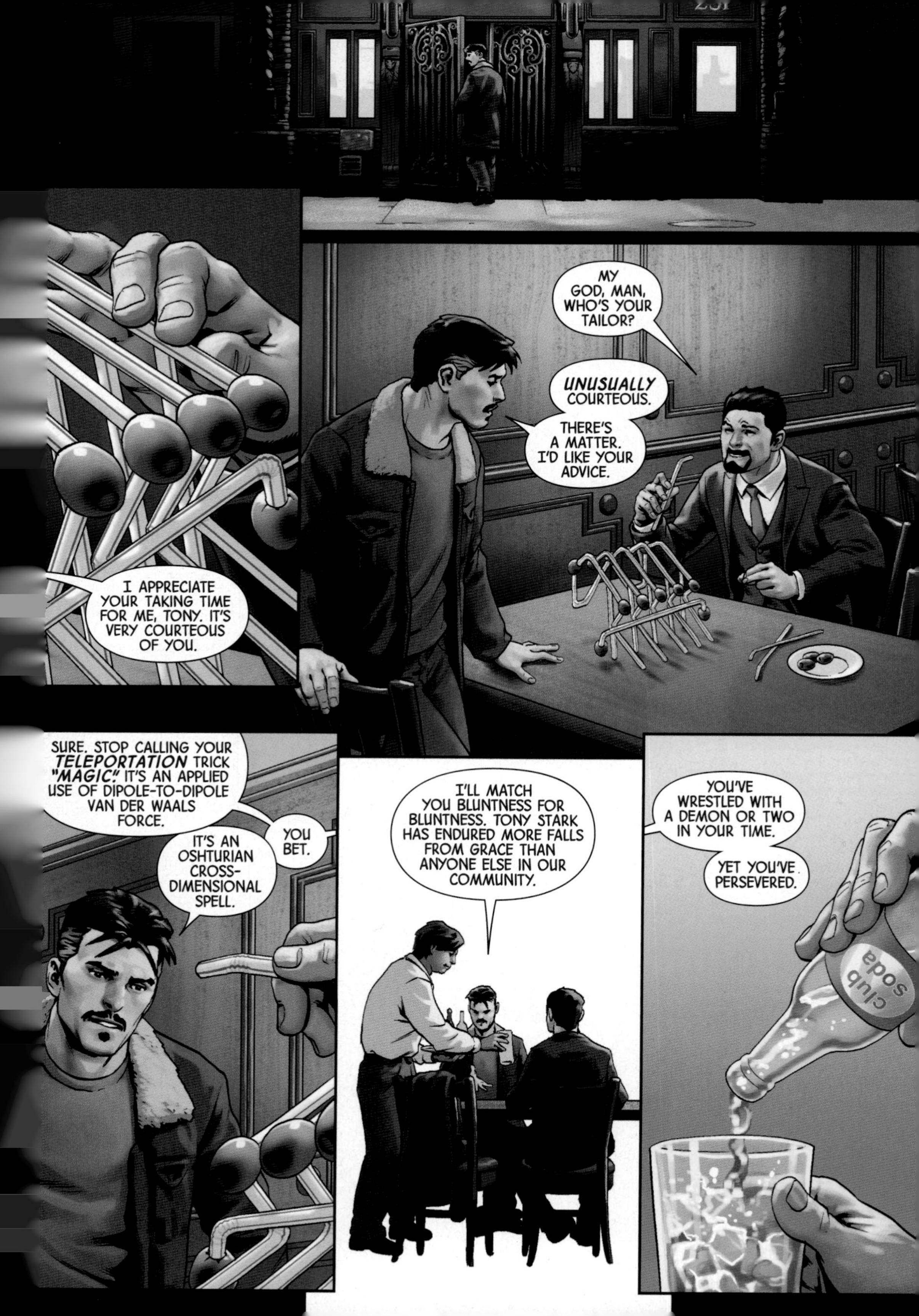
I APPRECIATE YOUR TAKING TIME FOR ME, TONY. IT'S VERY COURTEOUS OF YOU.
MY GOD, MAN, WHO'S YOUR TAILOR?
UNUSUALLY COURTEOUS.
THERE'S A MATTER. I'D LIKE YOUR ADVICE.
SURE. STOP CALLING YOUR TELEPORTATION TRICK "MAGIC." IT'S AN APPLIED USE OF DIPOLE-TO-DIPOLE VAN DER WAALS FORCE.
IT'S AN OSHTURIAN CROSS-DIMENSIONAL SPELL.
YOU BET.
I'LL MATCH YOU BLUNTNESS FOR BLUNTNESS. TONY STARK HAS ENDURED MORE FALLS FROM GRACE THAN ANYONE ELSE IN OUR COMMUNITY.
YOU'VE WRESTLED WITH A DEMON OR TWO IN YOUR TIME.
YET YOU'VE PERSEVERED.
club soda

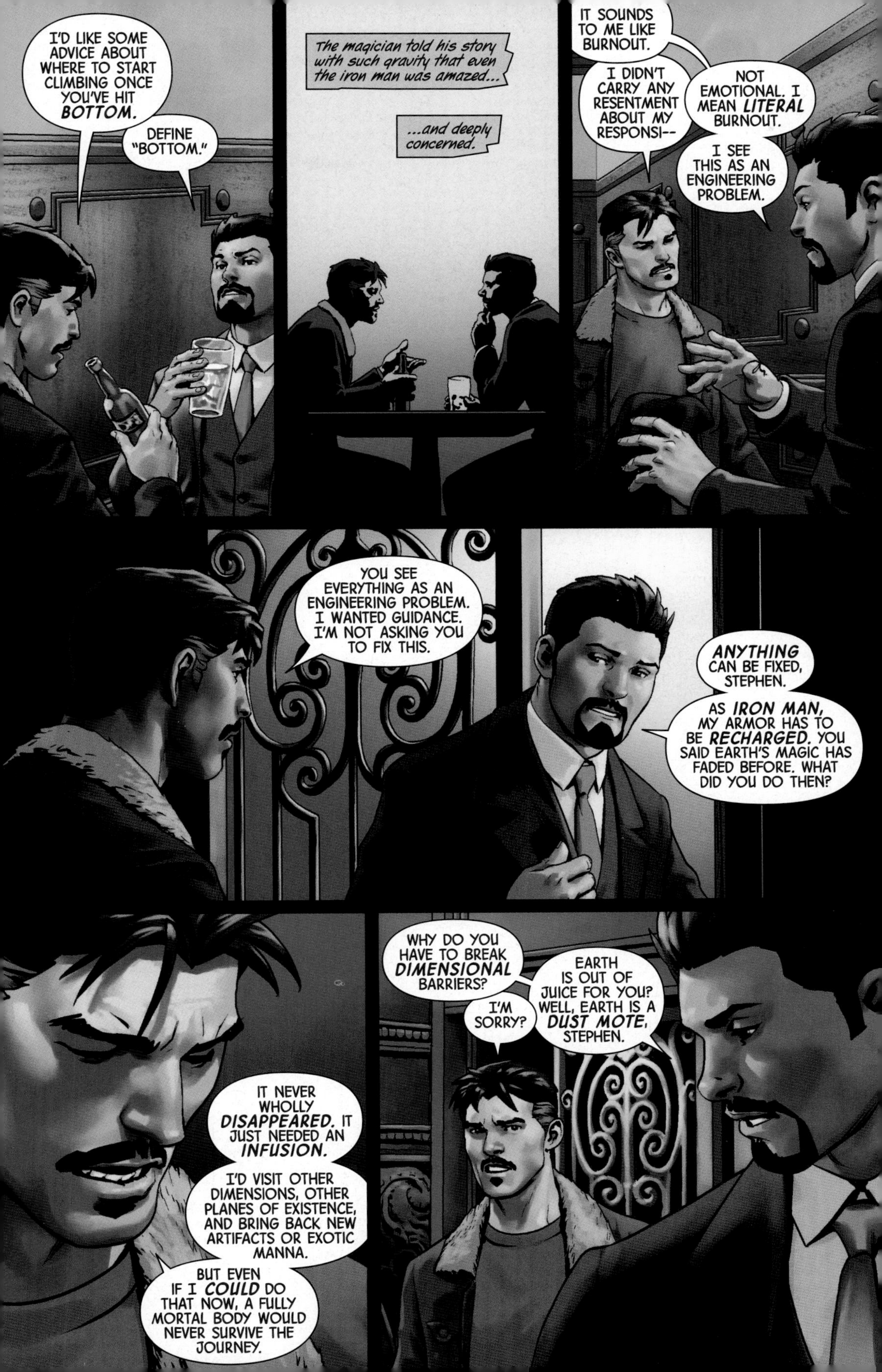
I'D LIKE SOME ADVICE ABOUT WHERE TO START CLIMBING ONCE YOU'VE HIT BOTTOM.
DEFINE "BOTTOM."
The magician told his story with such gravity that even the iron man was amazed...
...and deeply concerned.
IT SOUNDS TO ME LIKE BURNOUT.
I DIDN'T CARRY ANY RESENTMENT ABOUT MY RESPONSI--
NOT EMOTIONAL. I MEAN LITERAL BURNOUT.
I SEE THIS AS AN ENGINEERING PROBLEM.
YOU SEE EVERYTHING AS AN ENGINEERING PROBLEM. I WANTED GUIDANCE. I'M NOT ASKING YOU TO FIX THIS.
ANYTHING CAN BE FIXED, STEPHEN.
AS IRON MAN, MY ARMOR HAS TO BE RECHARGED. YOU SAID EARTH'S MAGIC HAS FADED BEFORE. WHAT DID YOU DO THEN?
IT NEVER WHOLLY DISAPPEARED. IT JUST NEEDED AN INFUSION.
I'D VISIT OTHER DIMENSIONS, OTHER PLANES OF EXISTENCE, AND BRING BACK NEW ARTIFACTS OR EXOTIC MANNA.
BUT EVEN IF I COULD DO THAT NOW, A FULLY MORTAL BODY WOULD NEVER SURVIVE THE JOURNEY.
WHY DO YOU HAVE TO BREAK DIMENSIONAL BARRIERS?
I'M SORRY?
EARTH IS OUT OF JUICE FOR YOU? WELL, EARTH IS A DUST MOTE, STEPHEN.

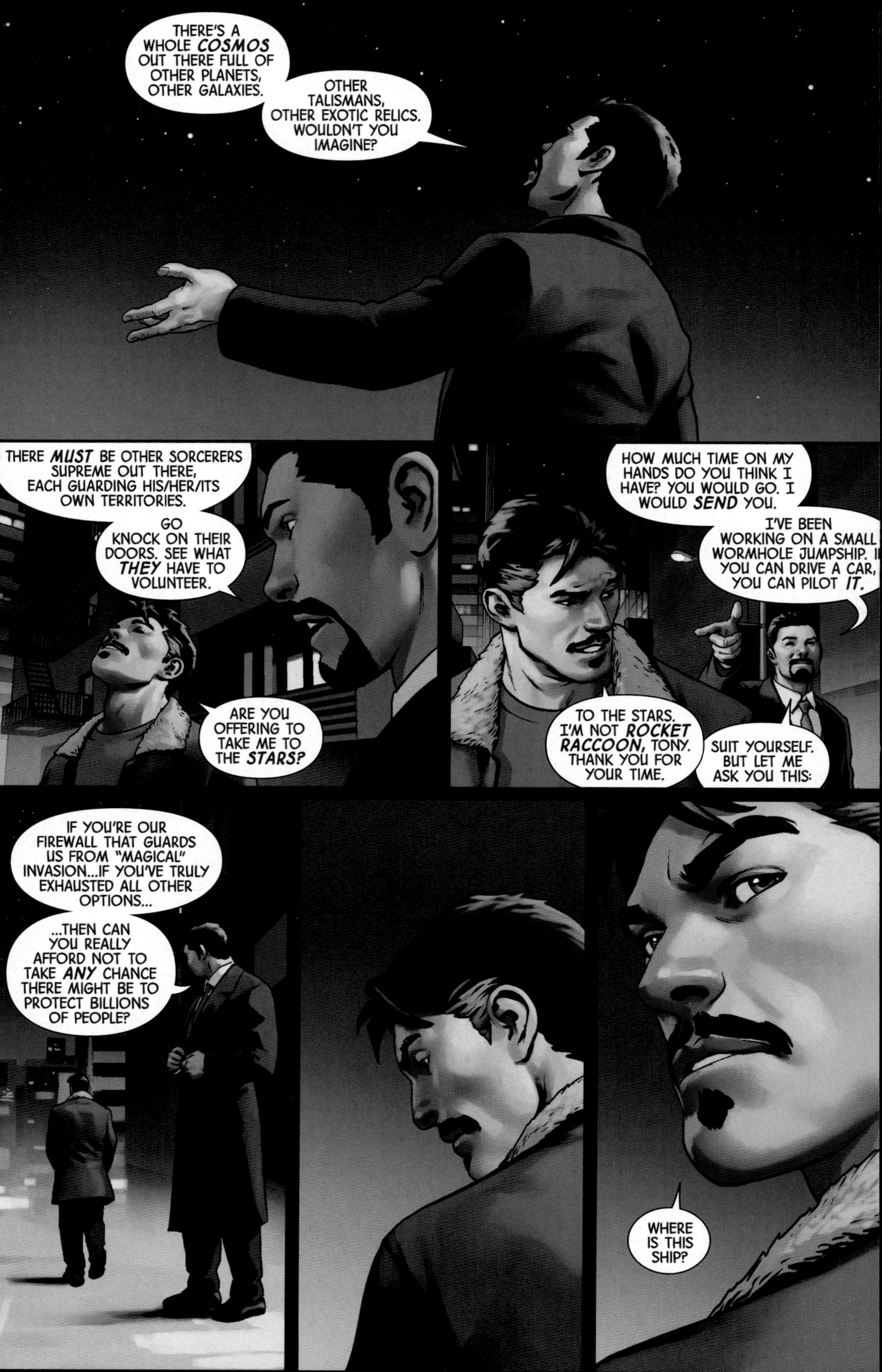
THERE'S A WHOLE COSMOS OUT THERE FULL OF OTHER PLANETS, OTHER GALAXIES.
OTHER TALISMANS, OTHER EXOTIC RELICS. WOULDN'T YOU IMAGINE?
THERE MUST BE OTHER SORCERERS SUPREME OUT THERE, EACH GUARDING HIS/HER/ITS OWN TERRITORIES.
GO KNOCK ON THEIR DOORS. SEE WHAT THEY HAVE TO VOLUNTEER.
ARE YOU OFFERING TO TAKE ME TO THE STARS?
HOW MUCH TIME ON MY HANDS DO YOU THINK I HAVE? YOU WOULD GO. I WOULD SEND YOU.
I'VE BEEN WORKING ON A SMALL WORMHOLE JUMPSHIP. IF YOU CAN DRIVE A CAR, YOU CAN PILOT IT.
TO THE STARS. I'M NOT ROCKET RACCOON, TONY. THANK YOU FOR YOUR TIME.
SUIT YOURSELF. BUT LET ME ASK YOU THIS:
IF YOU'RE OUR FIREWALL THAT GUARDS US FROM "MAGICAL" INVASION...IF YOU'VE TRULY EXHAUSTED ALL OTHER OPTIONS...
...THEN CAN YOU REALLY AFFORD NOT TO TAKE ANY CHANCE THERE MIGHT BE TO PROTECT BILLIONS OF PEOPLE?
WHERE IS THIS SHIP?

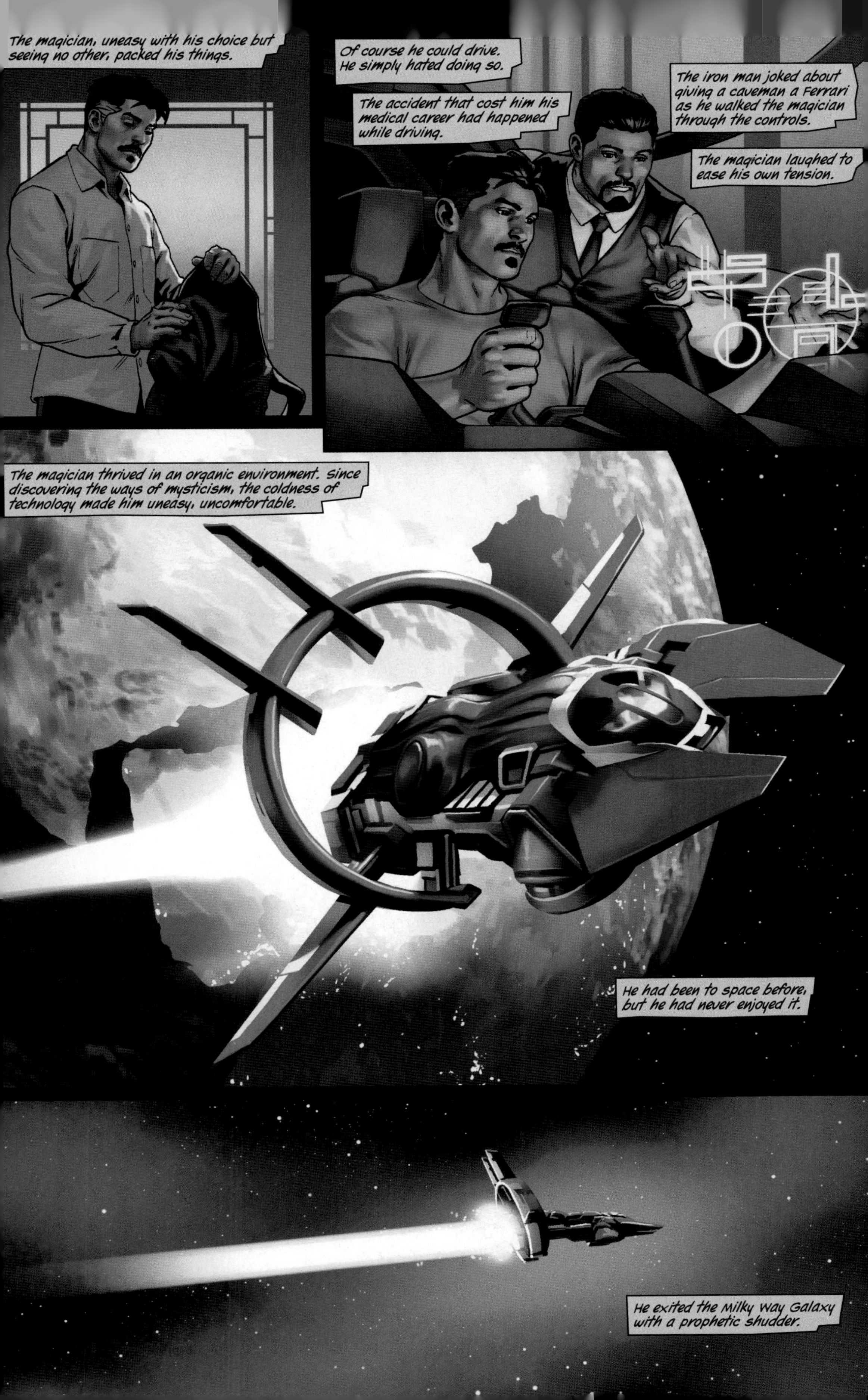
The magician, uneasy with his choice but seeing no other, packed his things.
Of course he could drive. He simply hated doing so.
The accident that cost him his medical career had happened while driving.
The iron man joked about giving a caveman a Ferrari as he walked the magician through the controls.
The magician laughed to ease his own tension.
The magician thrived in an organic environment. Since discovering the ways of mysticism, the coldness of technology made him uneasy, uncomfortable.
He had been to space before, but he had never enjoyed it.
He exited the Milky Way Galaxy with a prophetic shudder.

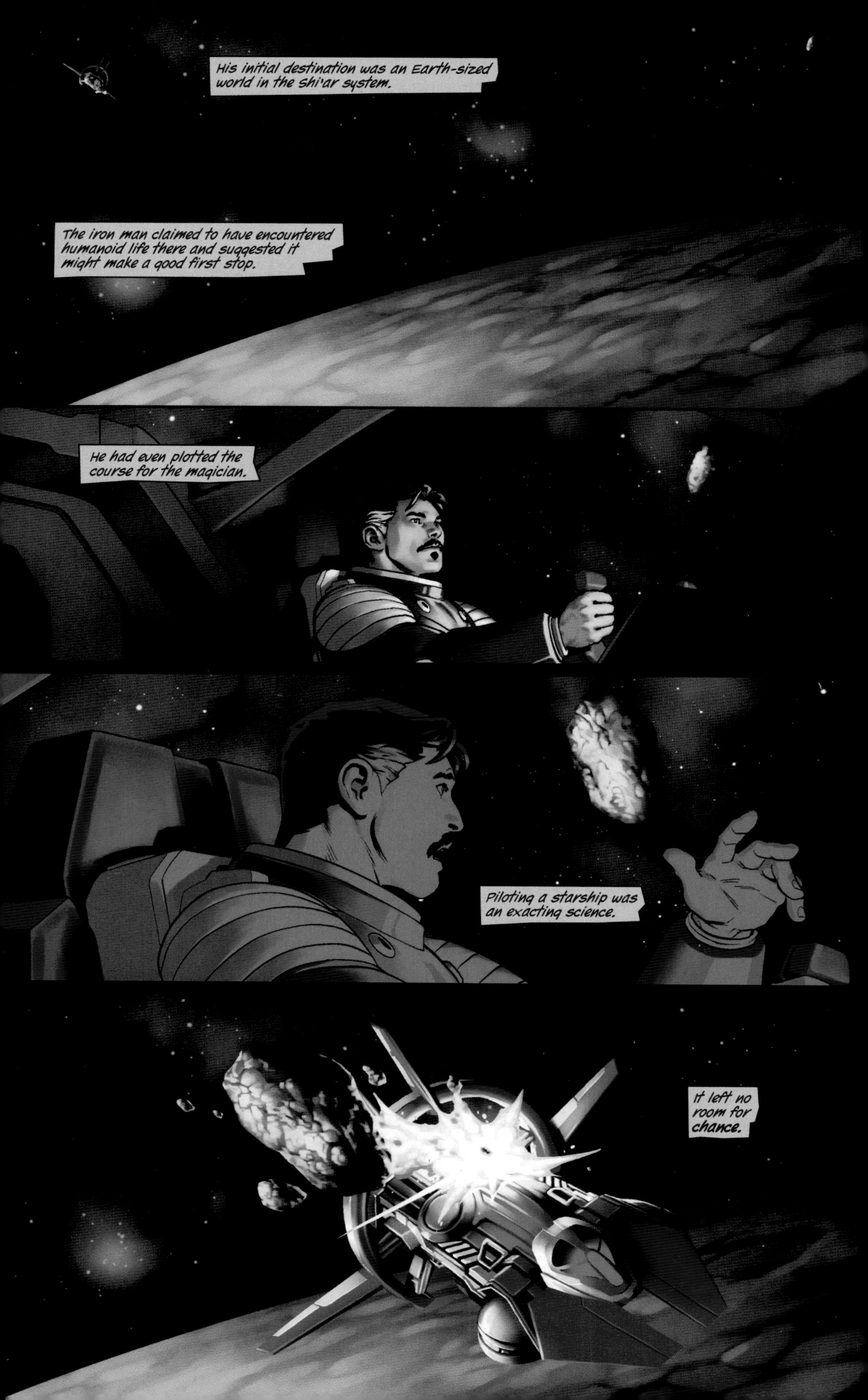
His initial destination was an Earth-sized world in the Shi'ar system.
The iron man claimed to have encountered humanoid life there and suggested it might make a good first stop.
He had even plotted the course for the magician.
Piloting a starship was an exacting science.
It left no room for chance.

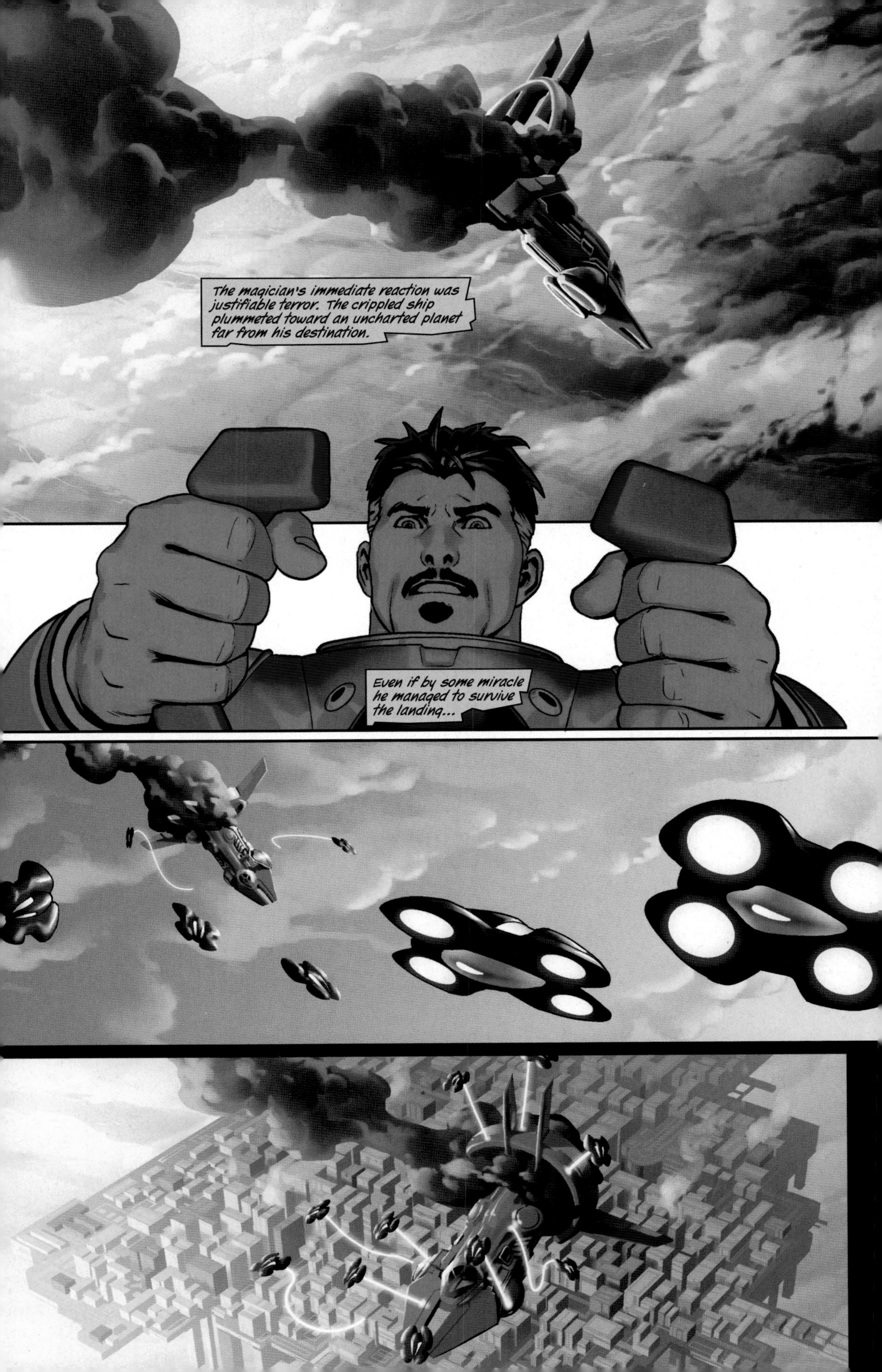
The magician's immediate reaction was justifiable terror. The crippled ship plummeted toward an uncharted planet far from his destination.
Even if by some miracle he managed to survive the landing...

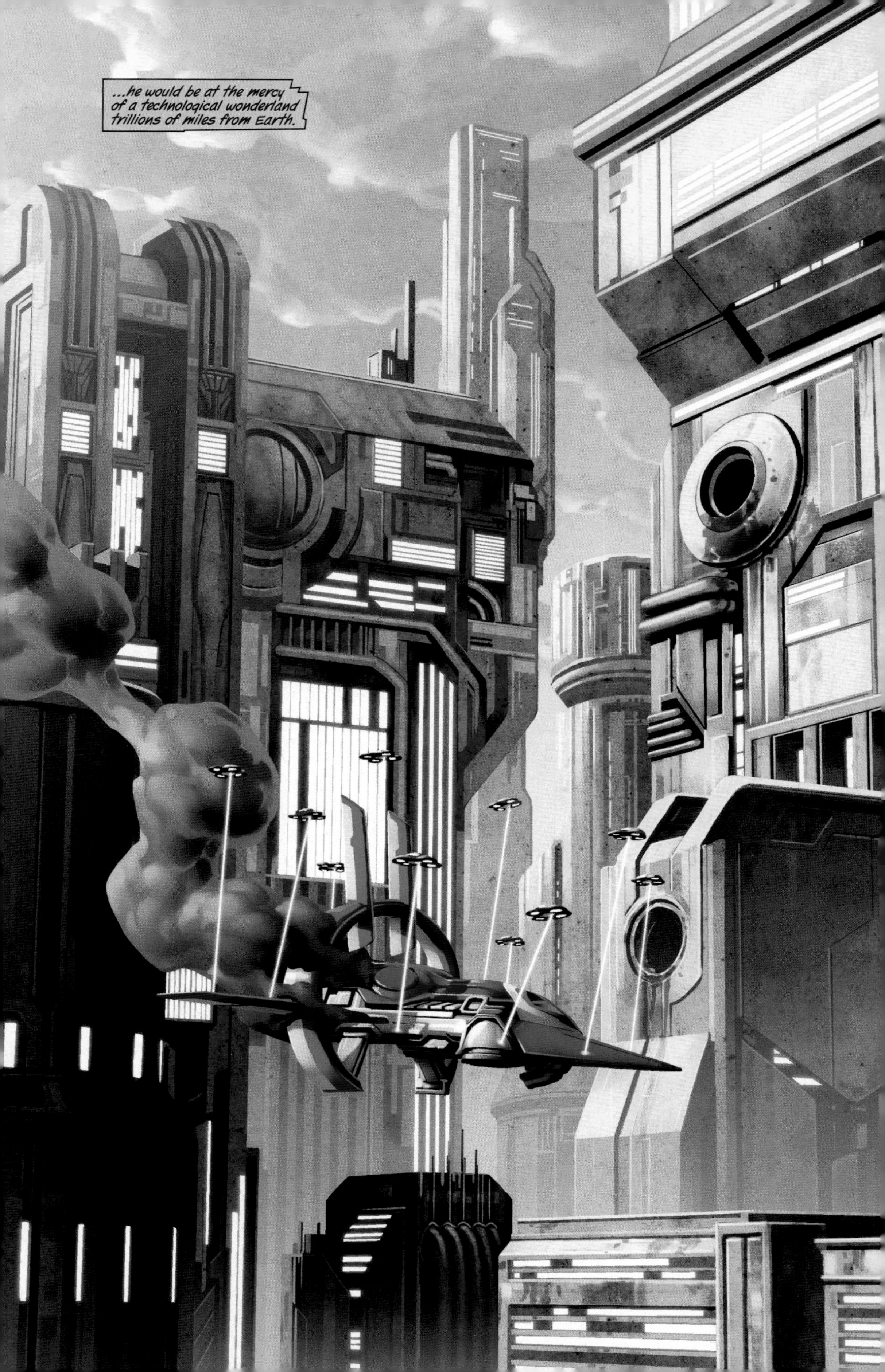
...he would be at the mercy of a technological wonderland trillions of miles from Earth.

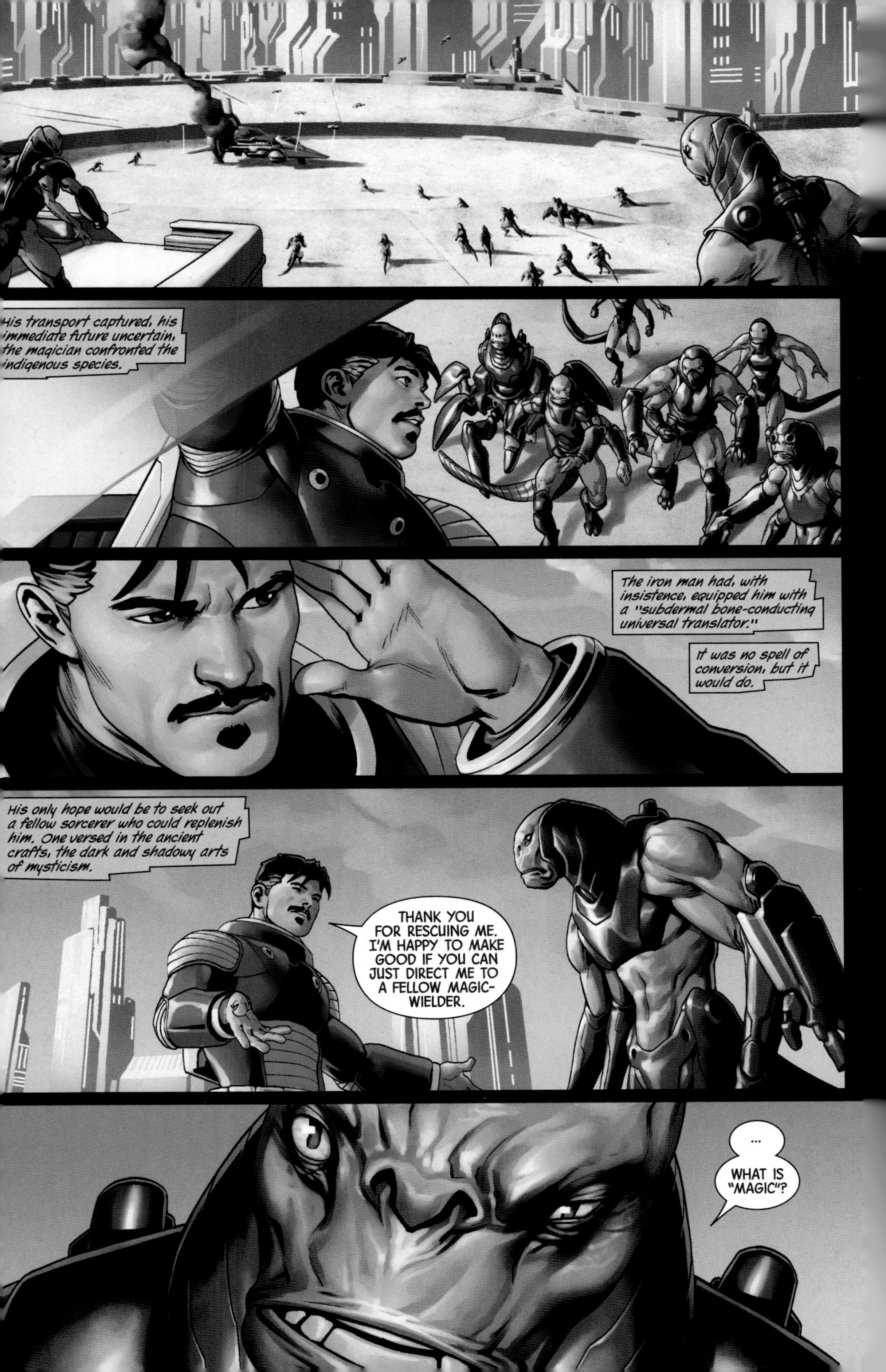
His transport captured, his immediate future uncertain, the magician confronted the indigenous species.
The iron man had, with insistence, equipped him with a "subdermal bone-conducting universal translator."
It was no spell of conversion, but it would do.
His only hope would be to seek out a fellow sorcerer who could replenish him. One versed in the ancient crafts, the dark and shadowy arts of mysticism.
THANK YOU FOR RESCUING ME. I'M HAPPY TO MAKE GOOD IF YOU CAN JUST DIRECT ME TO A FELLOW MAGIC-WIELDER.
...
WHAT IS "MAGIC"?

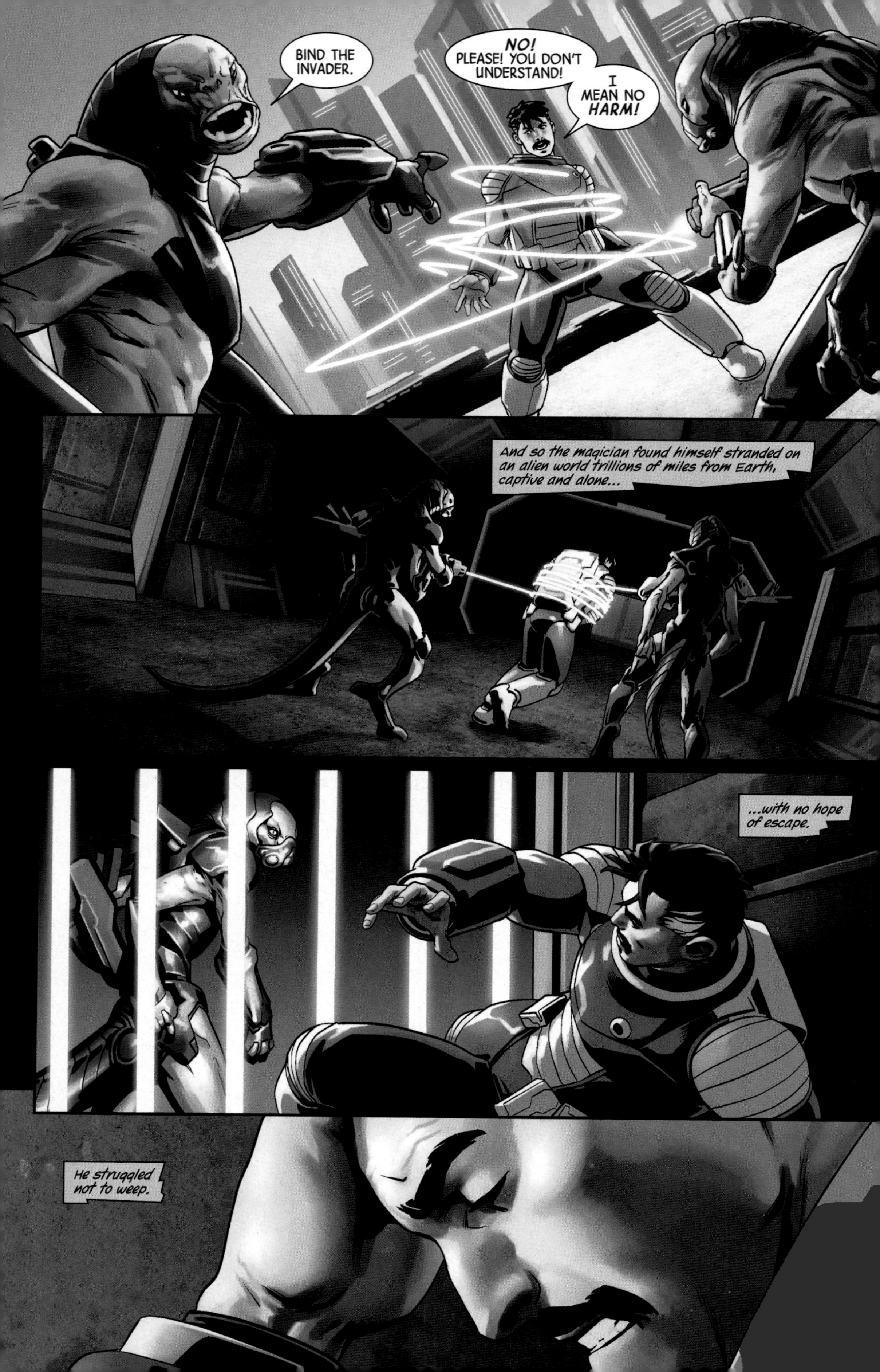
BIND THE INVADER.
NO! PLEASE! YOU DON'T UNDERSTAND!
I MEAN NO HARM!
And so the magician found himself stranded on an alien world trillions of miles from Earth, captive and alone...
...with no hope of escape.
He struggled not to weep.

2

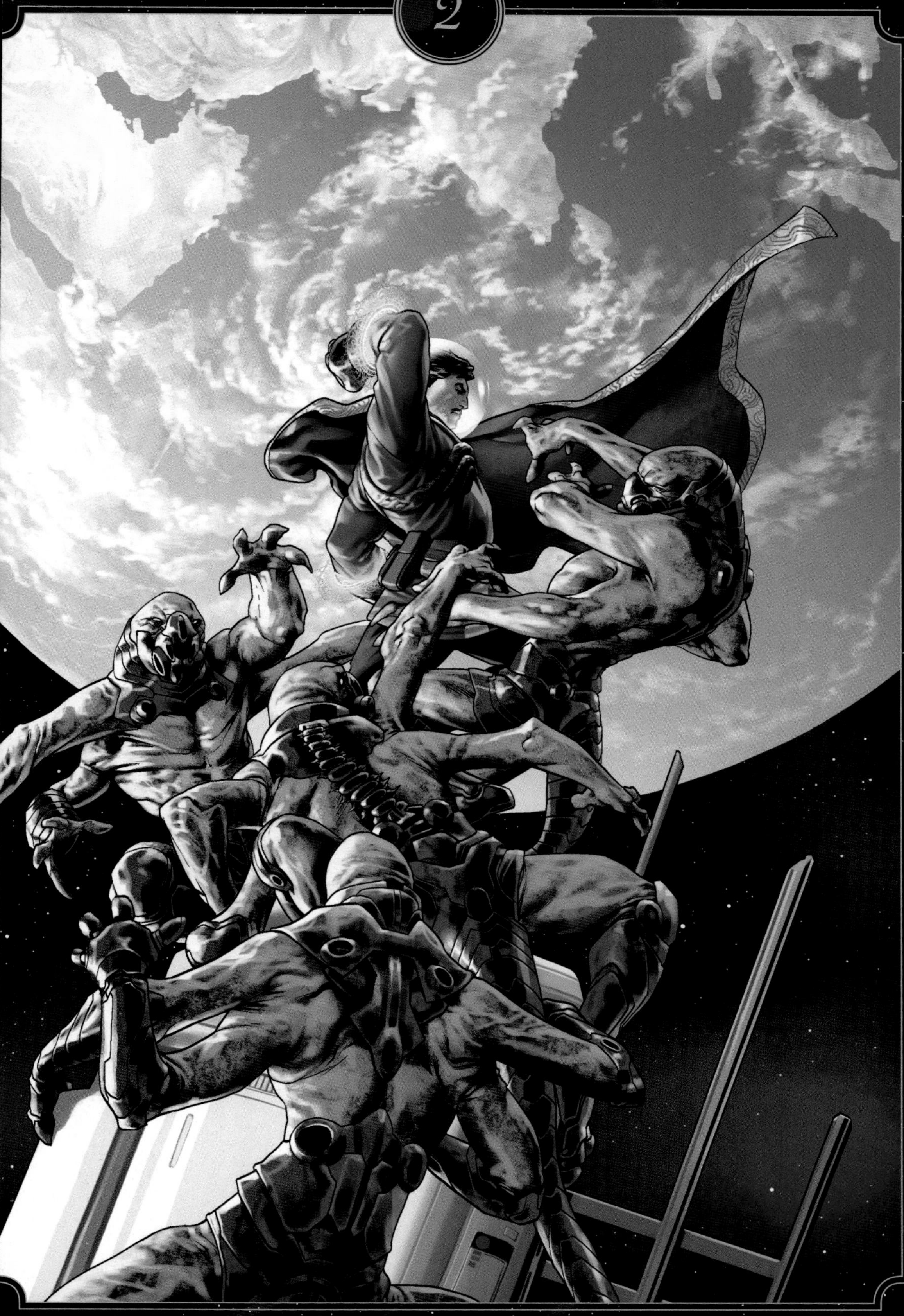

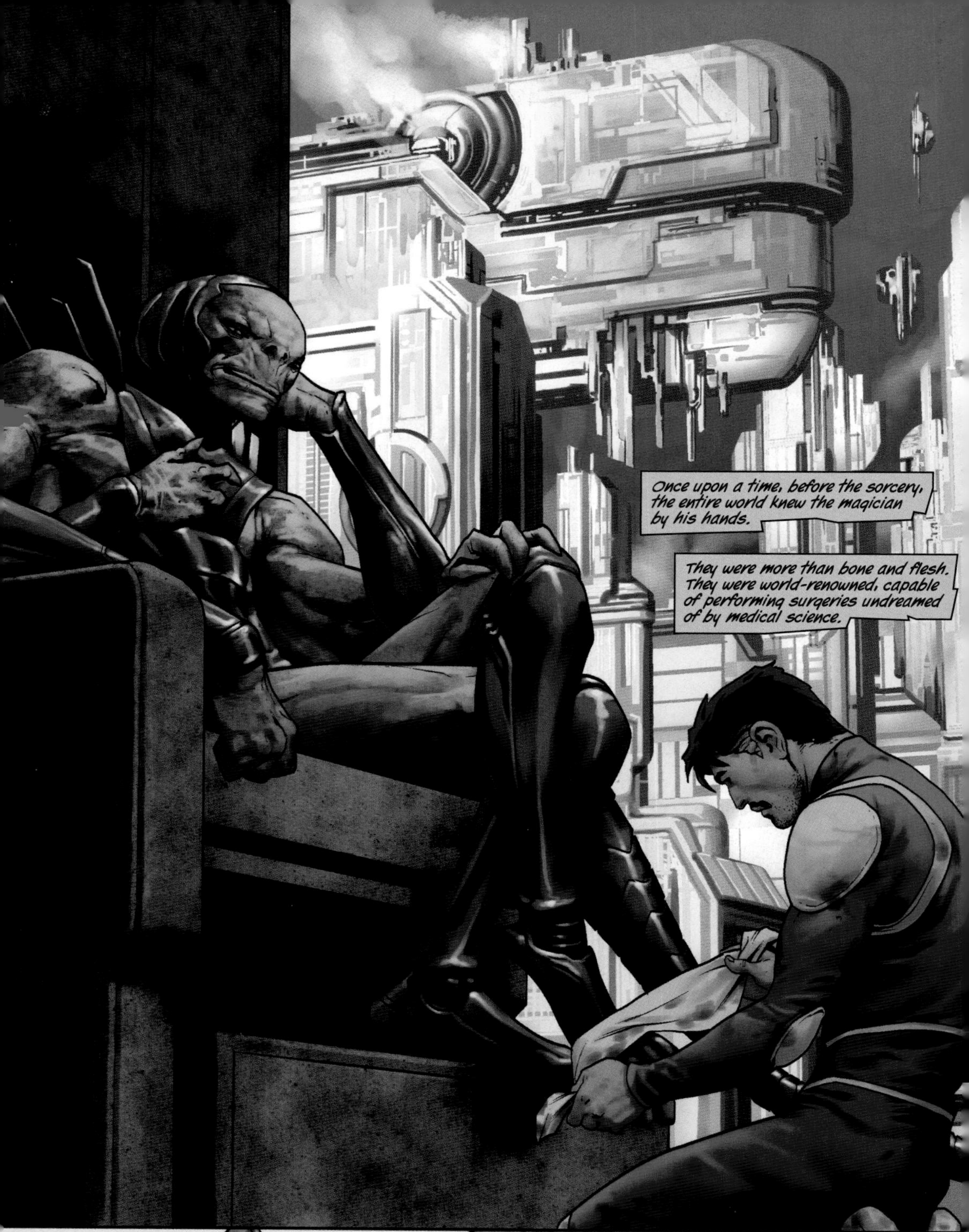
Once upon a time, before the sorcery, the entire world knew the magician by his hands.
They were more than bone and flesh. They were world-renowned, capable of performing surgeries undreamed of by medical science.

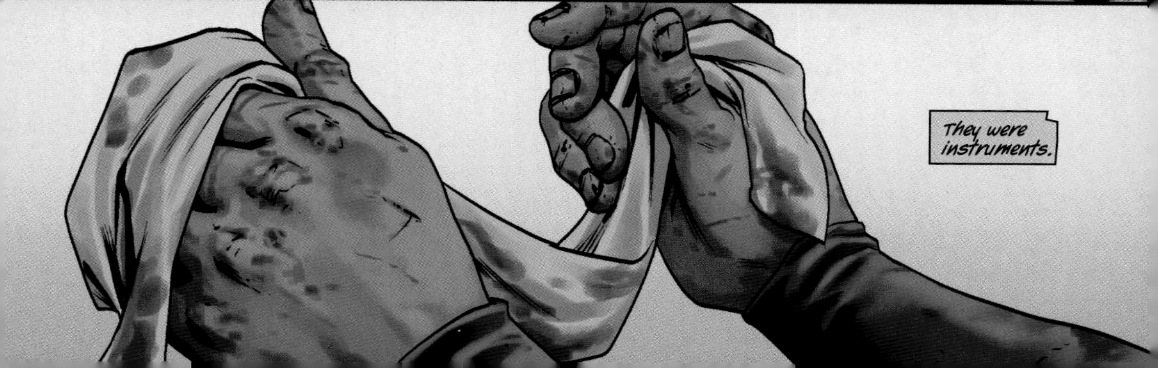
They were instruments.

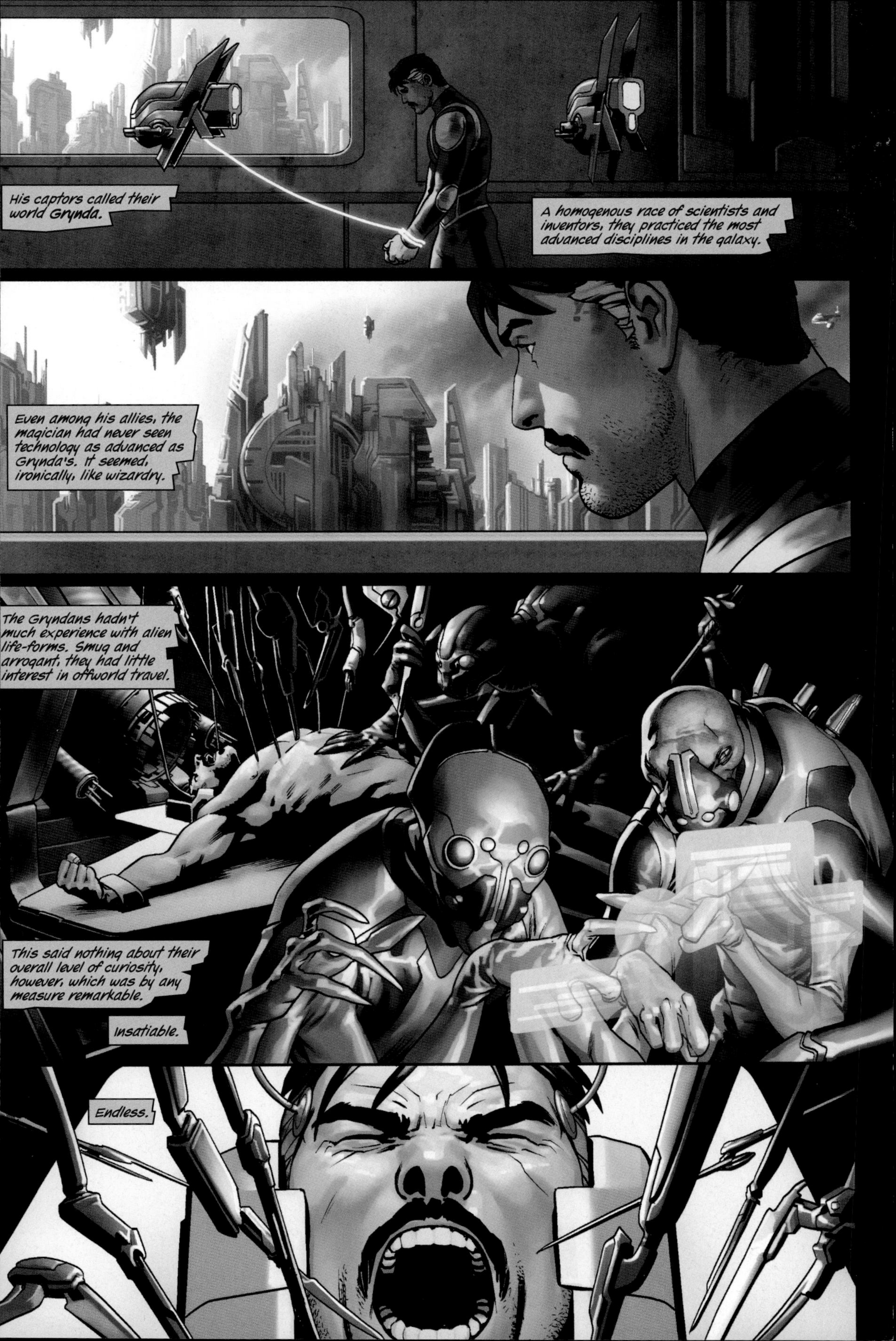
His captors called their world Grynda.
A homogenous race of scientists and inventors, they practiced the most advanced disciplines in the galaxy.
Even among his allies, the magician had never seen technology as advanced as Grynda's. It seemed, ironically, like wizardry.
The Gryndans hadn't much experience with alien life-forms. Smug and arrogant, they had little interest in offworld travel.
This said nothing about their overall level of curiosity, however, which was by any measure remarkable.
Insatiable.
Endless.

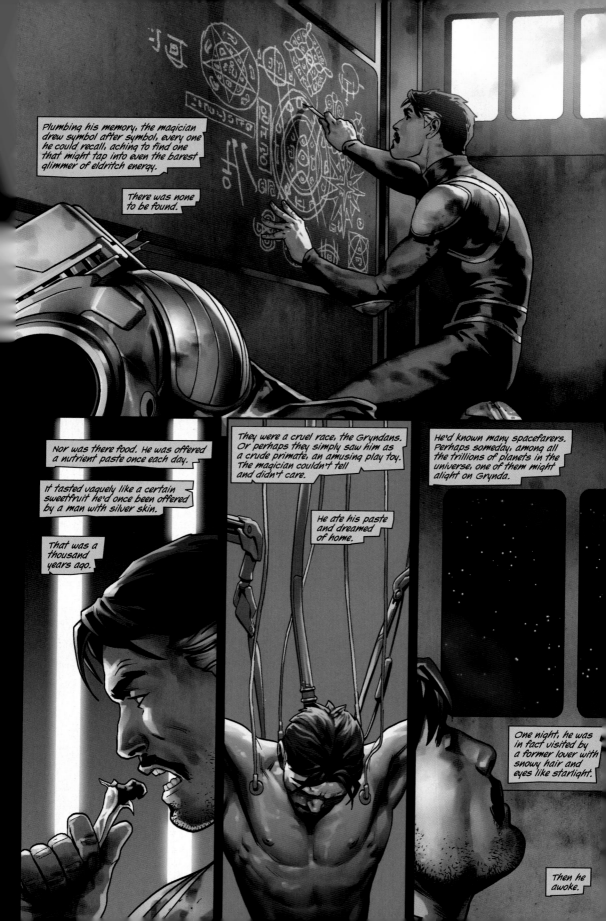

Plumbing his memory, the magician drew symbol after symbol, every one he could recall, aching to find one that might tap into even the barest glimmer of eldritch energy.

There was none to be found.

Nor was there food. He was offered a nutrient paste once each day.

It tasted vaguely like a certain sweetfruit he'd once been offered by a man with silver skin.

That was a thousand years ago.

They were a cruel race, the Gryndans. Or perhaps they simply saw him as a crude primate, an amusing play toy. The magician couldn't tell and didn't care.

He ate his paste and dreamed of home.

He'd known many spacefarers. Perhaps someday, among all the trillions of planets in the universe, one of them might alight on Grynda.

One night, he was in fact visited by a former lover with snowy hair and eyes like starlight.

Then he awoke.

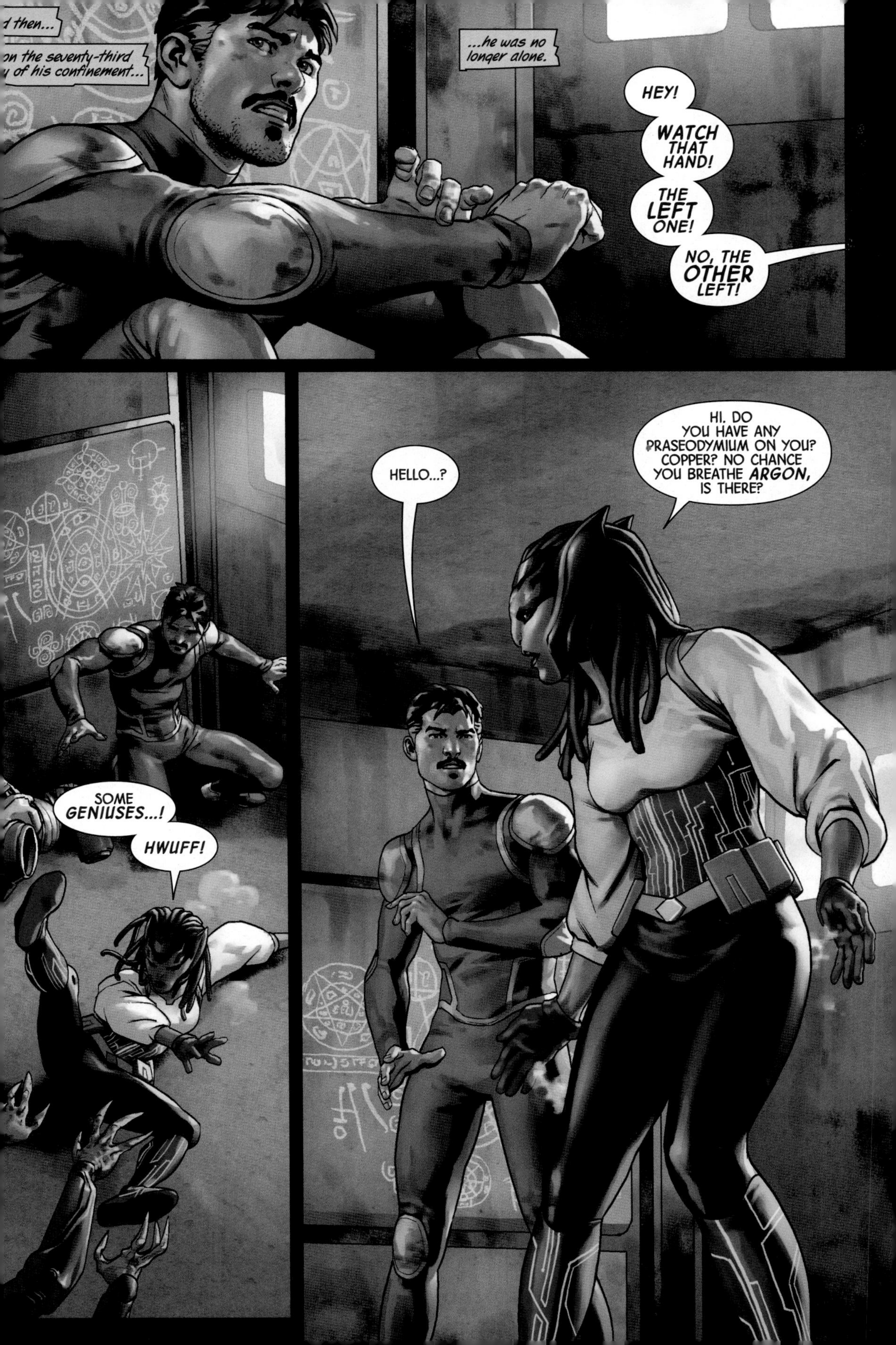

...d then...
...on the seventy-third ...y of his confinement...
...he was no longer alone.
HEY!
WATCH THAT HAND!
THE LEFT ONE!
NO, THE OTHER LEFT!
SOME GENIUSES...!
HWUFF!
HELLO...?
HI. DO YOU HAVE ANY PRASEODYMIUM ON YOU? COPPER? NO CHANCE YOU BREATHE ARGON, IS THERE?

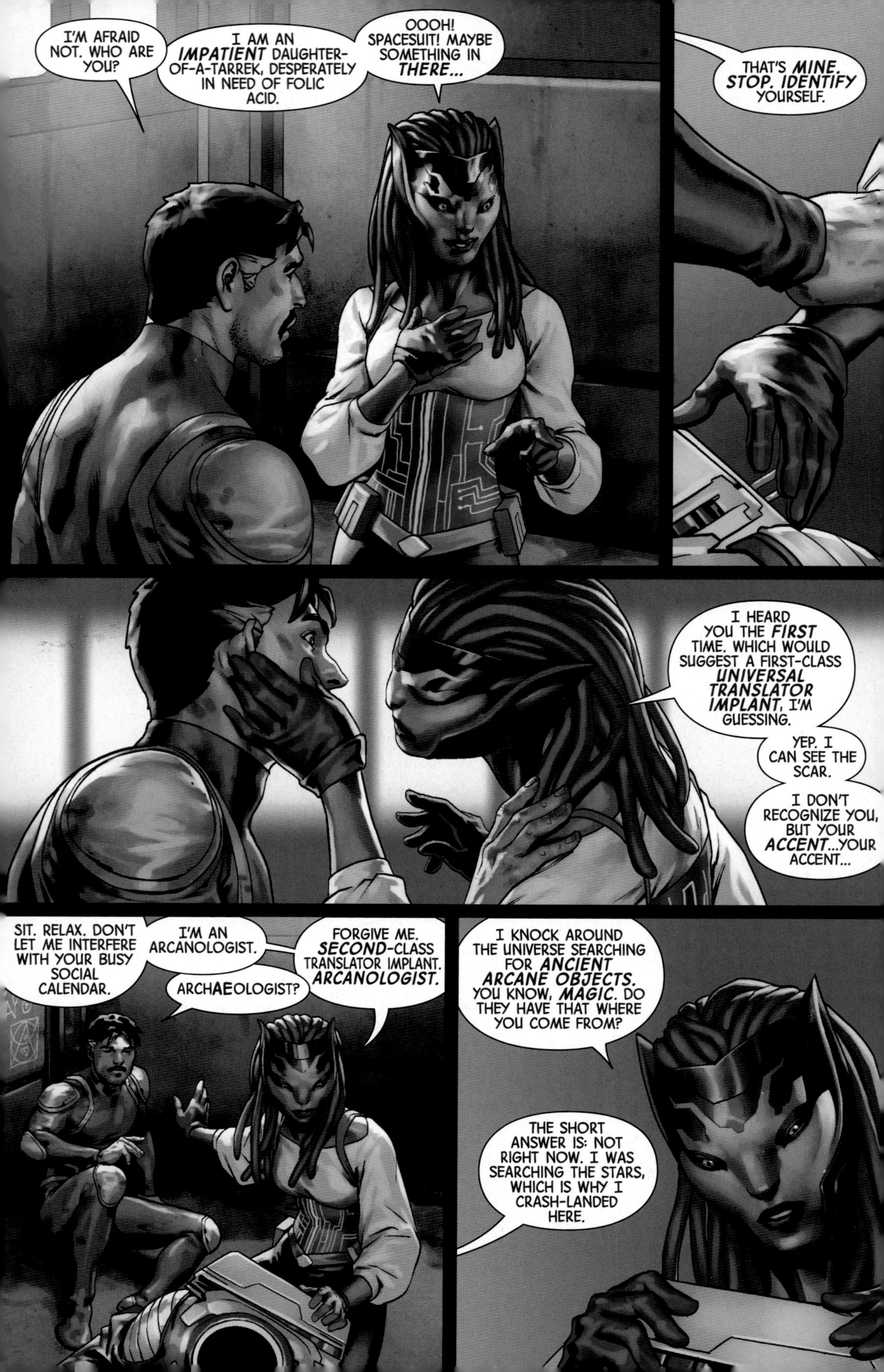
I'M AFRAID NOT. WHO ARE YOU?
I AM AN IMPATIENT DAUGHTER-OF-A-TARREK, DESPERATELY IN NEED OF FOLIC ACID.
OOOH! SPACESUIT! MAYBE SOMETHING IN THERE...
THAT'S MINE. STOP. IDENTIFY YOURSELF.
I HEARD YOU THE FIRST TIME. WHICH WOULD SUGGEST A FIRST-CLASS UNIVERSAL TRANSLATOR IMPLANT, I'M GUESSING.
YEP. I CAN SEE THE SCAR.
I DON'T RECOGNIZE YOU, BUT YOUR ACCENT...YOUR ACCENT...
SIT. RELAX. DON'T LET ME INTERFERE WITH YOUR BUSY SOCIAL CALENDAR.
I'M AN ARCANOLOGIST.
ARCHAEOLOGIST?
FORGIVE ME. SECOND-CLASS TRANSLATOR IMPLANT. ARCANOLOGIST.
I KNOCK AROUND THE UNIVERSE SEARCHING FOR ANCIENT ARCANE OBJECTS. YOU KNOW, MAGIC. DO THEY HAVE THAT WHERE YOU COME FROM?
THE SHORT ANSWER IS: NOT RIGHT NOW. I WAS SEARCHING THE STARS, WHICH IS WHY I CRASH-LANDED HERE.

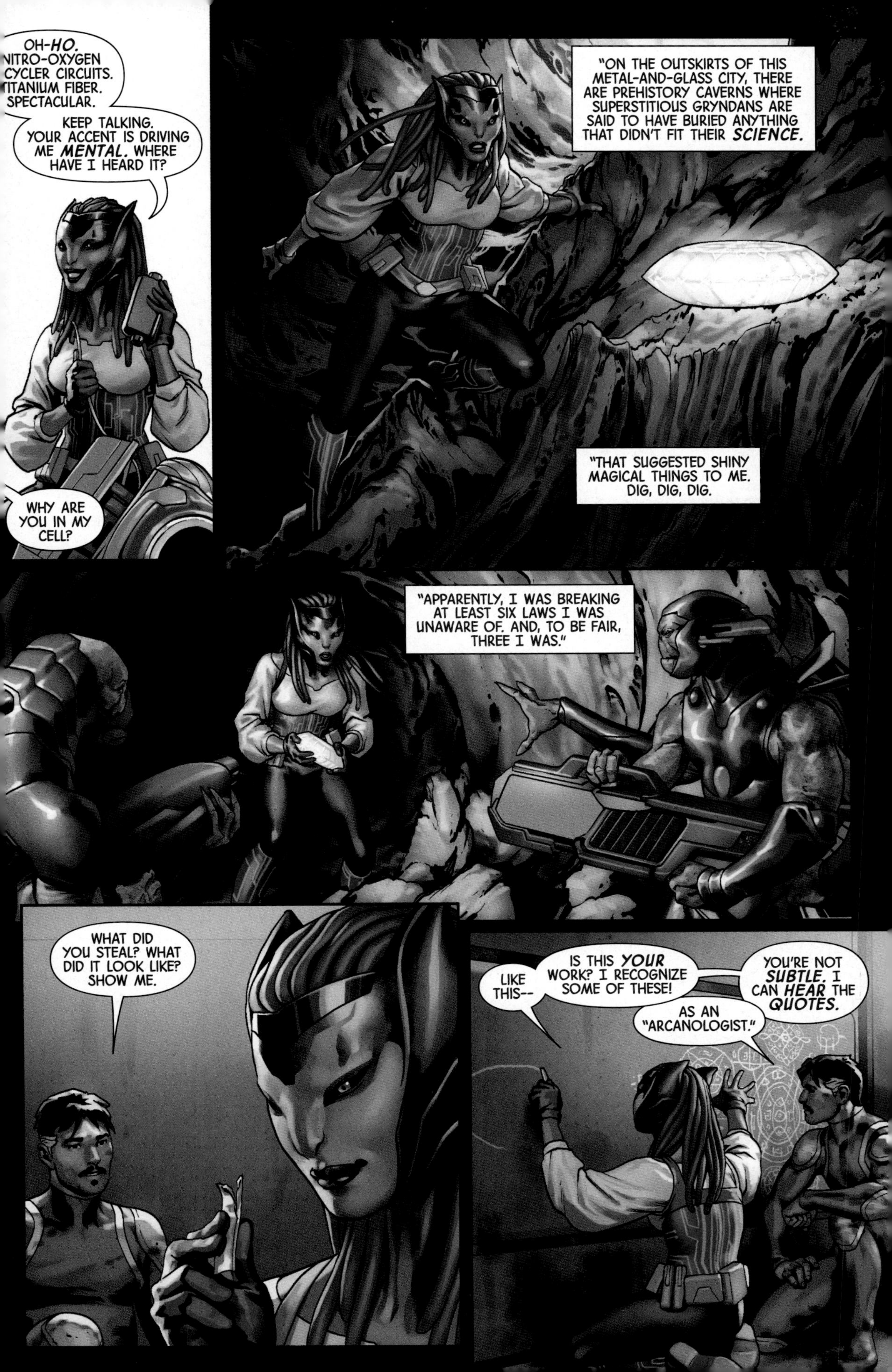
OH-HO. NITRO-OXYGEN CYCLER CIRCUITS. TITANIUM FIBER. SPECTACULAR.
KEEP TALKING. YOUR ACCENT IS DRIVING ME MENTAL. WHERE HAVE I HEARD IT?
WHY ARE YOU IN MY CELL?
"ON THE OUTSKIRTS OF THIS METAL-AND-GLASS CITY, THERE ARE PREHISTORY CAVERNS WHERE SUPERSTITIOUS GRYNDANS ARE SAID TO HAVE BURIED ANYTHING THAT DIDN'T FIT THEIR SCIENCE.
"THAT SUGGESTED SHINY MAGICAL THINGS TO ME. DIG, DIG, DIG.
"APPARENTLY, I WAS BREAKING AT LEAST SIX LAWS I WAS UNAWARE OF. AND, TO BE FAIR, THREE I WAS."
WHAT DID YOU STEAL? WHAT DID IT LOOK LIKE? SHOW ME.
LIKE THIS--
IS THIS YOUR WORK? I RECOGNIZE SOME OF THESE!
AS AN "ARCANOLOGIST."
YOU'RE NOT SUBTLE. I CAN HEAR THE QUOTES.

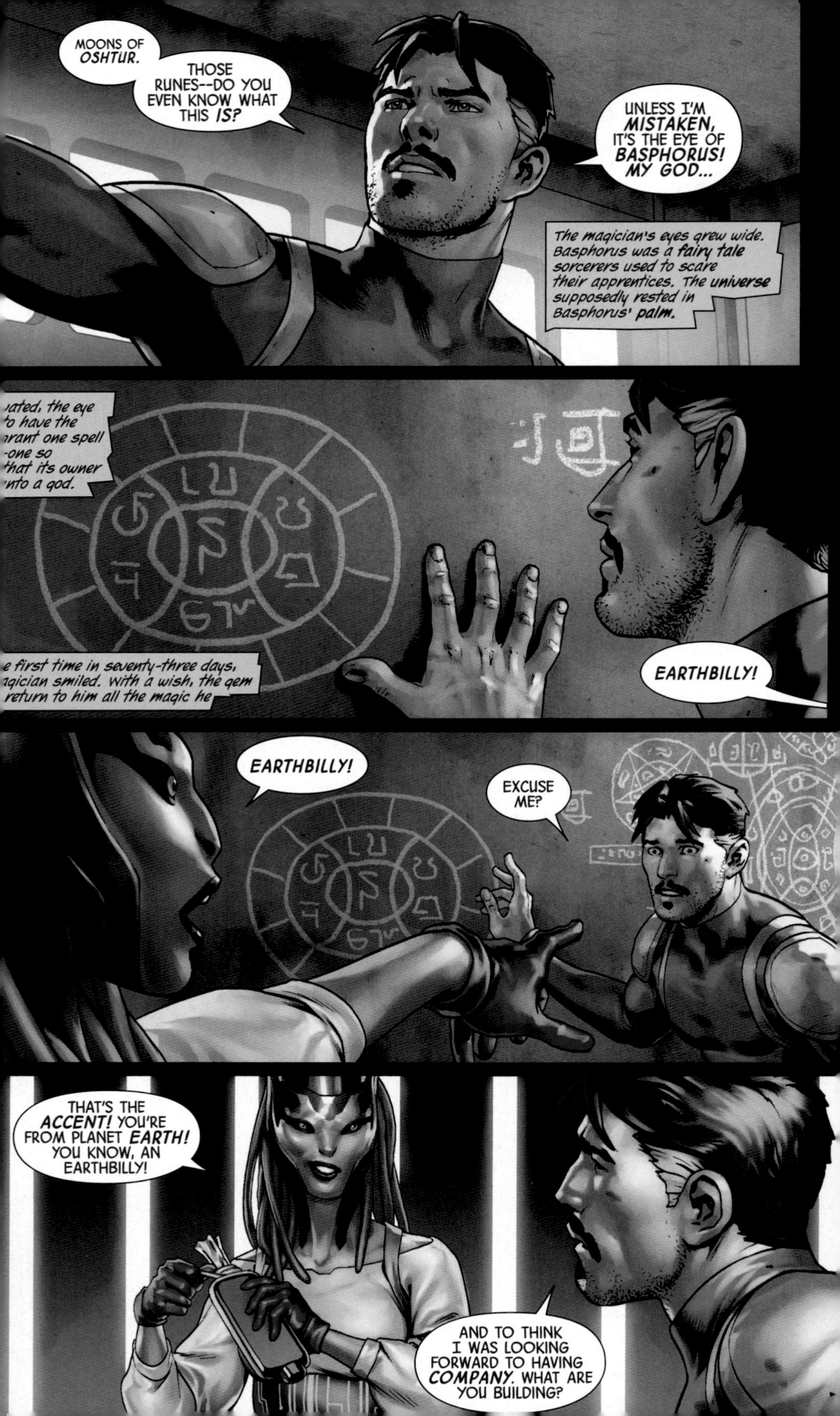

MOONS OF OSHTUR.
THOSE RUNES--DO YOU EVEN KNOW WHAT THIS IS?
UNLESS I'M MISTAKEN, IT'S THE EYE OF BASPHORUS! MY GOD...
The magician's eyes grew wide. Basphorus was a fairy tale sorcerers used to scare their apprentices. The universe supposedly rested in Basphorus' palm.
uated, the eye to have the grant one spell -one so that its owner into a god.
e first time in seventy-three days, agician smiled. With a wish, the gem return to him all the magic he
EARTHBILLY!
EARTHBILLY!
EXCUSE ME?
THAT'S THE ACCENT! YOU'RE FROM PLANET EARTH! YOU KNOW, AN EARTHBILLY!
AND TO THINK I WAS LOOKING FORWARD TO HAVING COMPANY. WHAT ARE YOU BUILDING?

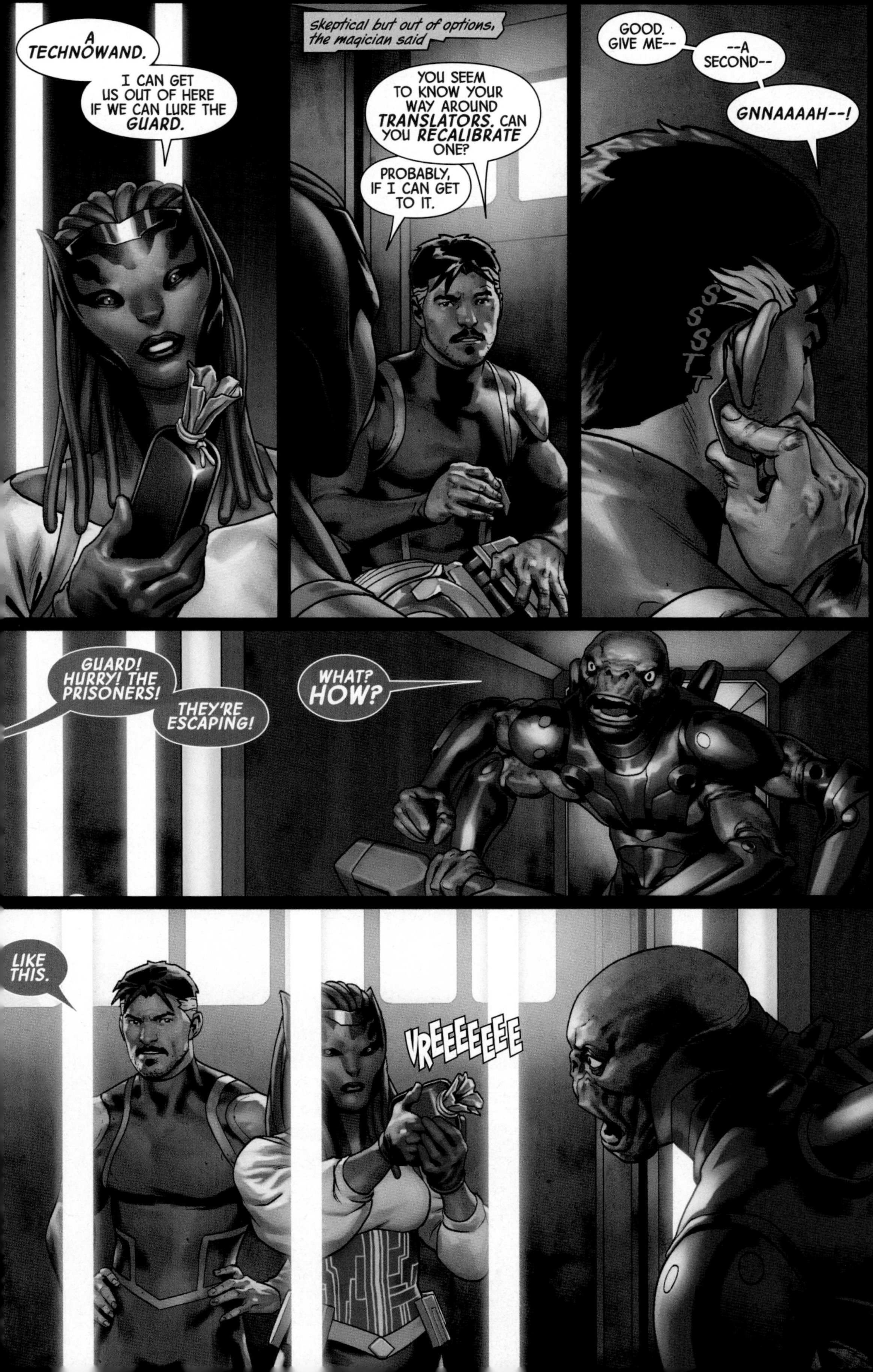
A TECHNOWAND.
I CAN GET US OUT OF HERE IF WE CAN LURE THE GUARD.
skeptical but out of options, the magician said
YOU SEEM TO KNOW YOUR WAY AROUND TRANSLATORS. CAN YOU RECALIBRATE ONE?
PROBABLY, IF I CAN GET TO IT.
GOOD. GIVE ME--
--A SECOND--
GNNAAAAH--!
SSST
GUARD! HURRY! THE PRISONERS!
THEY'RE ESCAPING!
WHAT? HOW?
LIKE THIS.
VREEEEEEE

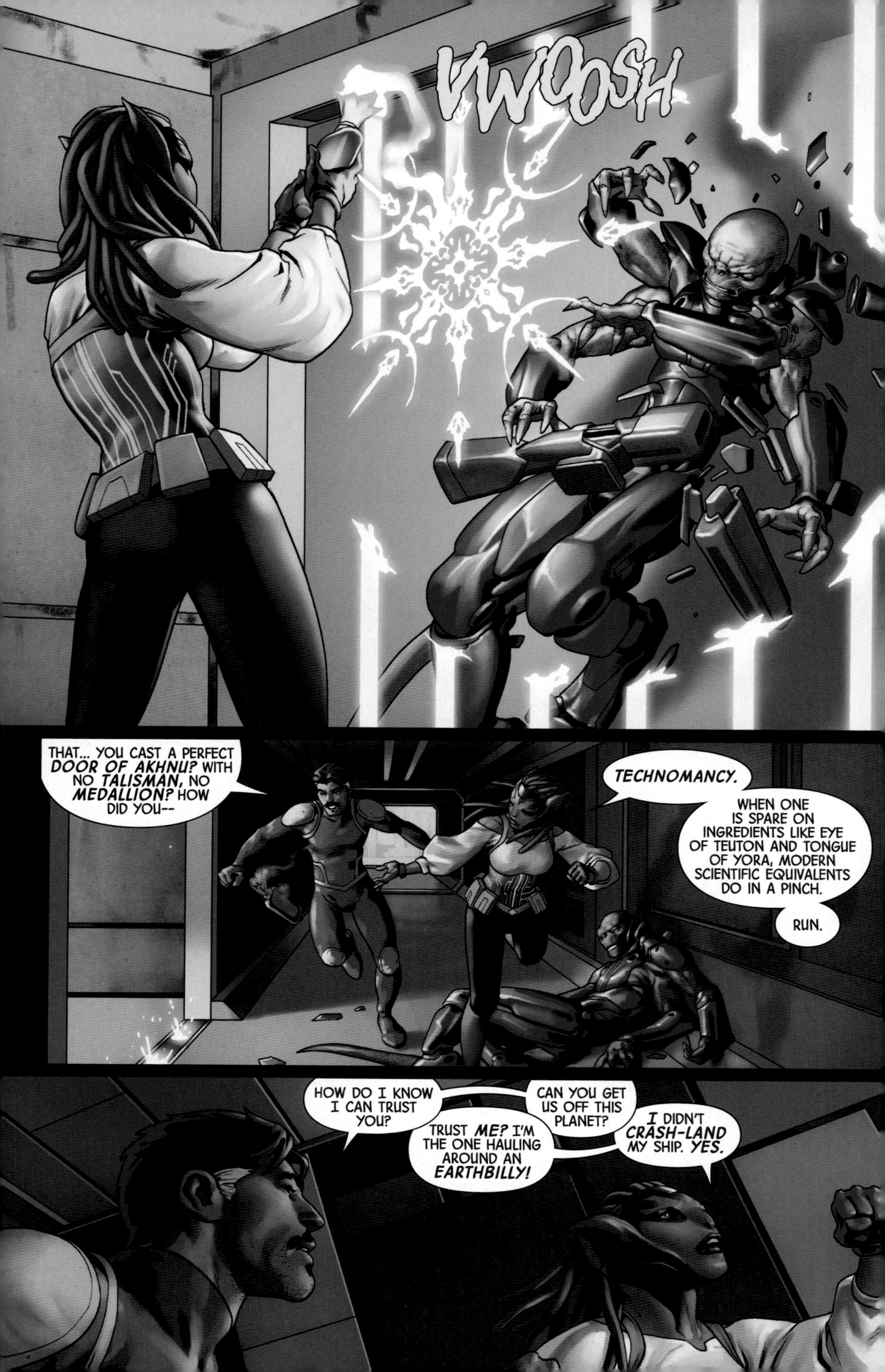

VWOOSH
THAT... YOU CAST A PERFECT DOOR OF AKHNU? WITH NO TALISMAN, NO MEDALLION? HOW DID YOU--
TECHNOMANCY.
WHEN ONE IS SPARE ON INGREDIENTS LIKE EYE OF TEUTON AND TONGUE OF YORA, MODERN SCIENTIFIC EQUIVALENTS DO IN A PINCH.
RUN.
HOW DO I KNOW I CAN TRUST YOU?
TRUST ME? I'M THE ONE HAULING AROUND AN EARTHBILLY!
CAN YOU GET US OFF THIS PLANET?
I DIDN'T CRASH-LAND MY SHIP. YES.

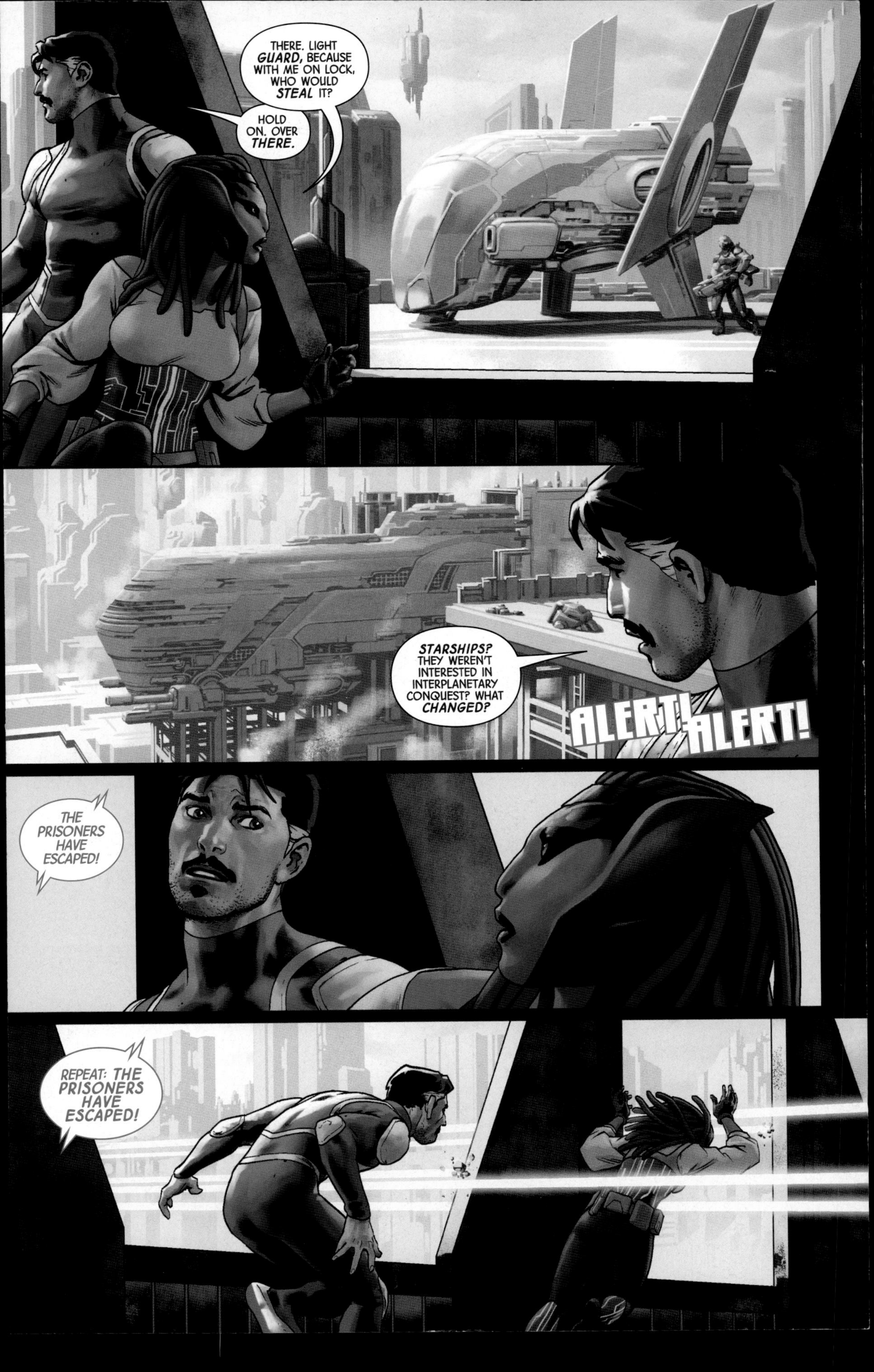
THERE. LIGHT GUARD, BECAUSE WITH ME ON LOCK, WHO WOULD STEAL IT?
HOLD ON. OVER THERE.
STARSHIPS? THEY WEREN'T INTERESTED IN INTERPLANETARY CONQUEST? WHAT CHANGED?
ALERT! ALERT!
THE PRISONERS HAVE ESCAPED!
REPEAT: THE PRISONERS HAVE ESCAPED!

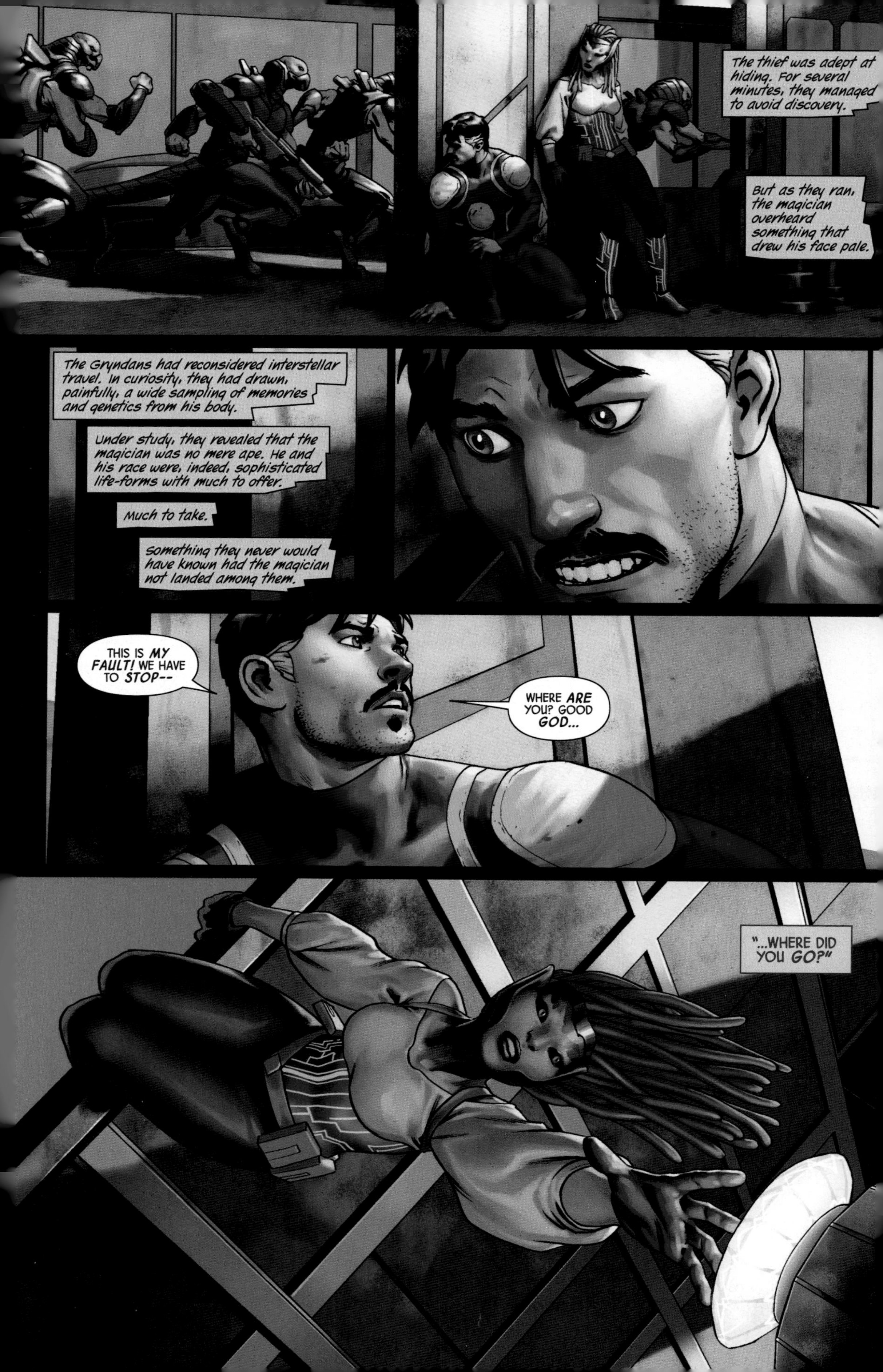
The thief was adept at hiding. For several minutes, they managed to avoid discovery.
But as they ran, the magician overheard something that drew his face pale.
The Gryndans had reconsidered interstellar travel. In curiosity, they had drawn, painfully, a wide sampling of memories and genetics from his body.
Under study, they revealed that the magician was no mere ape. He and his race were, indeed, sophisticated life-forms with much to offer.
Much to take.
Something they never would have known had the magician not landed among them.
THIS IS MY FAULT! WE HAVE TO STOP--
WHERE ARE YOU? GOOD GOD...
"...WHERE DID YOU GO?"

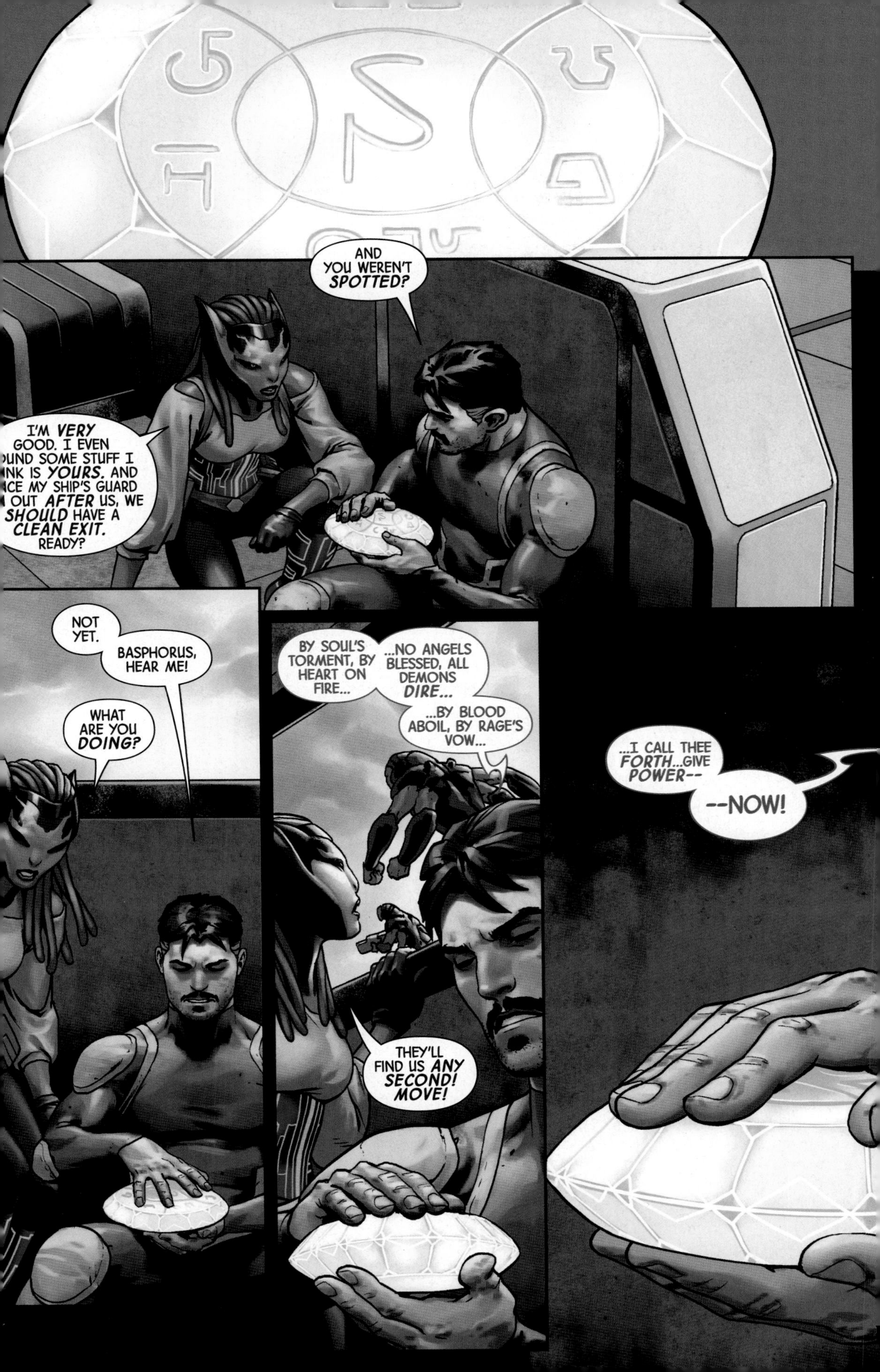
AND YOU WEREN'T SPOTTED?
I'M VERY GOOD. I EVEN
OUND SOME STUFF I
NK IS YOURS. AND
CE MY SHIP'S GUARD
OUT AFTER US, WE
SHOULD HAVE A CLEAN EXIT. READY?
NOT YET.
BASPHORUS, HEAR ME!
WHAT ARE YOU DOING?
BY SOUL'S TORMENT, BY HEART ON FIRE...
...NO ANGELS BLESSED, ALL DEMONS DIRE...
...BY BLOOD ABOIL, BY RAGE'S VOW...
THEY'LL FIND US ANY SECOND! MOVE!
...I CALL THEE FORTH...GIVE POWER--
--NOW!

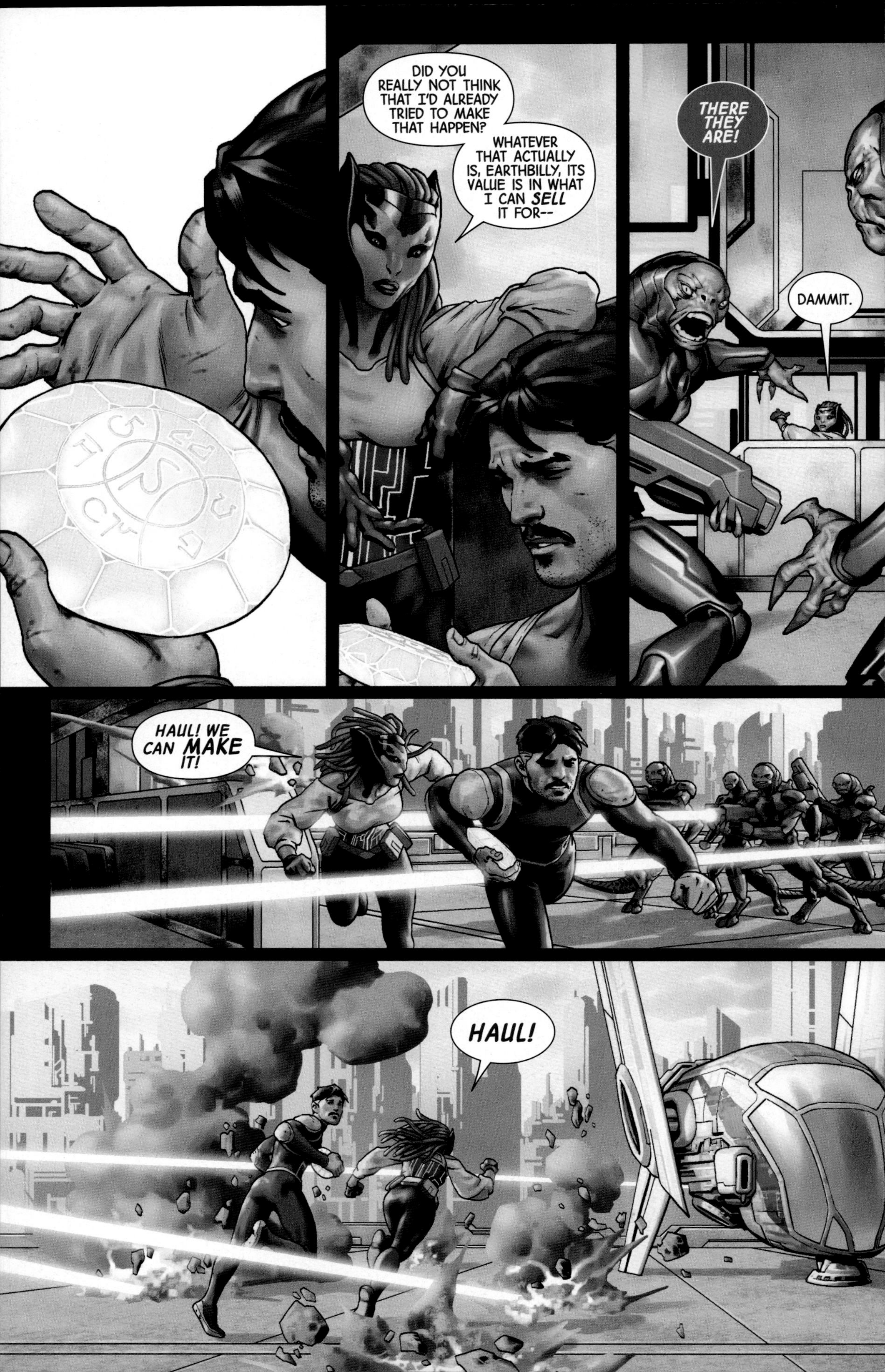
DID YOU REALLY NOT THINK THAT I'D ALREADY TRIED TO MAKE THAT HAPPEN?
WHATEVER THAT ACTUALLY IS, EARTHBILLY, ITS VALUE IS IN WHAT I CAN SELL IT FOR--
THERE THEY ARE!
DAMMIT.
HAUL! WE CAN MAKE IT!
HAUL!

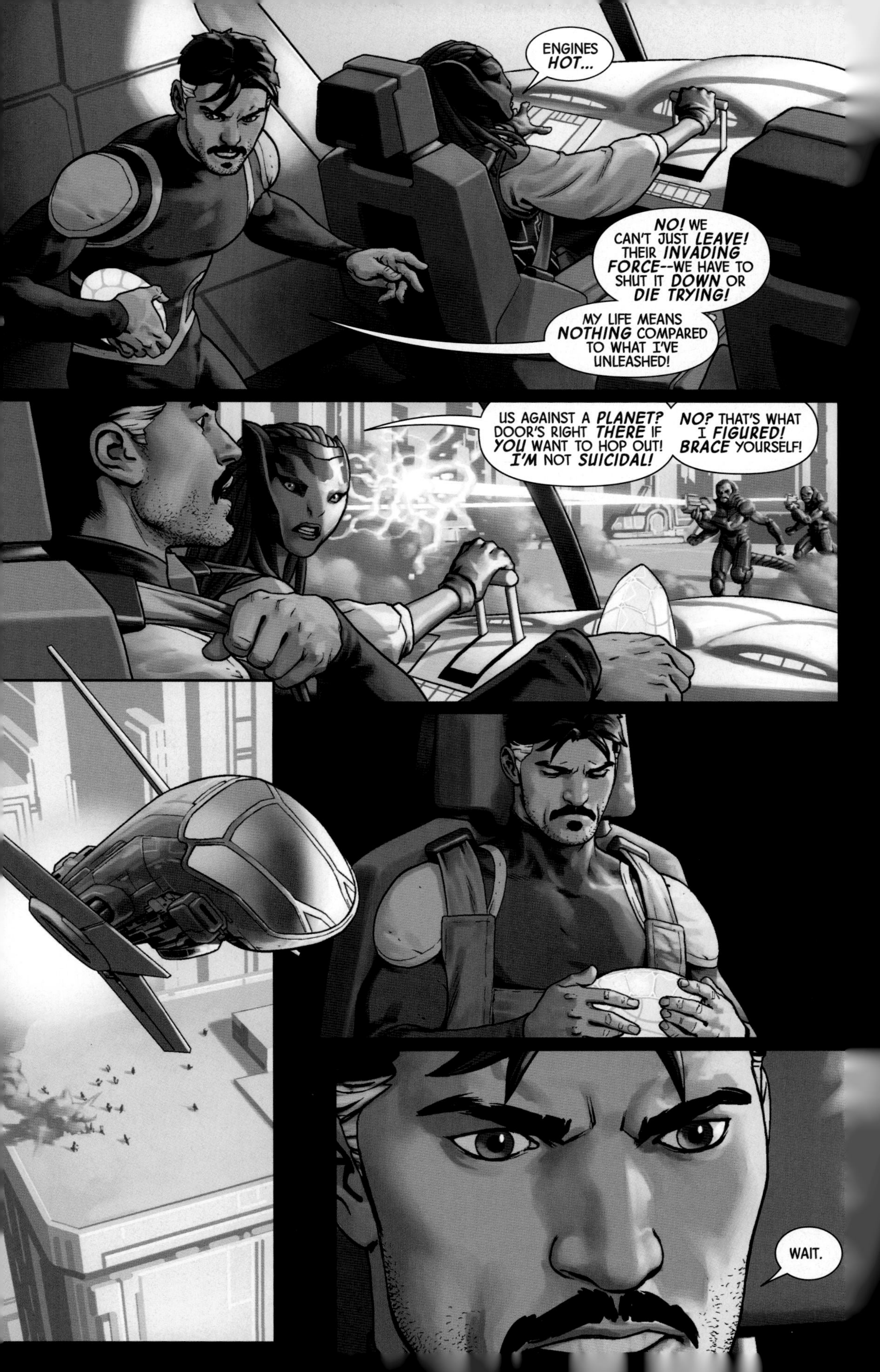
ENGINES HOT...
NO! WE CAN'T JUST LEAVE! THEIR INVADING FORCE--WE HAVE TO SHUT IT DOWN OR DIE TRYING!
MY LIFE MEANS NOTHING COMPARED TO WHAT I'VE UNLEASHED!
US AGAINST A PLANET? DOOR'S RIGHT THERE IF YOU WANT TO HOP OUT! I'M NOT SUICIDAL!
NO? THAT'S WHAT I FIGURED! BRACE YOURSELF!
WAIT.

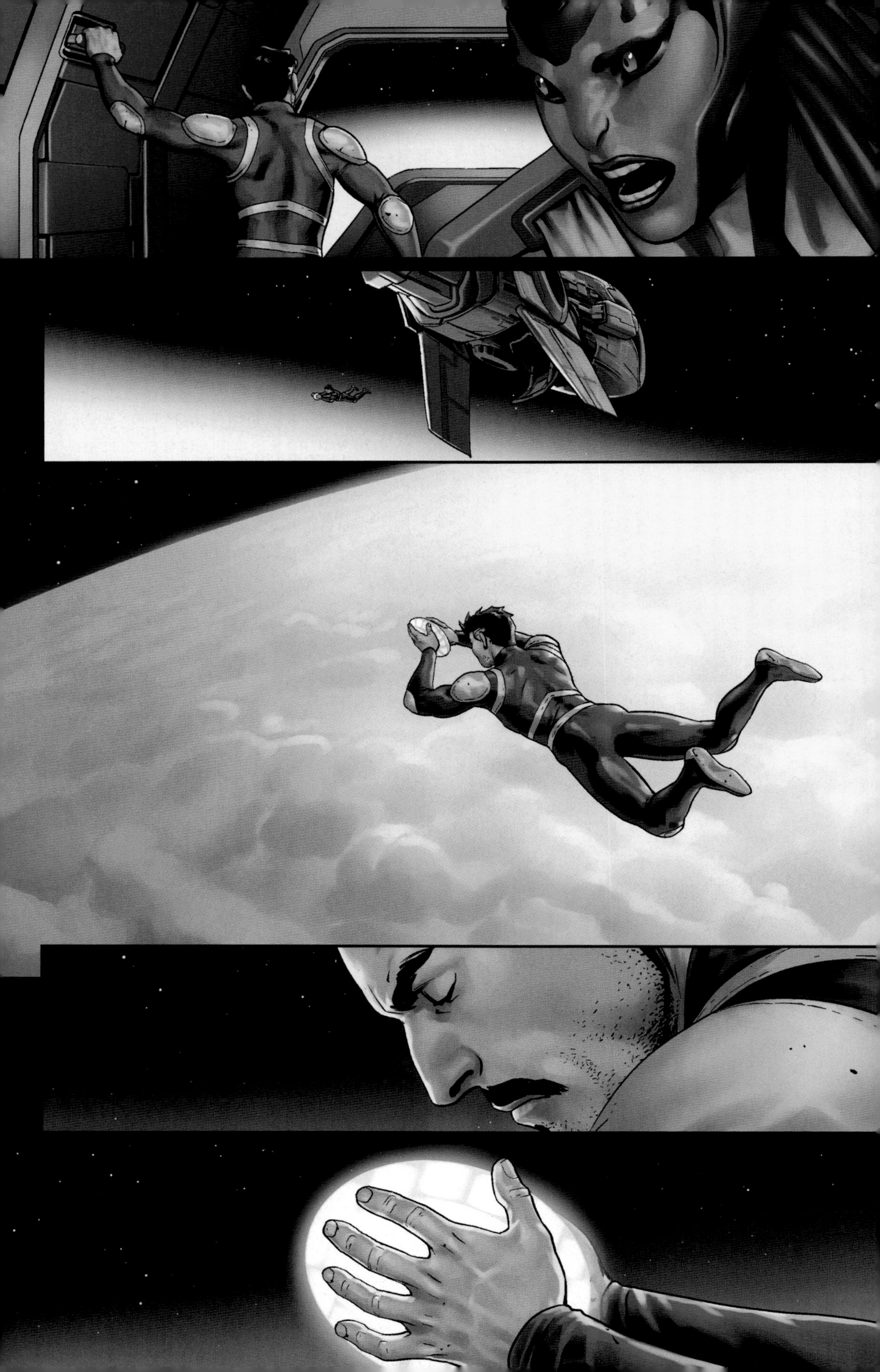

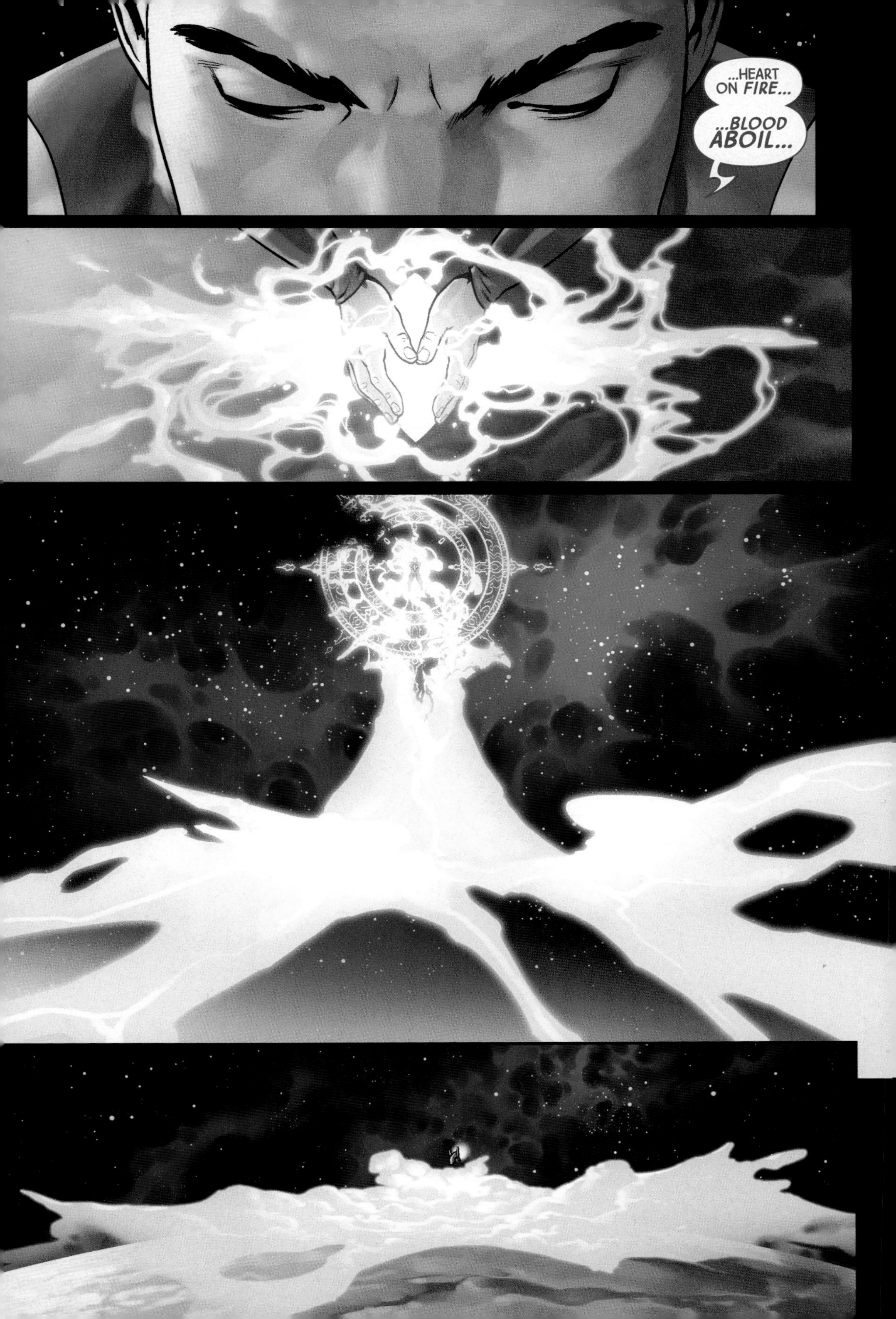
...HEART ON FIRE...
...BLOOD ABOIL...

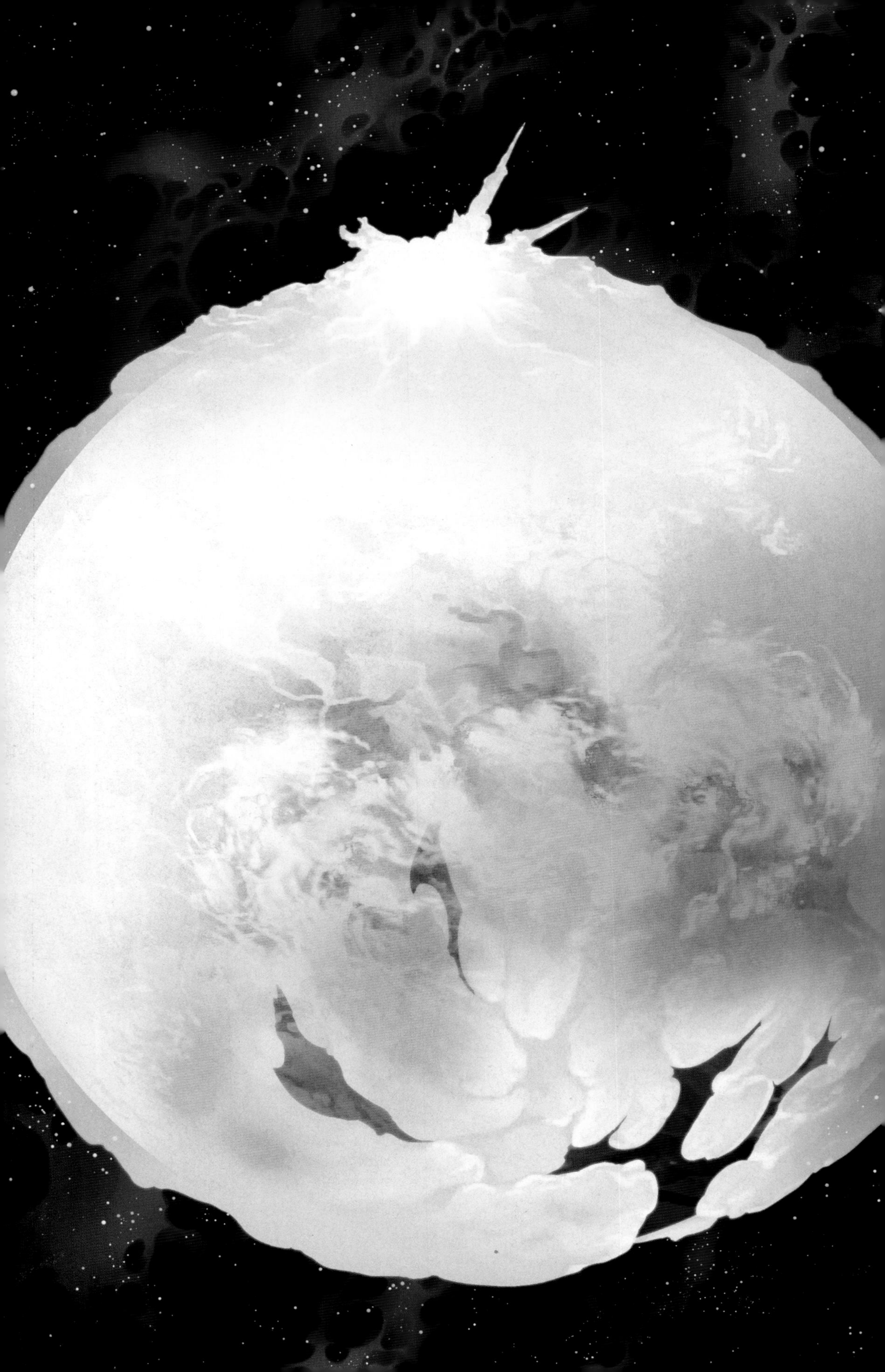

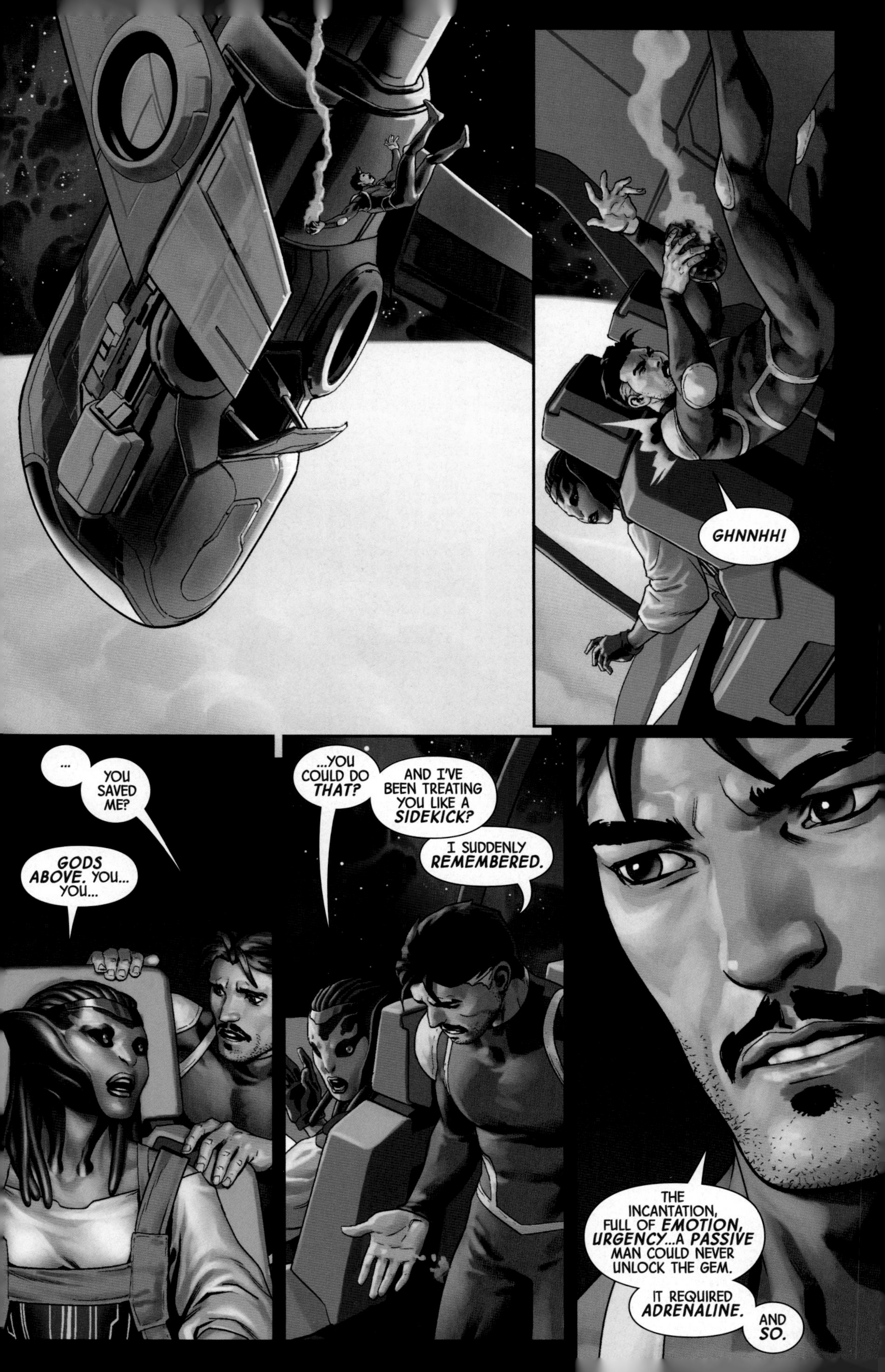
GHNNHH!
...
YOU SAVED ME?
GODS ABOVE. YOU... YOU...
...YOU COULD DO THAT?
AND I'VE BEEN TREATING YOU LIKE A SIDEKICK?
I SUDDENLY REMEMBERED.
THE INCANTATION, FULL OF EMOTION, URGENCY...A PASSIVE MAN COULD NEVER UNLOCK THE GEM.
IT REQUIRED ADRENALINE.
AND SO.

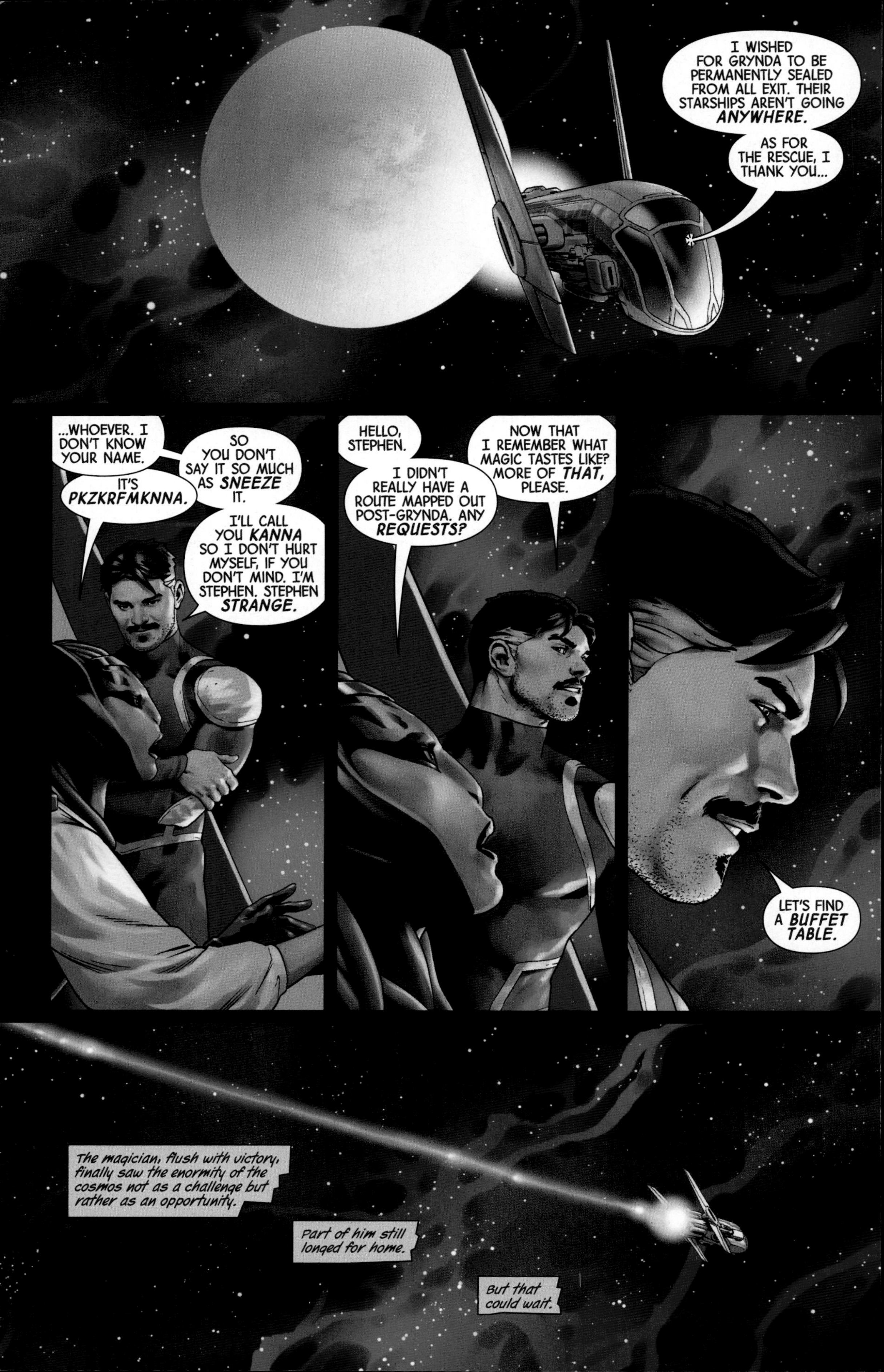
I WISHED FOR GRYNDA TO BE PERMANENTLY SEALED FROM ALL EXIT. THEIR STARSHIPS AREN'T GOING ANYWHERE.
AS FOR THE RESCUE, I THANK YOU...
...WHOEVER. I DON'T KNOW YOUR NAME.
IT'S PKZKRFMKNNA.
SO YOU DON'T SAY IT SO MUCH AS SNEEZE IT.
I'LL CALL YOU KANNA SO I DON'T HURT MYSELF, IF YOU DON'T MIND. I'M STEPHEN. STEPHEN STRANGE.
HELLO, STEPHEN.
I DIDN'T REALLY HAVE A ROUTE MAPPED OUT POST-GRYNDA. ANY REQUESTS?
NOW THAT I REMEMBER WHAT MAGIC TASTES LIKE? MORE OF THAT, PLEASE.
LET'S FIND A BUFFET TABLE.
The magician, flush with victory, finally saw the enormity of the cosmos not as a challenge but rather as an opportunity.
Part of him still longed for home.
But that could wait.

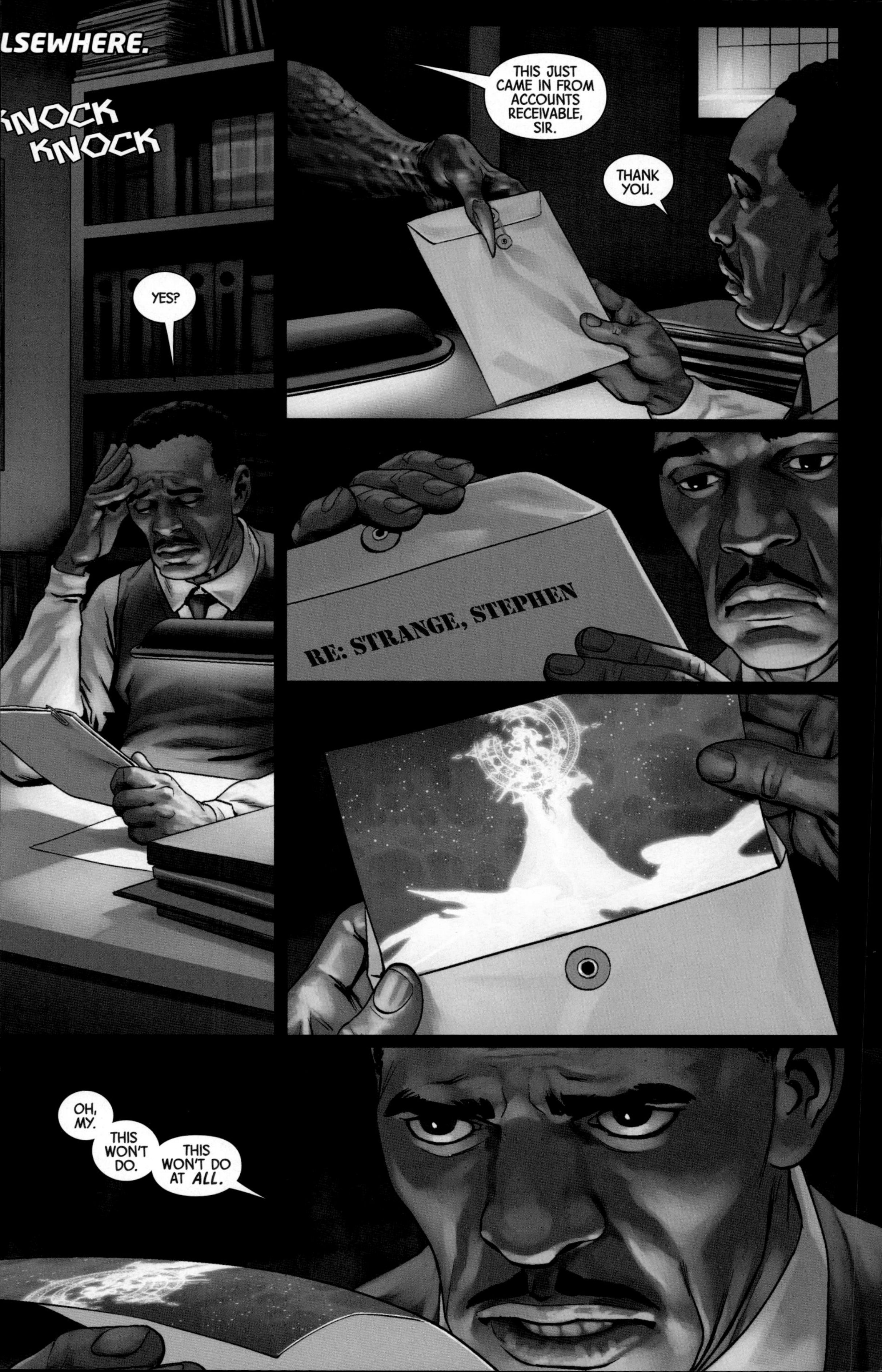

LSEWHERE.
KNOCK KNOCK
YES?
THIS JUST CAME IN FROM ACCOUNTS RECEIVABLE, SIR.
THANK YOU.
RE: STRANGE, STEPHEN
OH, MY.
THIS WON'T DO.
THIS WON'T DO AT ALL.

3

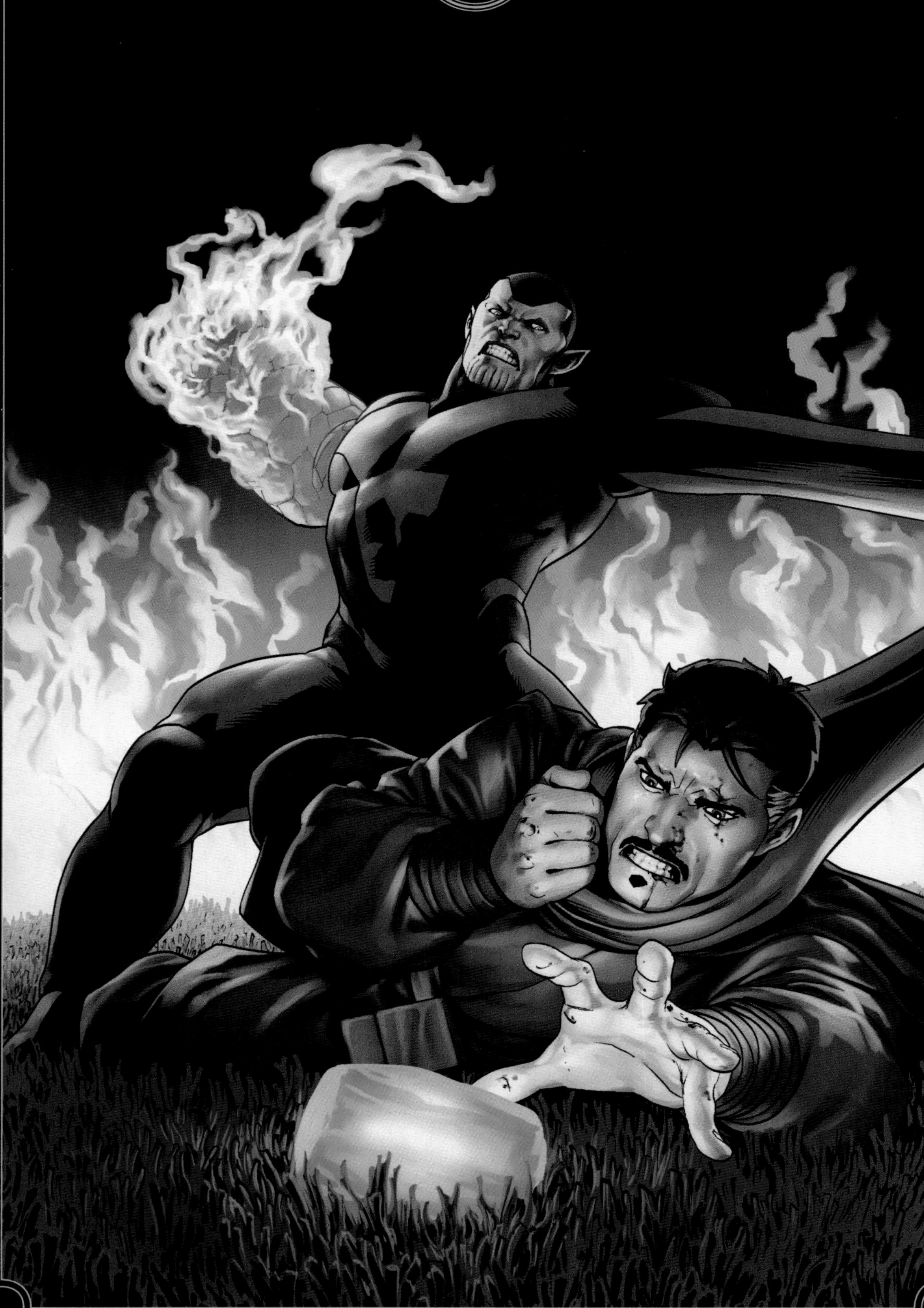

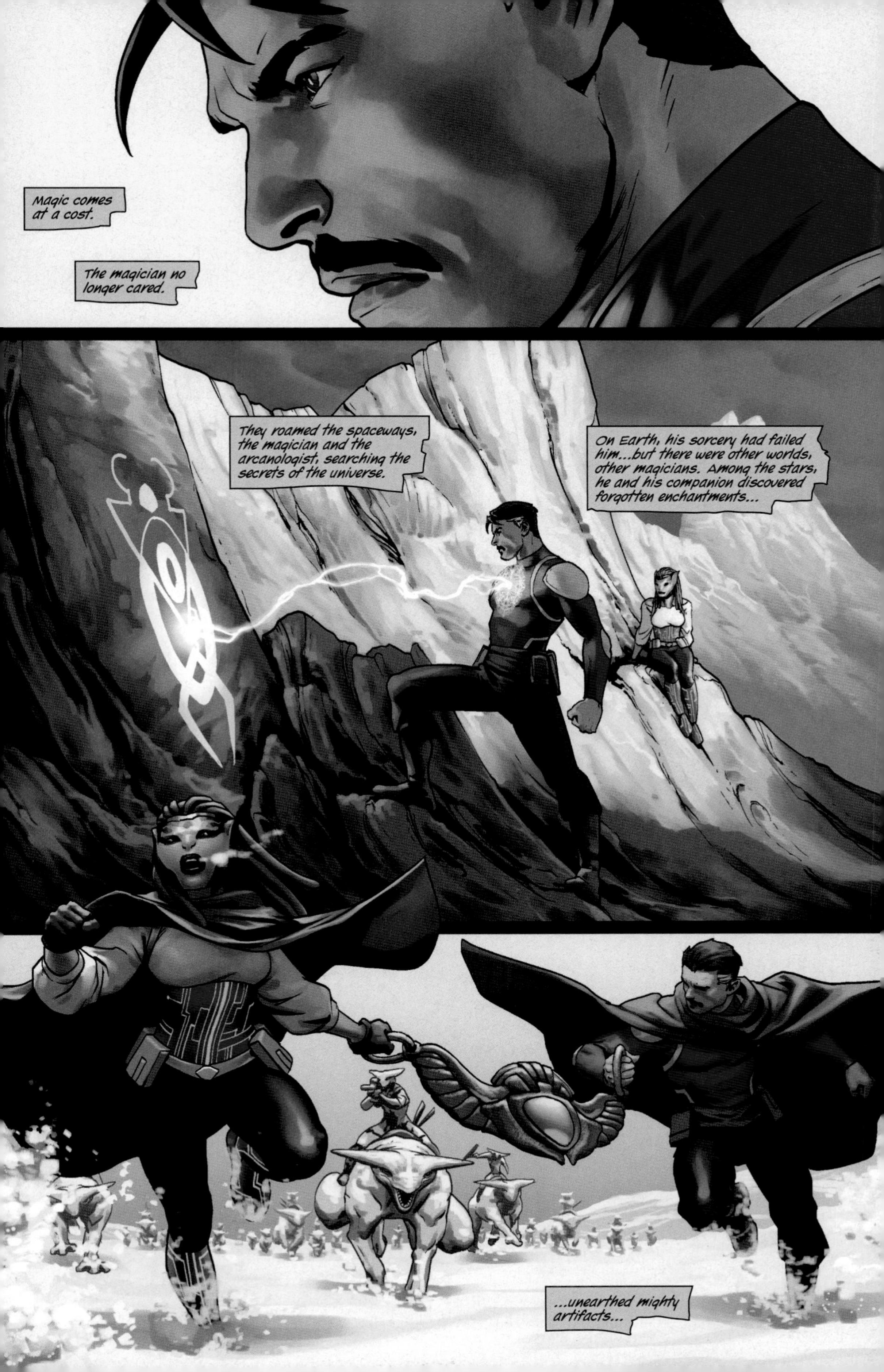
Magic comes at a cost.
The magician no longer cared.
They roamed the spaceways, the magician and the arcanologist, searching the secrets of the universe.
On Earth, his sorcery had failed him...but there were other worlds, other magicians. Among the stars, he and his companion discovered forgotten enchantments...
...unearthed mighty artifacts...

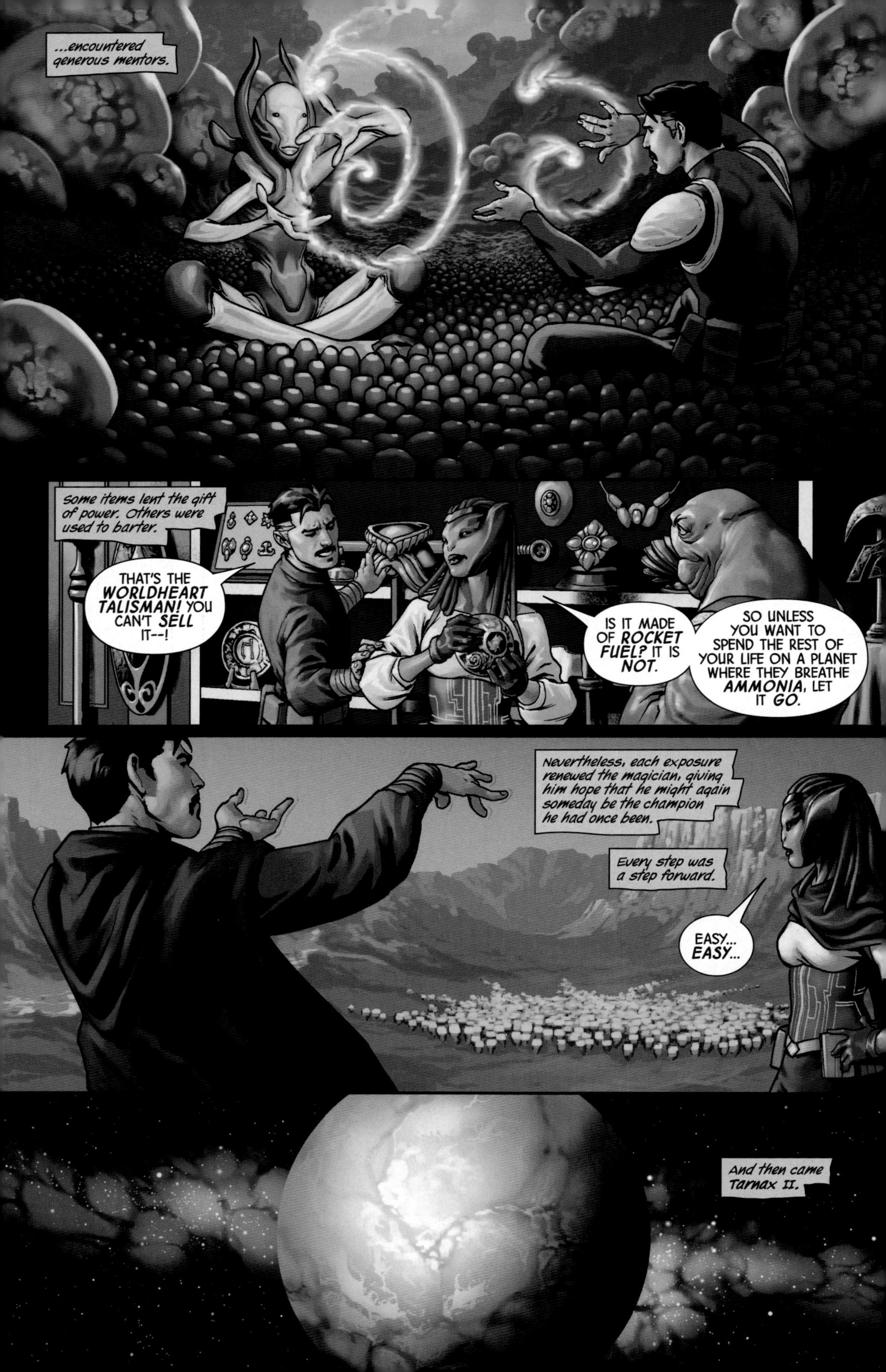
...encountered generous mentors.
Some items lent the gift of power. Others were used to barter.
THAT'S THE WORLDHEART TALISMAN! YOU CAN'T SELL IT--!
IS IT MADE OF ROCKET FUEL? IT IS NOT.
SO UNLESS YOU WANT TO SPEND THE REST OF YOUR LIFE ON A PLANET WHERE THEY BREATHE AMMONIA, LET IT GO.
Nevertheless, each exposure renewed the magician, giving him hope that he might again someday be the champion he had once been.
Every step was a step forward.
EASY... EASY...
And then came Tarnax II.

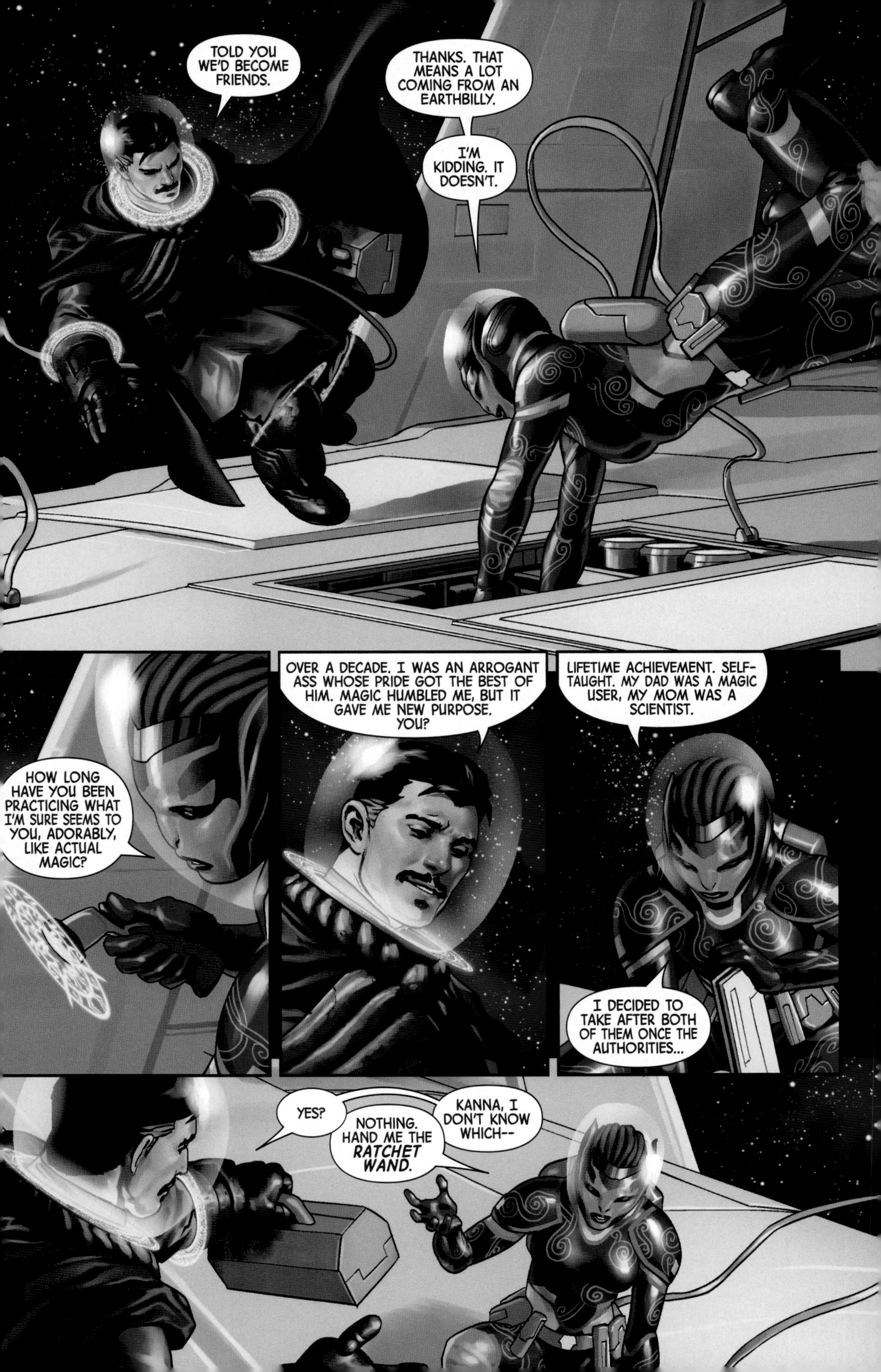
TOLD YOU WE'D BECOME FRIENDS.
THANKS. THAT MEANS A LOT COMING FROM AN EARTHBILLY.
I'M KIDDING. IT DOESN'T.
HOW LONG HAVE YOU BEEN PRACTICING WHAT I'M SURE SEEMS TO YOU, ADORABLY, LIKE ACTUAL MAGIC?
OVER A DECADE. I WAS AN ARROGANT ASS WHOSE PRIDE GOT THE BEST OF HIM. MAGIC HUMBLED ME, BUT IT GAVE ME NEW PURPOSE. YOU?
LIFETIME ACHIEVEMENT. SELF-TAUGHT. MY DAD WAS A MAGIC USER, MY MOM WAS A SCIENTIST.
I DECIDED TO TAKE AFTER BOTH OF THEM ONCE THE AUTHORITIES...
KANNA, I DON'T KNOW WHICH--
YES?
NOTHING. HAND ME THE *RATCHET WAND.*

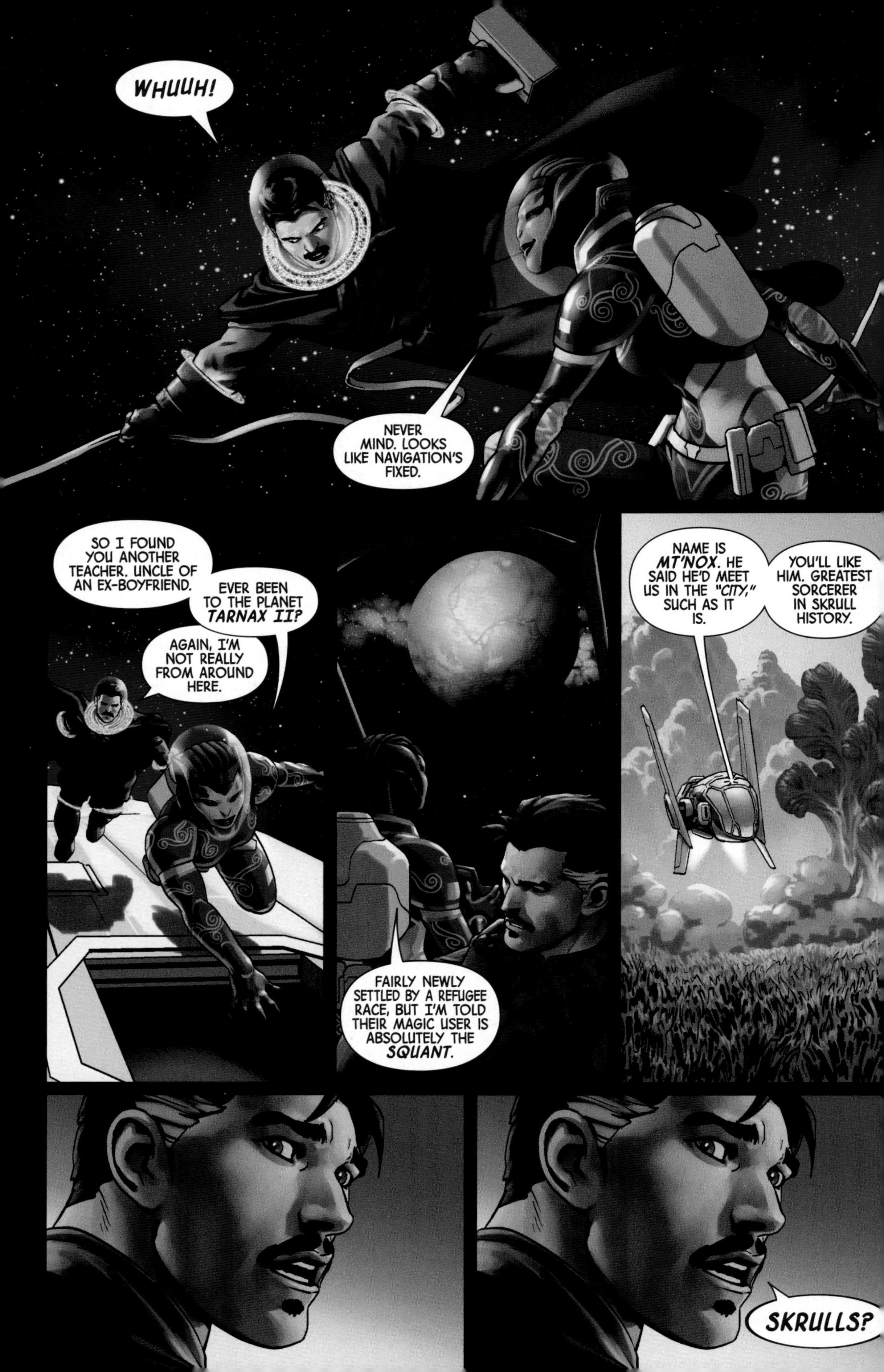
WHUUH!
NEVER MIND. LOOKS LIKE NAVIGATION'S FIXED.
SO I FOUND YOU ANOTHER TEACHER. UNCLE OF AN EX-BOYFRIEND.
EVER BEEN TO THE PLANET TARNAX II?
AGAIN, I'M NOT REALLY FROM AROUND HERE.
FAIRLY NEWLY SETTLED BY A REFUGEE RACE, BUT I'M TOLD THEIR MAGIC USER IS ABSOLUTELY THE SQUANT.
NAME IS MT'NOX. HE SAID HE'D MEET US IN THE "CITY," SUCH AS IT IS.
YOU'LL LIKE HIM. GREATEST SORCERER IN SKRULL HISTORY.
SKRULLS?

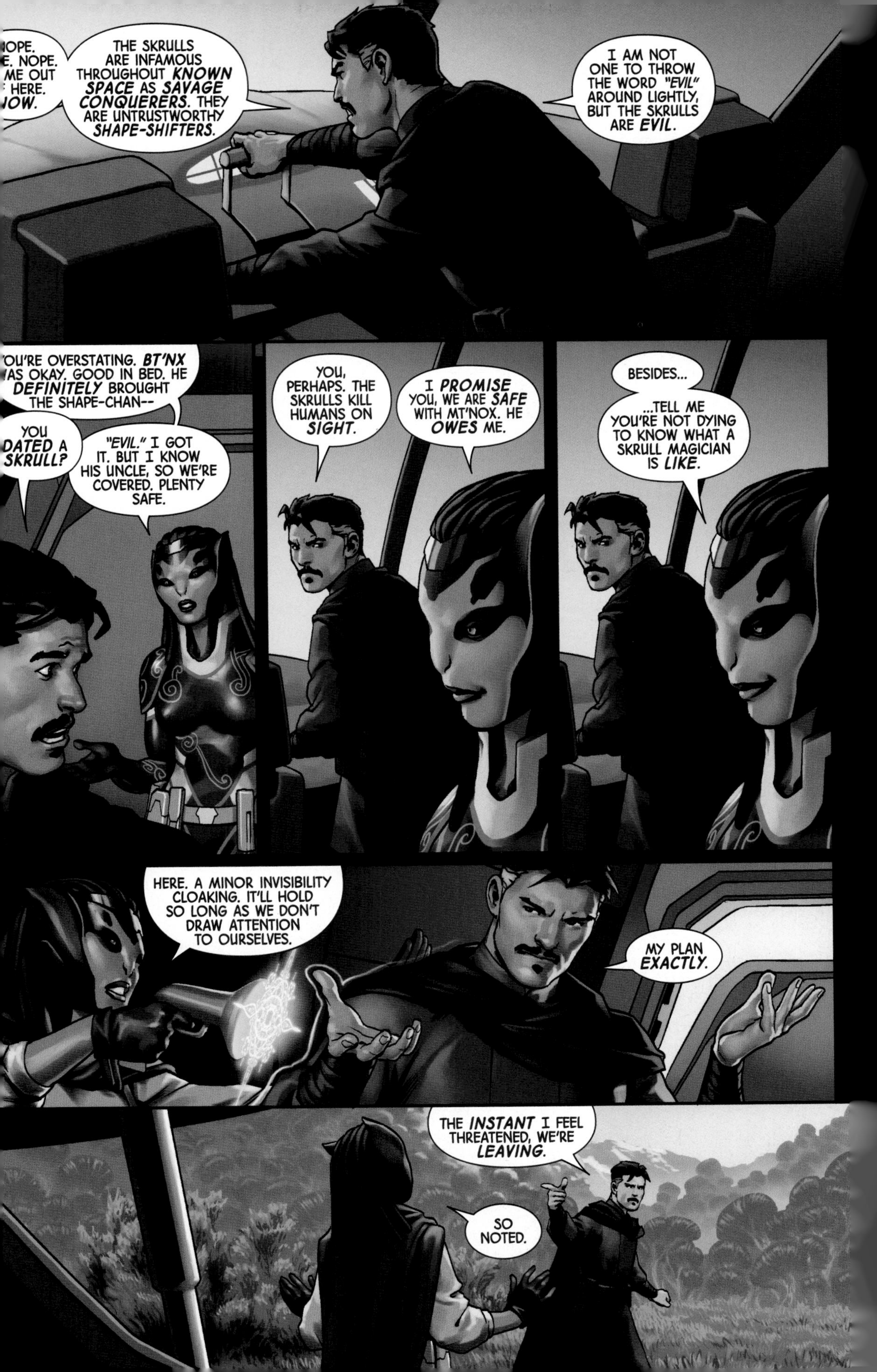
NOPE.
E. NOPE.
ME OUT
F HERE.
NOW.
THE SKRULLS ARE INFAMOUS THROUGHOUT KNOWN SPACE AS SAVAGE CONQUERERS. THEY ARE UNTRUSTWORTHY SHAPE-SHIFTERS.
I AM NOT ONE TO THROW THE WORD "EVIL" AROUND LIGHTLY, BUT THE SKRULLS ARE EVIL.
OU'RE OVERSTATING. BT'NX
AS OKAY. GOOD IN BED. HE DEFINITELY BROUGHT THE SHAPE-CHAN--
YOU DATED A SKRULL?
"EVIL." I GOT IT. BUT I KNOW HIS UNCLE, SO WE'RE COVERED. PLENTY SAFE.
YOU, PERHAPS. THE SKRULLS KILL HUMANS ON SIGHT.
I PROMISE YOU, WE ARE SAFE WITH MT'NOX. HE OWES ME.
BESIDES...
...TELL ME YOU'RE NOT DYING TO KNOW WHAT A SKRULL MAGICIAN IS LIKE.
HERE. A MINOR INVISIBILITY CLOAKING. IT'LL HOLD SO LONG AS WE DON'T DRAW ATTENTION TO OURSELVES.
MY PLAN EXACTLY.
THE INSTANT I FEEL THREATENED, WE'RE LEAVING.
SO NOTED.

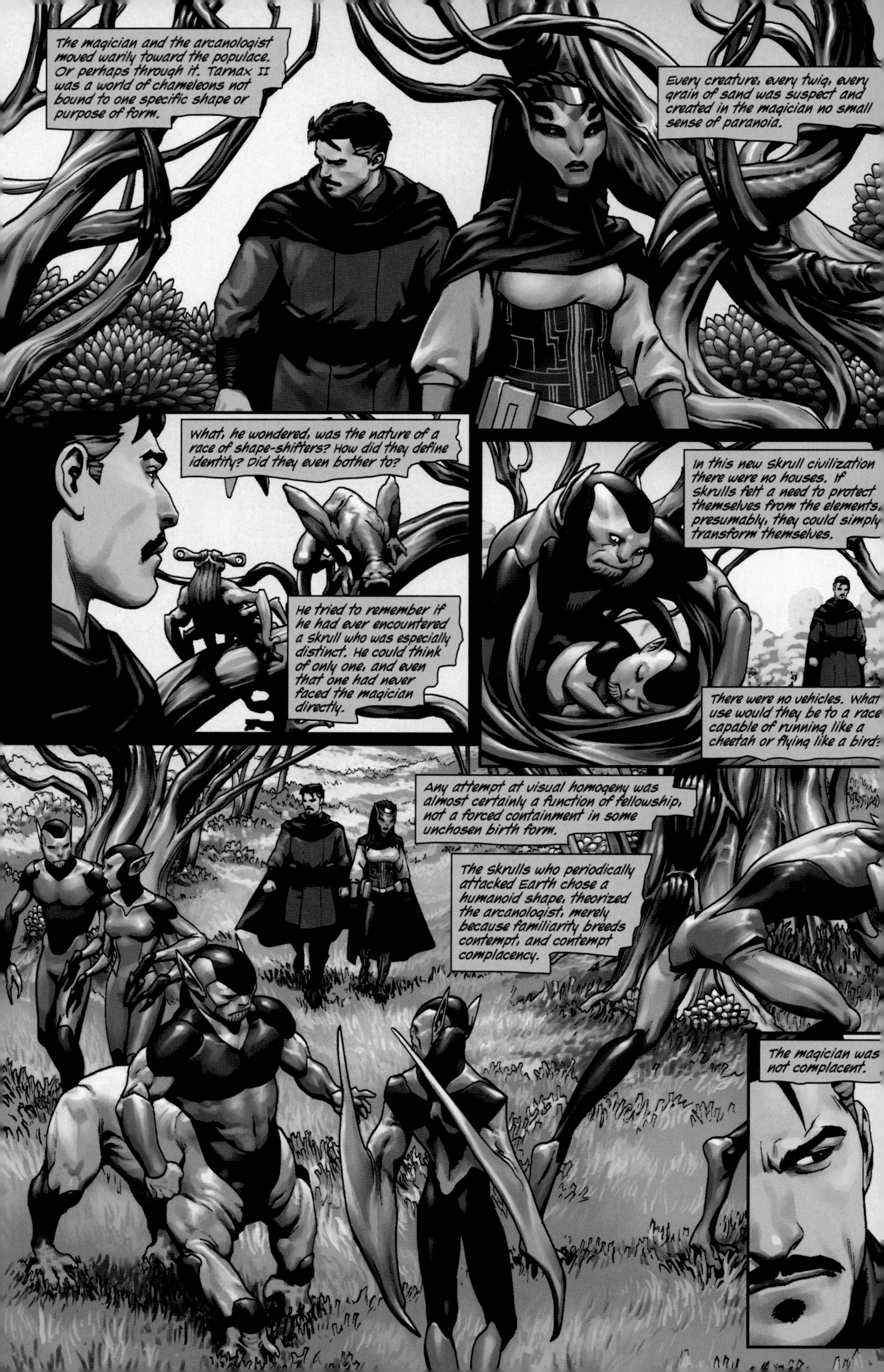
The magician and the arcanologist moved warily toward the populace. Or perhaps through it. Tarnax II was a world of chameleons not bound to one specific shape or purpose of form.
Every creature, every twig, every grain of sand was suspect and created in the magician no small sense of paranoia.
What, he wondered, was the nature of a race of shape-shifters? How did they define identity? Did they even bother to?
He tried to remember if he had ever encountered a skrull who was especially distinct. He could think of only one, and even that one had never faced the magician directly.
In this new skrull civilization there were no houses. If skrulls felt a need to protect themselves from the elements, presumably, they could simply transform themselves.
There were no vehicles. What use would they be to a race capable of running like a cheetah or flying like a bird?
Any attempt at visual homogeny was almost certainly a function of fellowship, not a forced containment in some unchosen birth form.
The skrulls who periodically attacked Earth chose a humanoid shape, theorized the arcanologist, merely because familiarity breeds contempt, and contempt complacency.
The magician was not complacent.

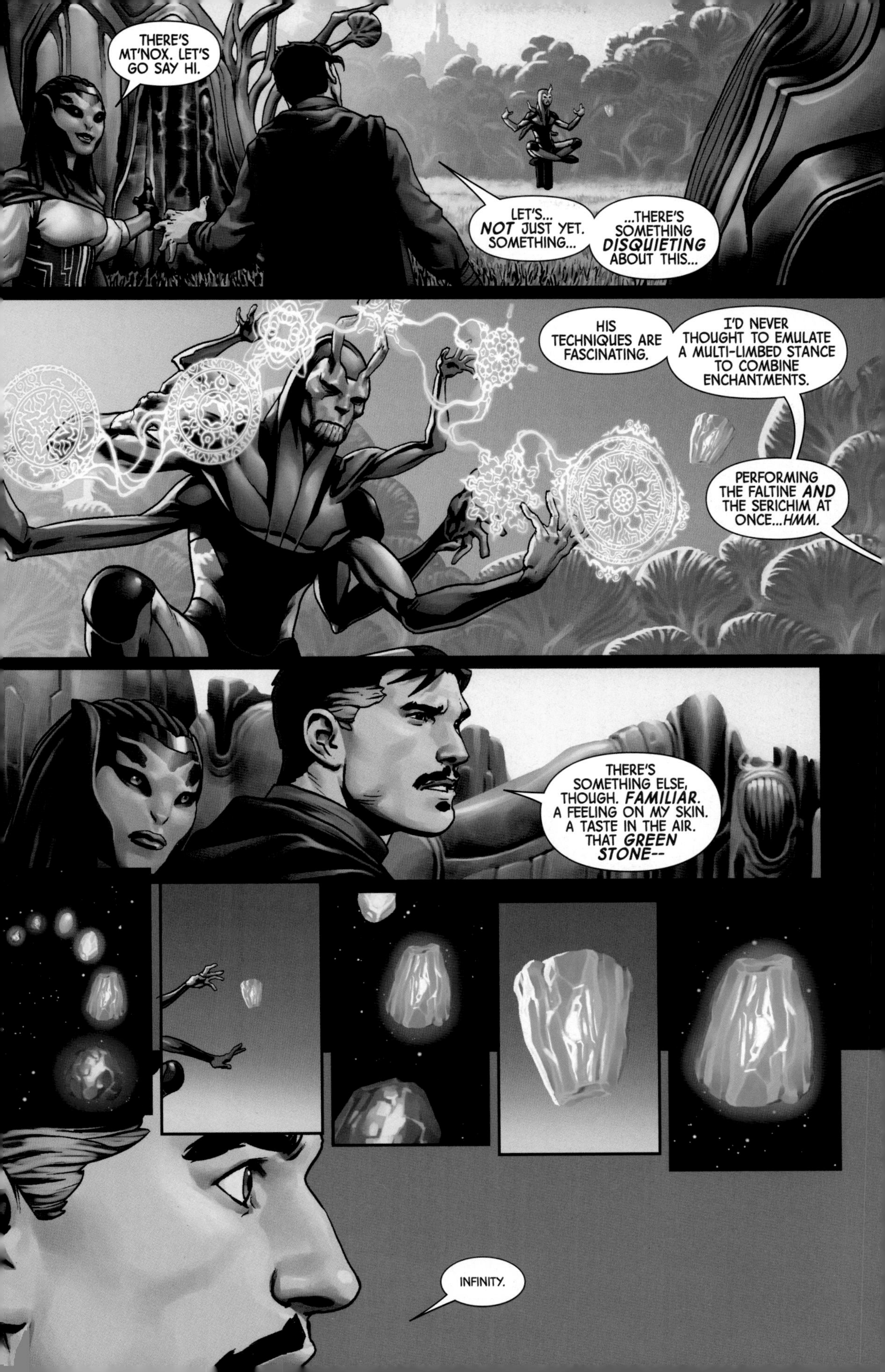
THERE'S MT'NOX. LET'S GO SAY HI.
LET'S... NOT JUST YET. SOMETHING...
...THERE'S SOMETHING DISQUIETING ABOUT THIS...
HIS TECHNIQUES ARE FASCINATING.
I'D NEVER THOUGHT TO EMULATE A MULTI-LIMBED STANCE TO COMBINE ENCHANTMENTS.
PERFORMING THE FALTINE AND THE SERICHIM AT ONCE...HMM.
THERE'S SOMETHING ELSE, THOUGH. FAMILIAR. A FEELING ON MY SKIN. A TASTE IN THE AIR. THAT GREEN STONE--
INFINITY.

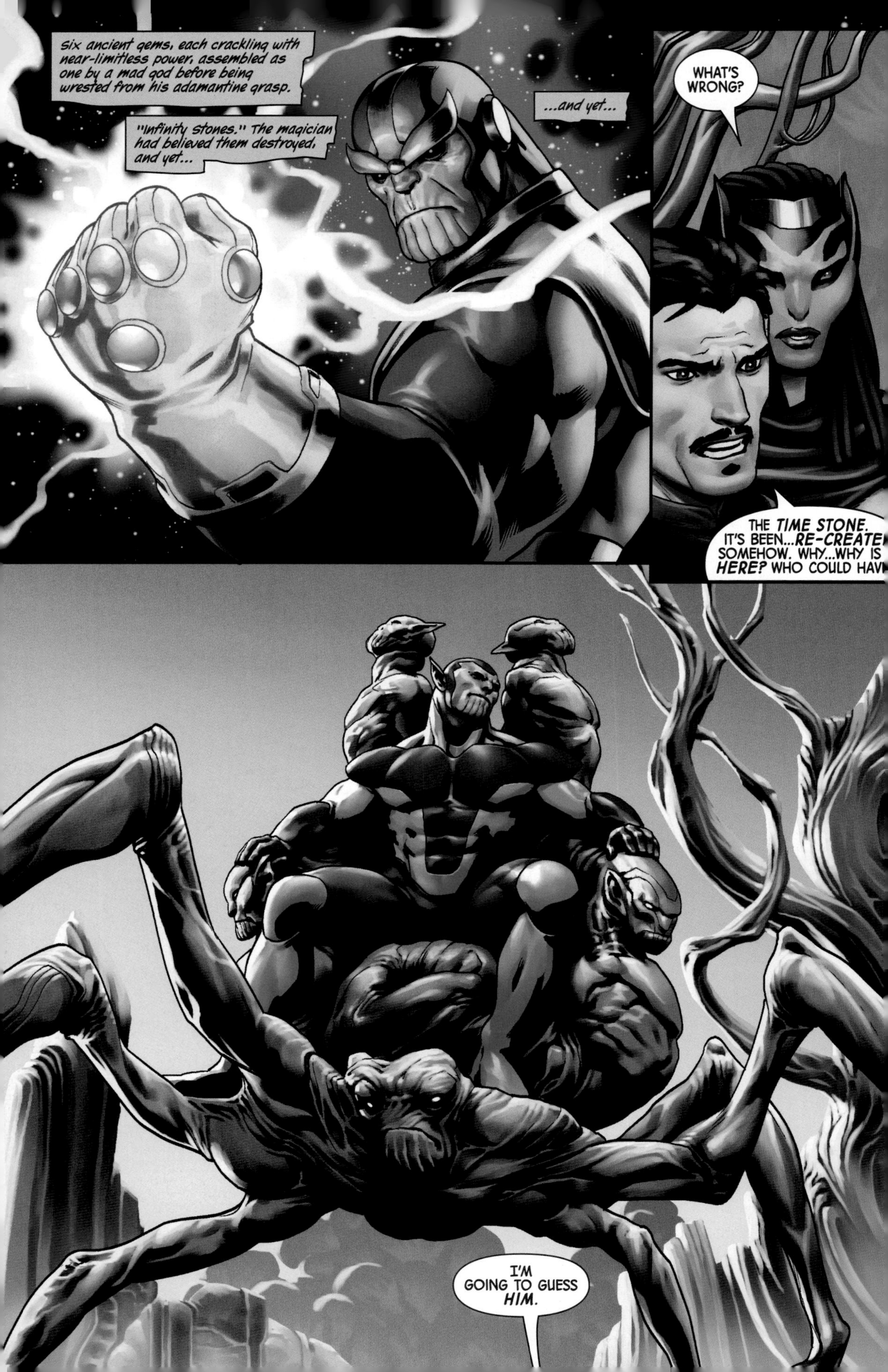
Six ancient gems, each crackling with near-limitless power, assembled as one by a mad god before being wrested from his adamantine grasp.
"Infinity stones." The magician had believed them destroyed, and yet...
...and yet...
WHAT'S WRONG?
THE TIME STONE. IT'S BEEN...RE-CREATE SOMEHOW. WHY...WHY IS HERE? WHO COULD HAV
I'M GOING TO GUESS HIM.

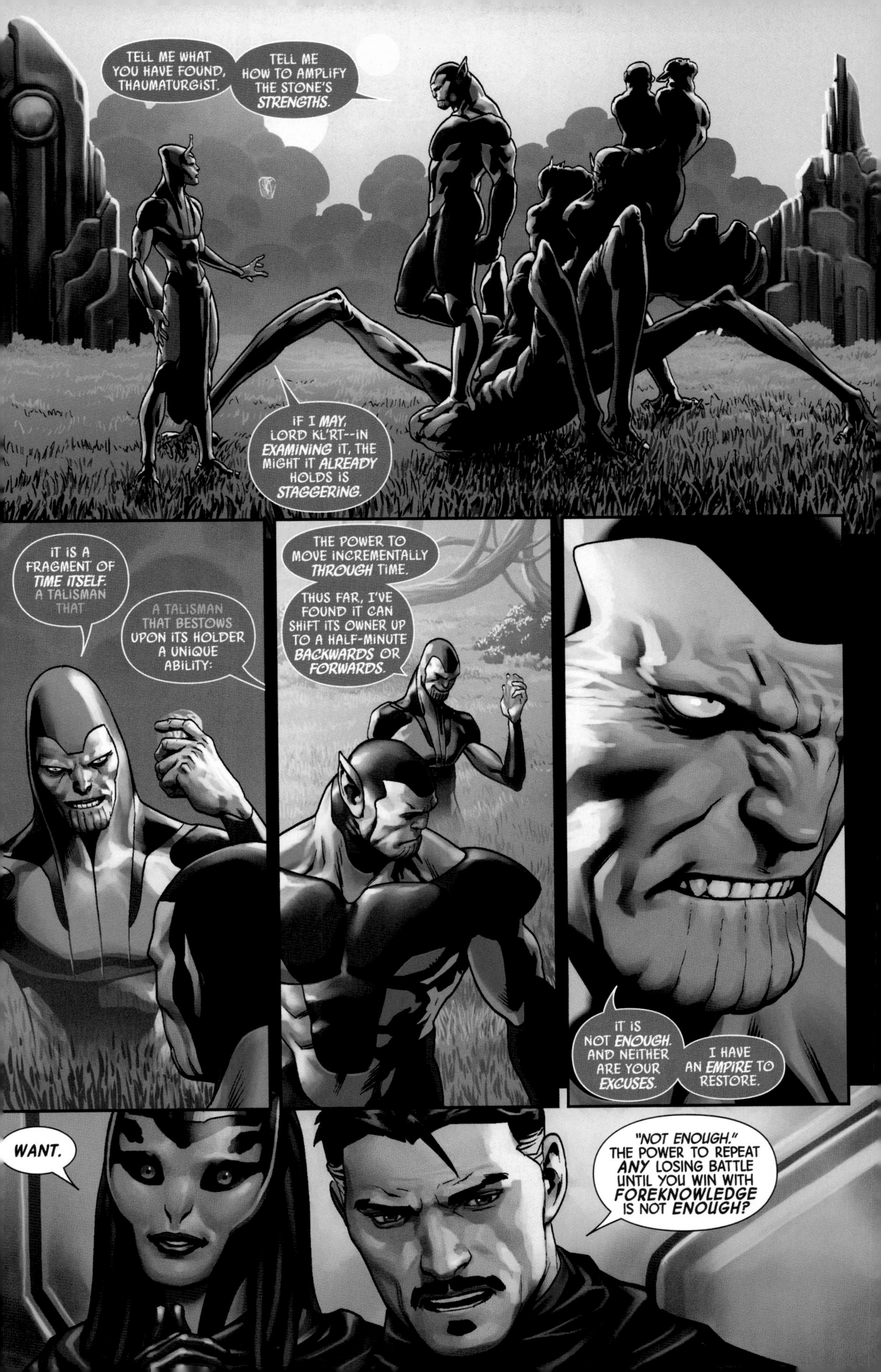
TELL ME WHAT YOU HAVE FOUND, THAUMATURGIST.
TELL ME HOW TO AMPLIFY THE STONE'S STRENGTHS.
IF I MAY, LORD KL'RT--IN EXAMINING IT, THE MIGHT IT ALREADY HOLDS IS STAGGERING.
IT IS A FRAGMENT OF TIME ITSELF. A TALISMAN THAT
A TALISMAN THAT BESTOWS UPON ITS HOLDER A UNIQUE ABILITY:
THE POWER TO MOVE INCREMENTALLY THROUGH TIME.
THUS FAR, I'VE FOUND IT CAN SHIFT ITS OWNER UP TO A HALF-MINUTE BACKWARDS OR FORWARDS.
IT IS NOT ENOUGH. AND NEITHER ARE YOUR EXCUSES.
I HAVE AN EMPIRE TO RESTORE.
WANT.
"NOT ENOUGH." THE POWER TO REPEAT ANY LOSING BATTLE UNTIL YOU WIN WITH FOREKNOWLEDGE IS NOT ENOUGH?

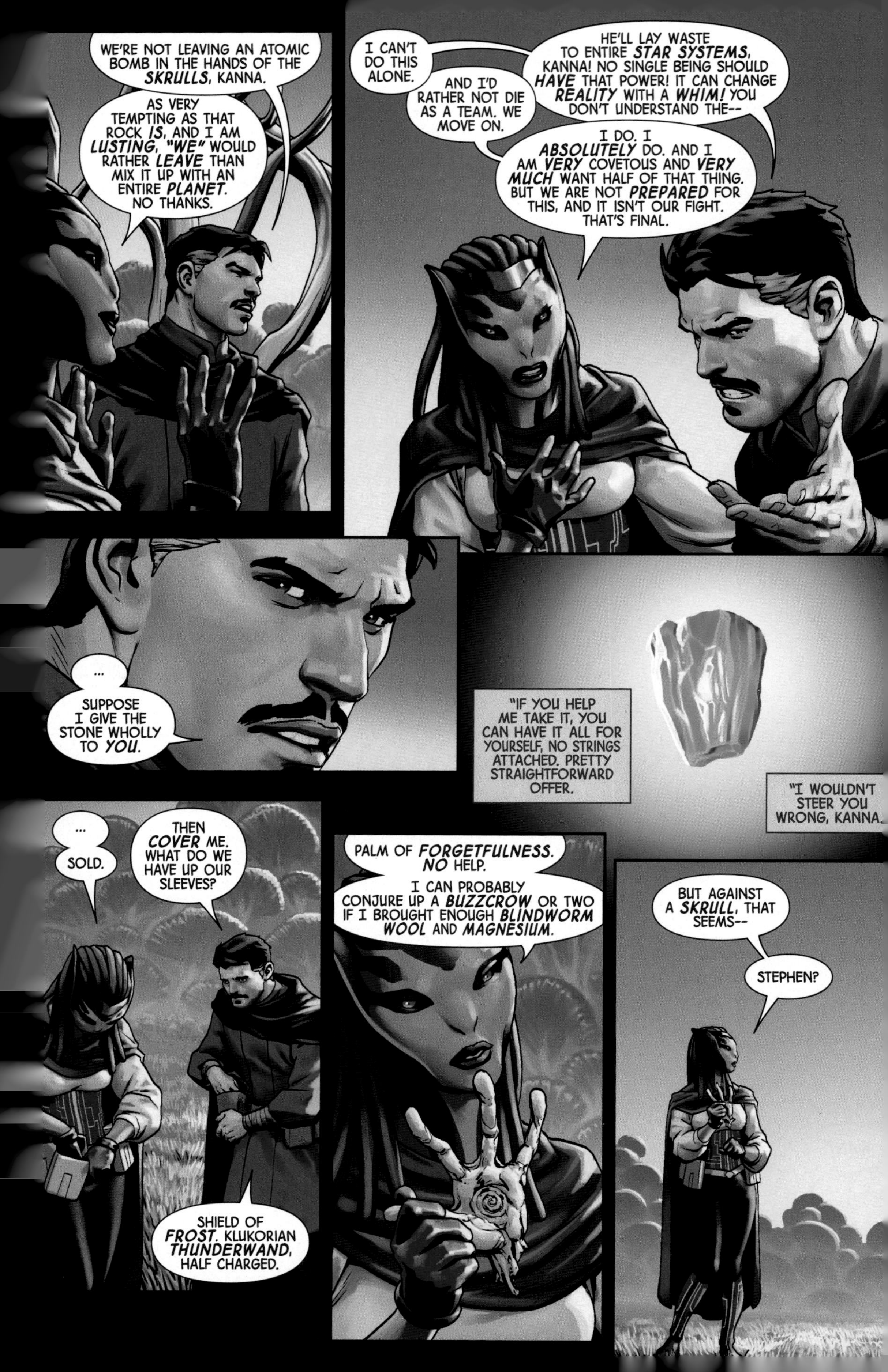
WE'RE NOT LEAVING AN ATOMIC BOMB IN THE HANDS OF THE SKRULLS, KANNA.
AS VERY TEMPTING AS THAT ROCK IS, AND I AM LUSTING, "WE" WOULD RATHER LEAVE THAN MIX IT UP WITH AN ENTIRE PLANET. NO THANKS.
I CAN'T DO THIS ALONE.
HE'LL LAY WASTE TO ENTIRE STAR SYSTEMS, KANNA! NO SINGLE BEING SHOULD HAVE THAT POWER! IT CAN CHANGE REALITY WITH A WHIM! YOU DON'T UNDERSTAND THE--
AND I'D RATHER NOT DIE AS A TEAM. WE MOVE ON.
I DO. I ABSOLUTELY DO. AND I AM VERY COVETOUS AND VERY MUCH WANT HALF OF THAT THING. BUT WE ARE NOT PREPARED FOR THIS, AND IT ISN'T OUR FIGHT. THAT'S FINAL.
...
SUPPOSE I GIVE THE STONE WHOLLY TO YOU.
"IF YOU HELP ME TAKE IT, YOU CAN HAVE IT ALL FOR YOURSELF, NO STRINGS ATTACHED. PRETTY STRAIGHTFORWARD OFFER.
"I WOULDN'T STEER YOU WRONG, KANNA.
...
SOLD.
THEN COVER ME. WHAT DO WE HAVE UP OUR SLEEVES?
SHIELD OF FROST. KLUKORIAN THUNDERWAND, HALF CHARGED.
PALM OF FORGETFULNESS. NO HELP.
I CAN PROBABLY CONJURE UP A BUZZCROW OR TWO IF I BROUGHT ENOUGH BLINDWORM WOOL AND MAGNESIUM.
BUT AGAINST A SKRULL, THAT SEEMS--
STEPHEN?

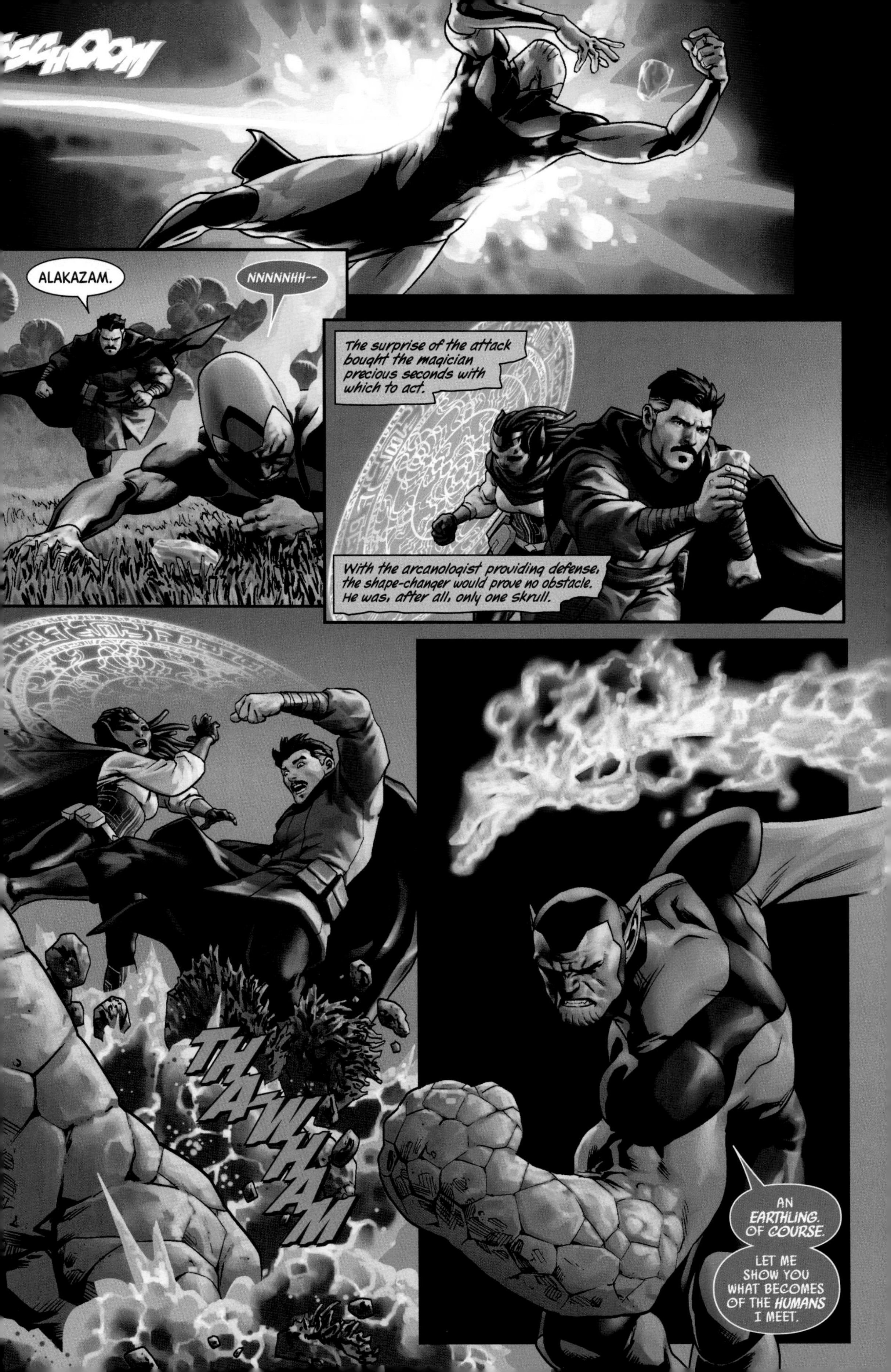
SCHOOM
ALAKAZAM.
NNNNNHH--
The surprise of the attack bought the magician precious seconds with which to act.
With the arcanologist providing defense, the shape-changer would prove no obstacle. He was, after all, only one skrull.
THAWHAM
AN EARTHLING. OF COURSE.
LET ME SHOW YOU WHAT BECOMES OF THE HUMANS I MEET.

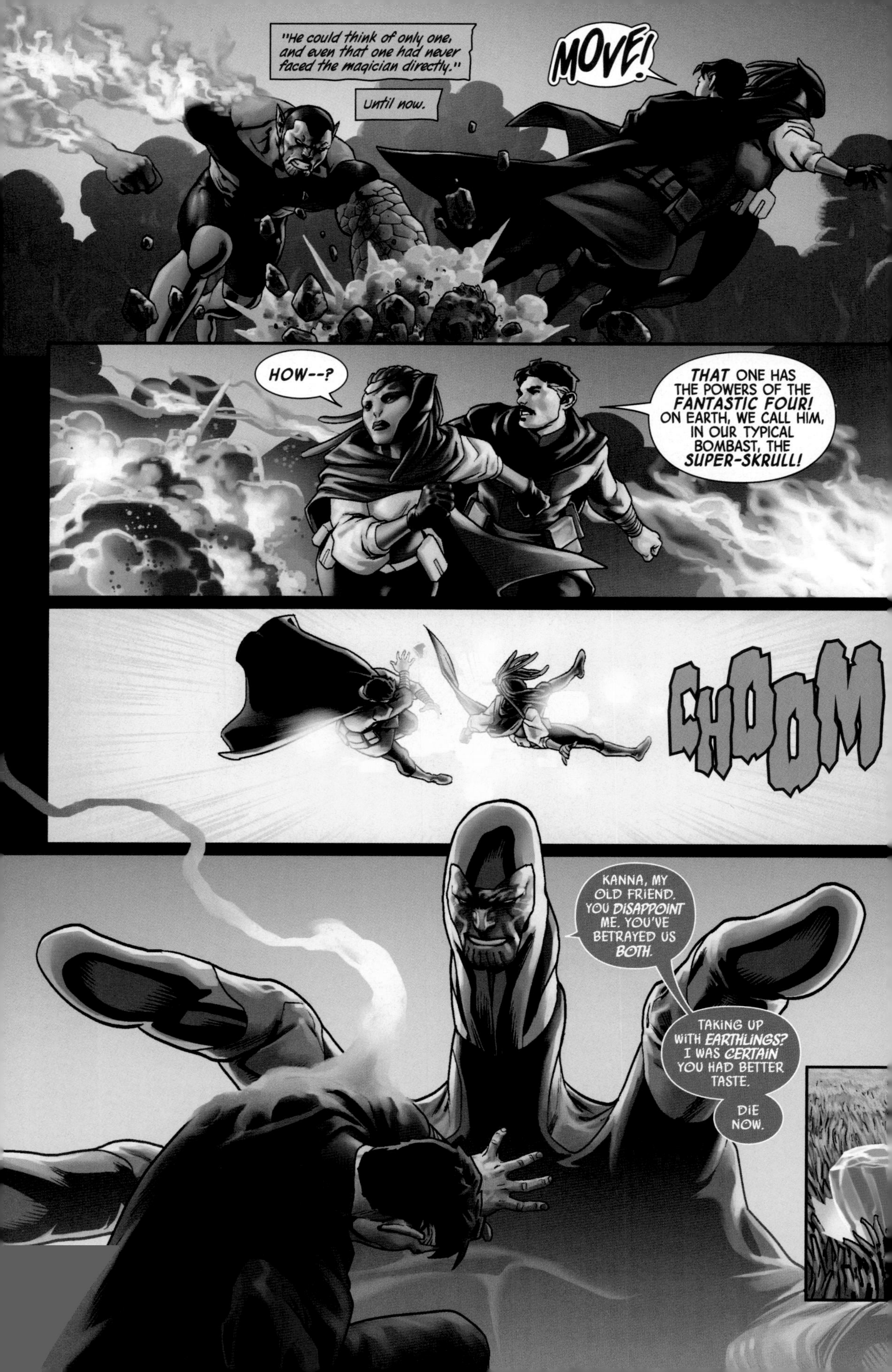
"He could think of only one, and even that one had never faced the magician directly."
Until now.
MOVE!
HOW--?
THAT ONE HAS THE POWERS OF THE FANTASTIC FOUR! ON EARTH, WE CALL HIM, IN OUR TYPICAL BOMBAST, THE SUPER-SKRULL!
CHOOM
KANNA, MY OLD FRIEND. YOU DISAPPOINT ME. YOU'VE BETRAYED US BOTH.
TAKING UP WITH EARTHLINGS? I WAS CERTAIN YOU HAD BETTER TASTE.
DIE NOW.

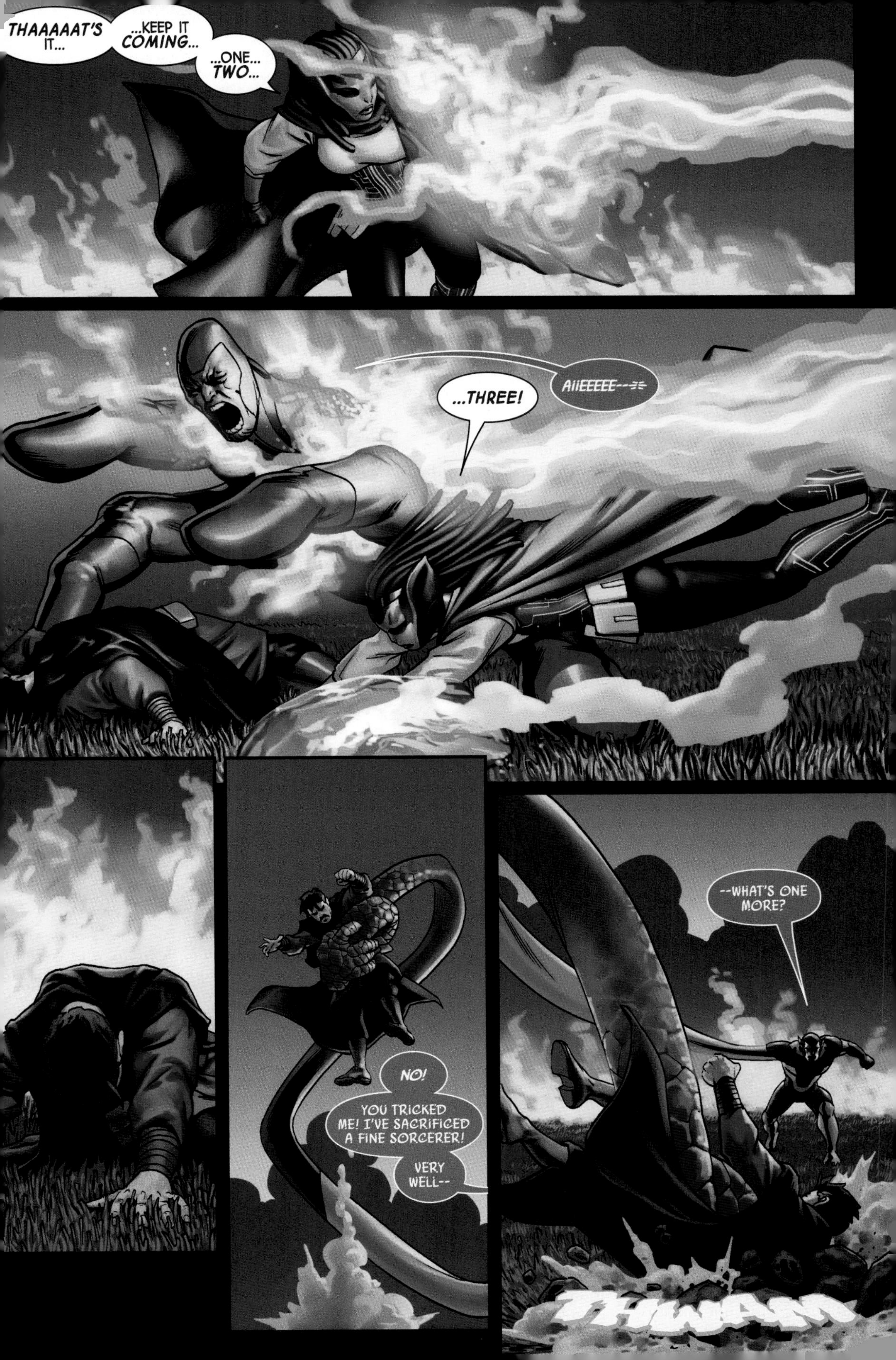
THAAAAAT'S IT...
...KEEP IT COMING...
...ONE... TWO...
AIIEEEEE--
...THREE!
NO!
YOU TRICKED ME! I'VE SACRIFICED A FINE SORCERER!
VERY WELL--
--WHAT'S ONE MORE?
THWAM

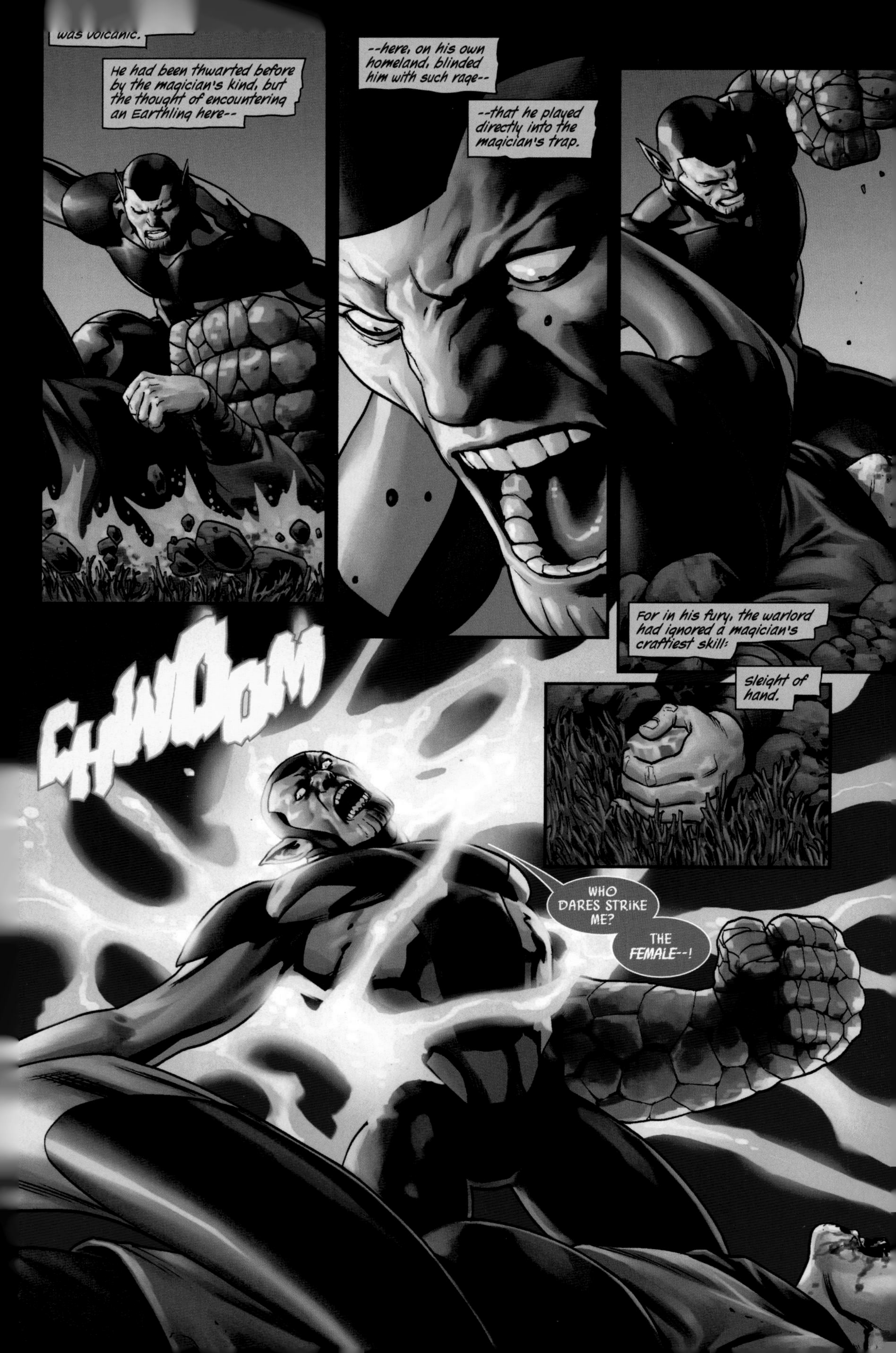
was volcanic.
He had been thwarted before by the magician's kind, but the thought of encountering an Earthling here--
--here, on his own homeland, blinded him with such rage--
--that he played directly into the magician's trap.
For in his fury, the warlord had ignored a magician's craftiest skill:
sleight of hand.
CHWOOM
WHO DARES STRIKE ME?
THE FEMALE--!

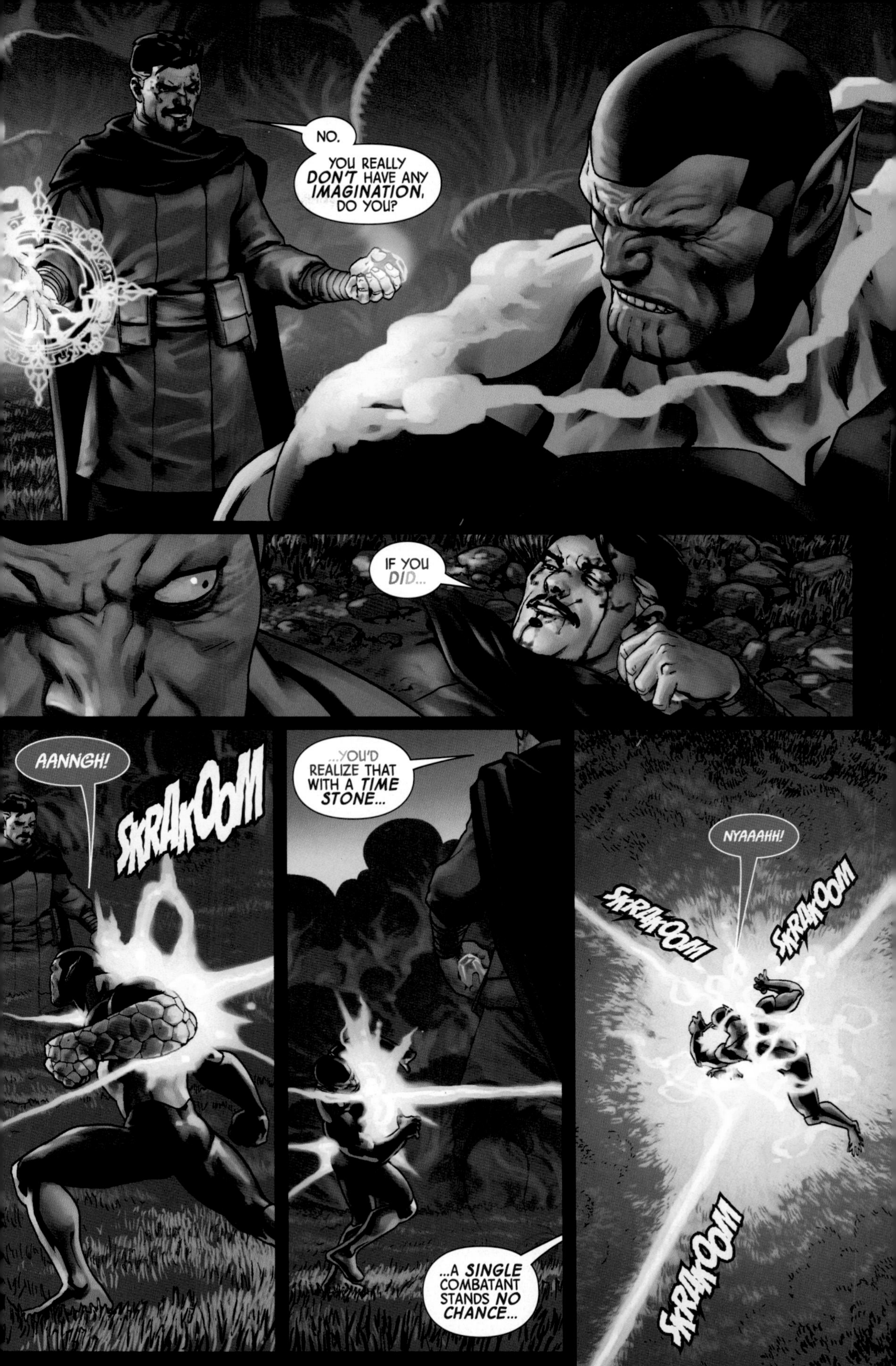

NO.
YOU REALLY DON'T HAVE ANY IMAGINATION, DO YOU?
IF YOU DID...
AANNGH!
SKRAKOOM
...YOU'D REALIZE THAT WITH A TIME STONE...
...A SINGLE COMBATANT STANDS NO CHANCE...
NYAAAHH!
SKRAKOOM
SKRAKOOM
SKRAKOOM

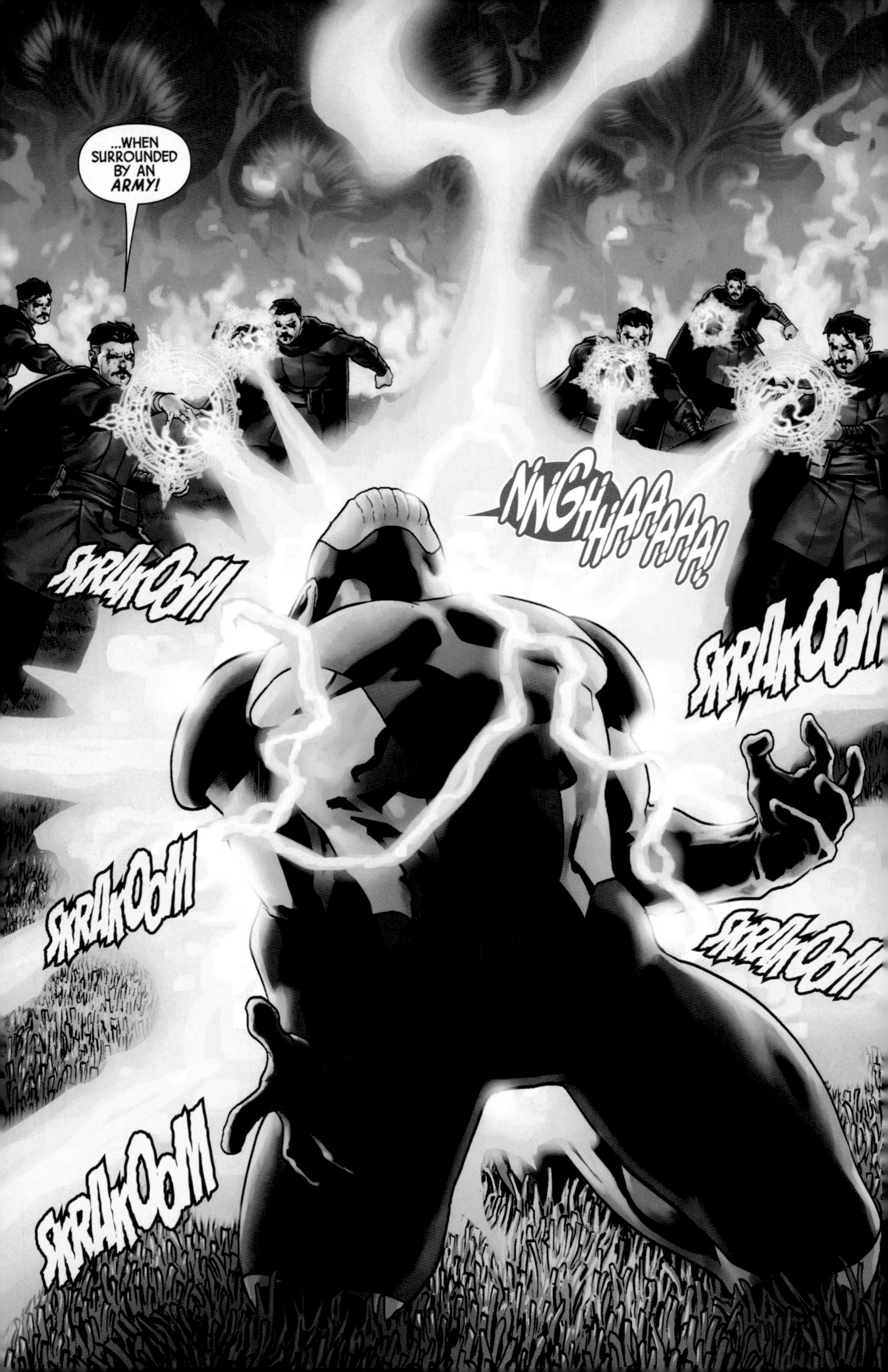
...WHEN SURROUNDED BY AN ARMY!
NNGHAAAAAA!
SKRAKOOM
SKRAKOOM
SKRAKOOM
SKRAKOOM
SKRAKOOM

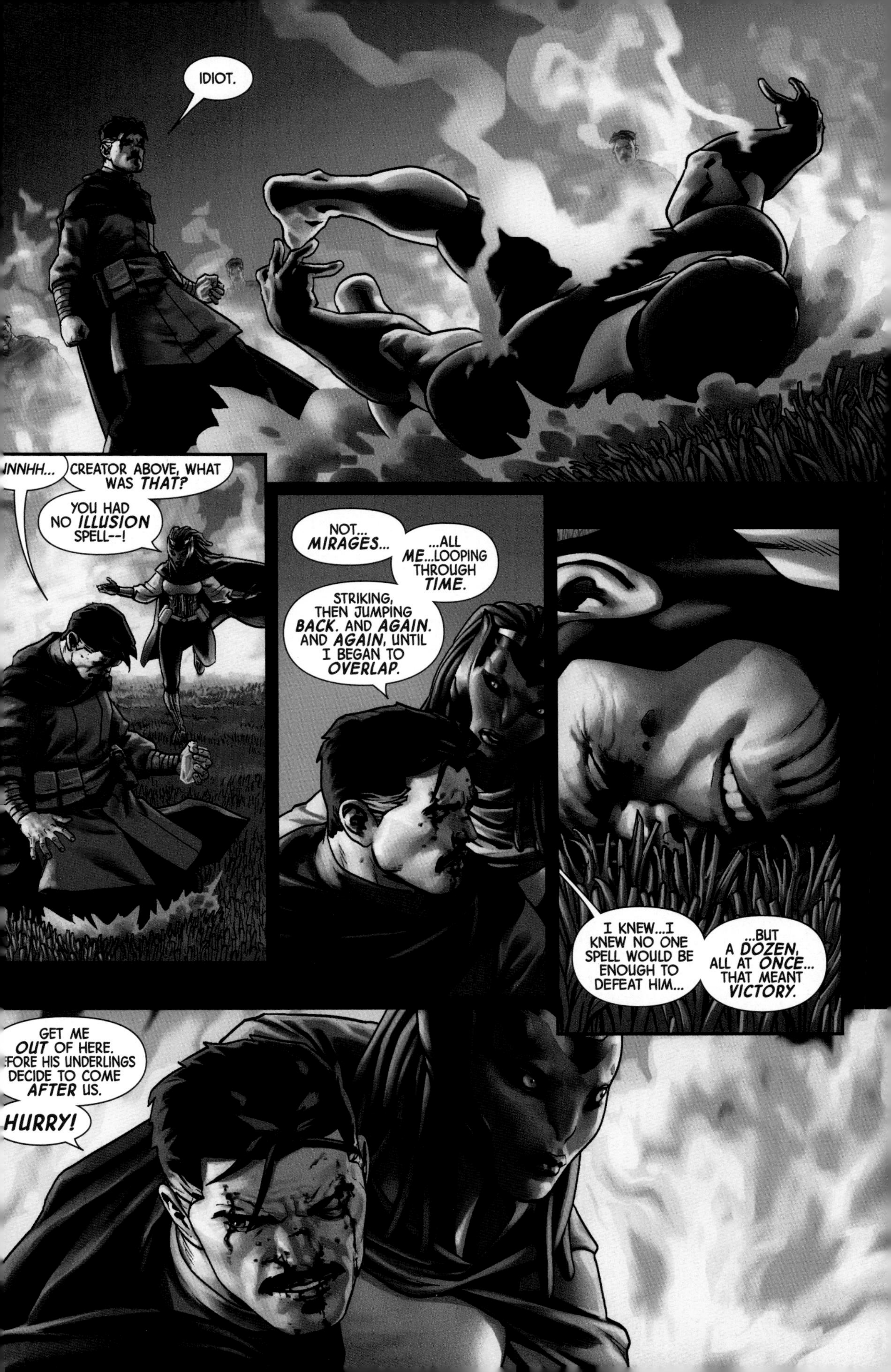
IDIOT.
NNHH...
CREATOR ABOVE, WHAT WAS THAT?
YOU HAD NO ILLUSION SPELL--!
NOT... MIRAGES...
...ALL ME...LOOPING THROUGH TIME.
STRIKING, THEN JUMPING BACK. AND AGAIN. AND AGAIN, UNTIL I BEGAN TO OVERLAP.
I KNEW...I KNEW NO ONE SPELL WOULD BE ENOUGH TO DEFEAT HIM...
...BUT A DOZEN, ALL AT ONCE... THAT MEANT VICTORY.
GET ME OUT OF HERE. FORE HIS UNDERLINGS DECIDE TO COME AFTER US.
HURRY!

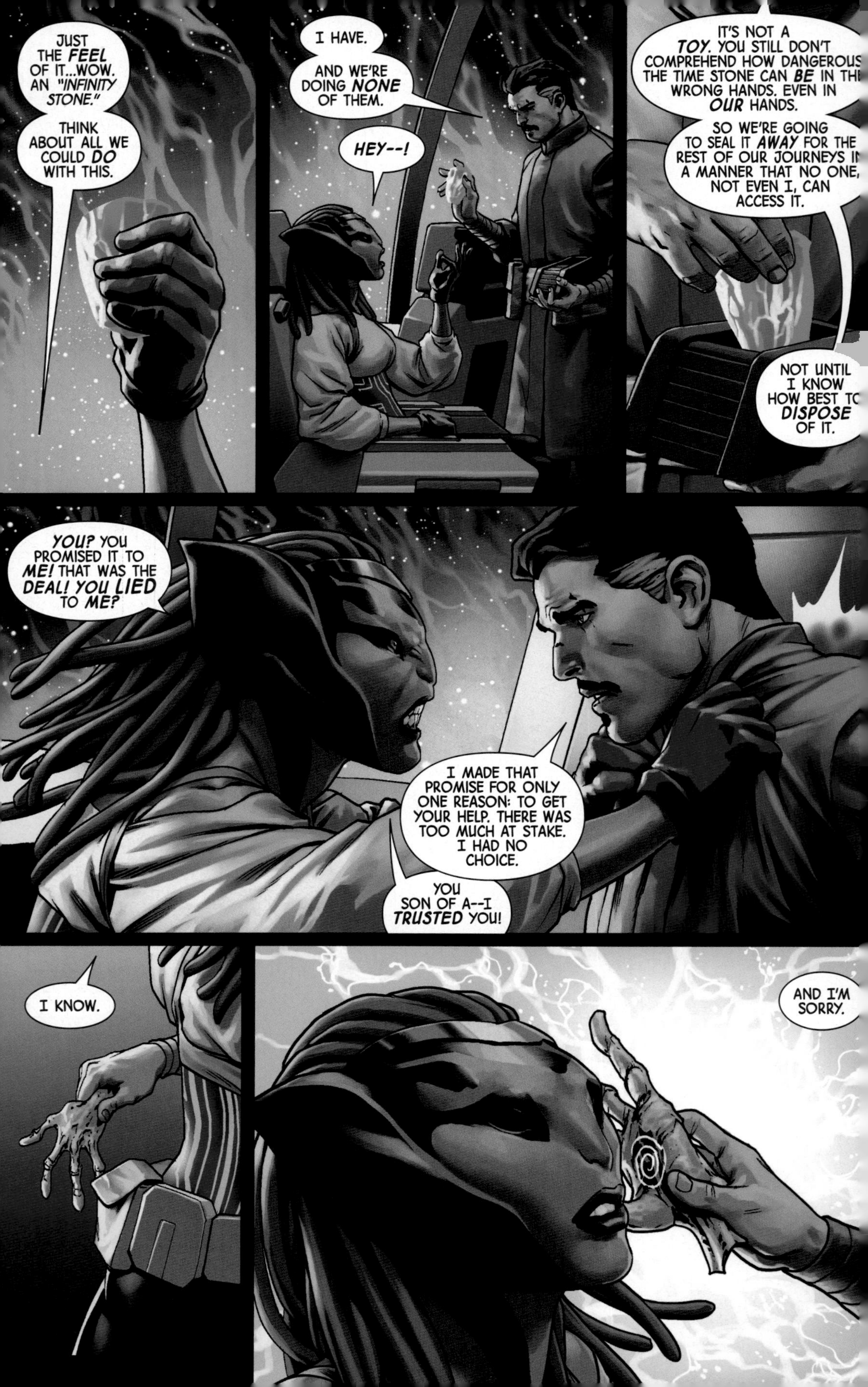
JUST THE FEEL OF IT...WOW. AN "INFINITY STONE."
THINK ABOUT ALL WE COULD DO WITH THIS.
I HAVE.
AND WE'RE DOING NONE OF THEM.
HEY--!
IT'S NOT A TOY. YOU STILL DON'T COMPREHEND HOW DANGEROUS THE TIME STONE CAN BE IN THE WRONG HANDS. EVEN IN OUR HANDS.
SO WE'RE GOING TO SEAL IT AWAY FOR THE REST OF OUR JOURNEYS IN A MANNER THAT NO ONE, NOT EVEN I, CAN ACCESS IT.
NOT UNTIL I KNOW HOW BEST TO DISPOSE OF IT.
YOU? YOU PROMISED IT TO ME! THAT WAS THE DEAL! YOU LIED TO ME?
I MADE THAT PROMISE FOR ONLY ONE REASON: TO GET YOUR HELP. THERE WAS TOO MUCH AT STAKE. I HAD NO CHOICE.
YOU SON OF A--I TRUSTED YOU!
I KNOW.
AND I'M SORRY.

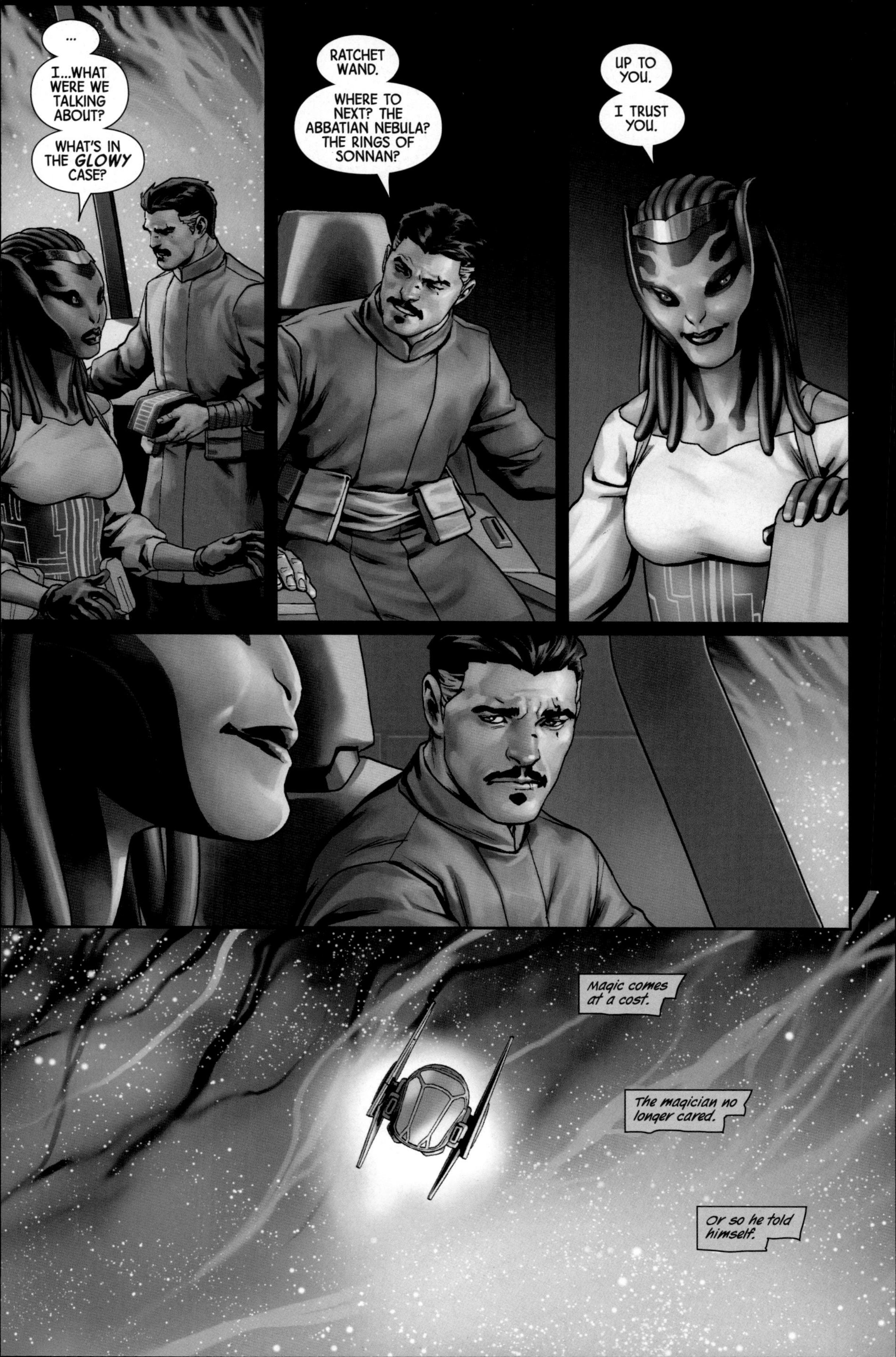
...
I...WHAT WERE WE TALKING ABOUT?
WHAT'S IN THE GLOWY CASE?
RATCHET WAND.
WHERE TO NEXT? THE ABBATIAN NEBULA? THE RINGS OF SONNAN?
UP TO YOU.
I TRUST YOU.
Magic comes at a cost.
The magician no longer cared.
Or so he told himself.

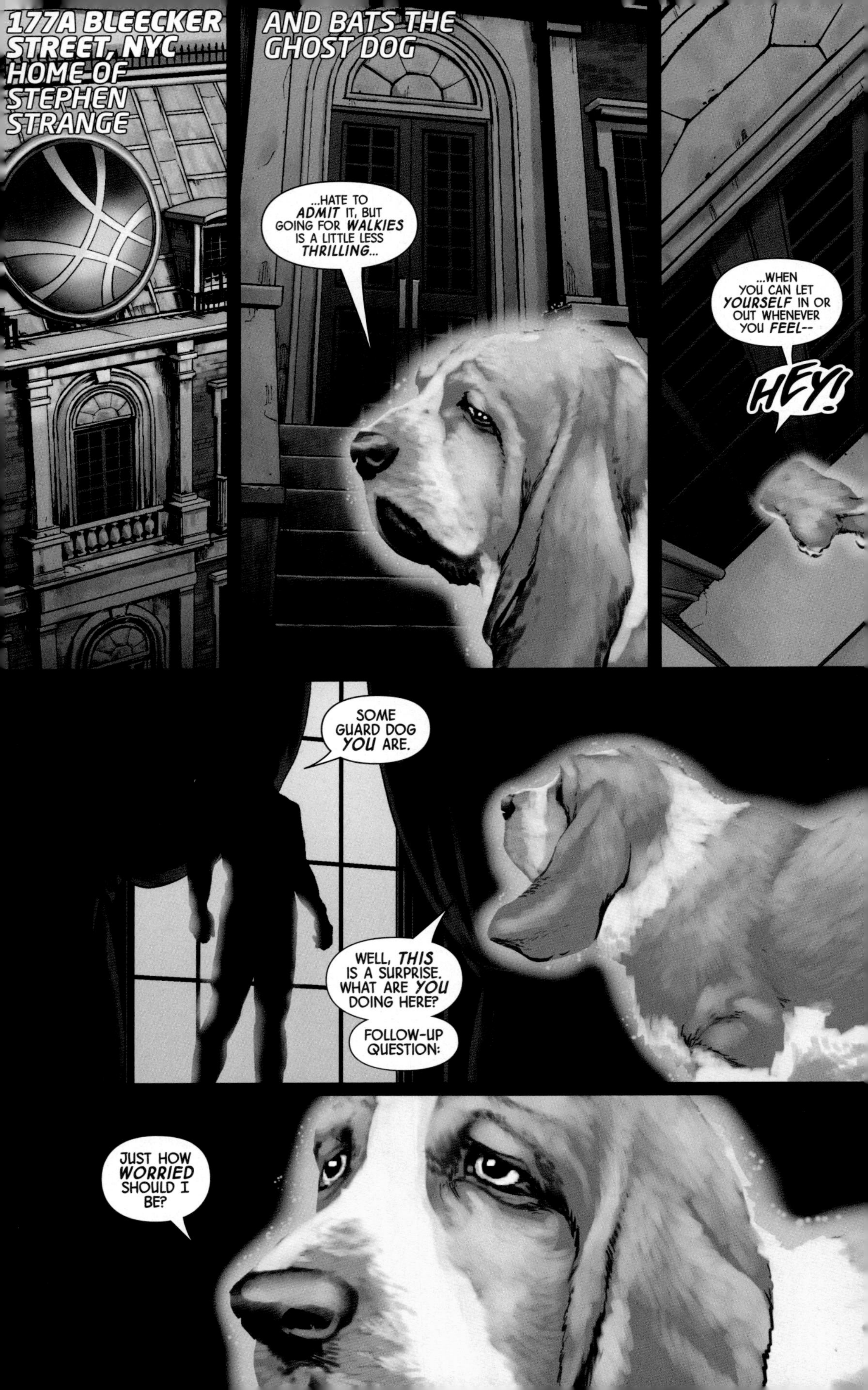
177A BLEECKER STREET, NYC
HOME OF STEPHEN STRANGE
AND BATS THE GHOST DOG
...HATE TO ADMIT IT, BUT GOING FOR WALKIES IS A LITTLE LESS THRILLING...
...WHEN YOU CAN LET YOURSELF IN OR OUT WHENEVER YOU FEEL--
HEY!
SOME GUARD DOG YOU ARE.
WELL, THIS IS A SURPRISE. WHAT ARE YOU DOING HERE?
FOLLOW-UP QUESTION:
JUST HOW WORRIED SHOULD I BE?

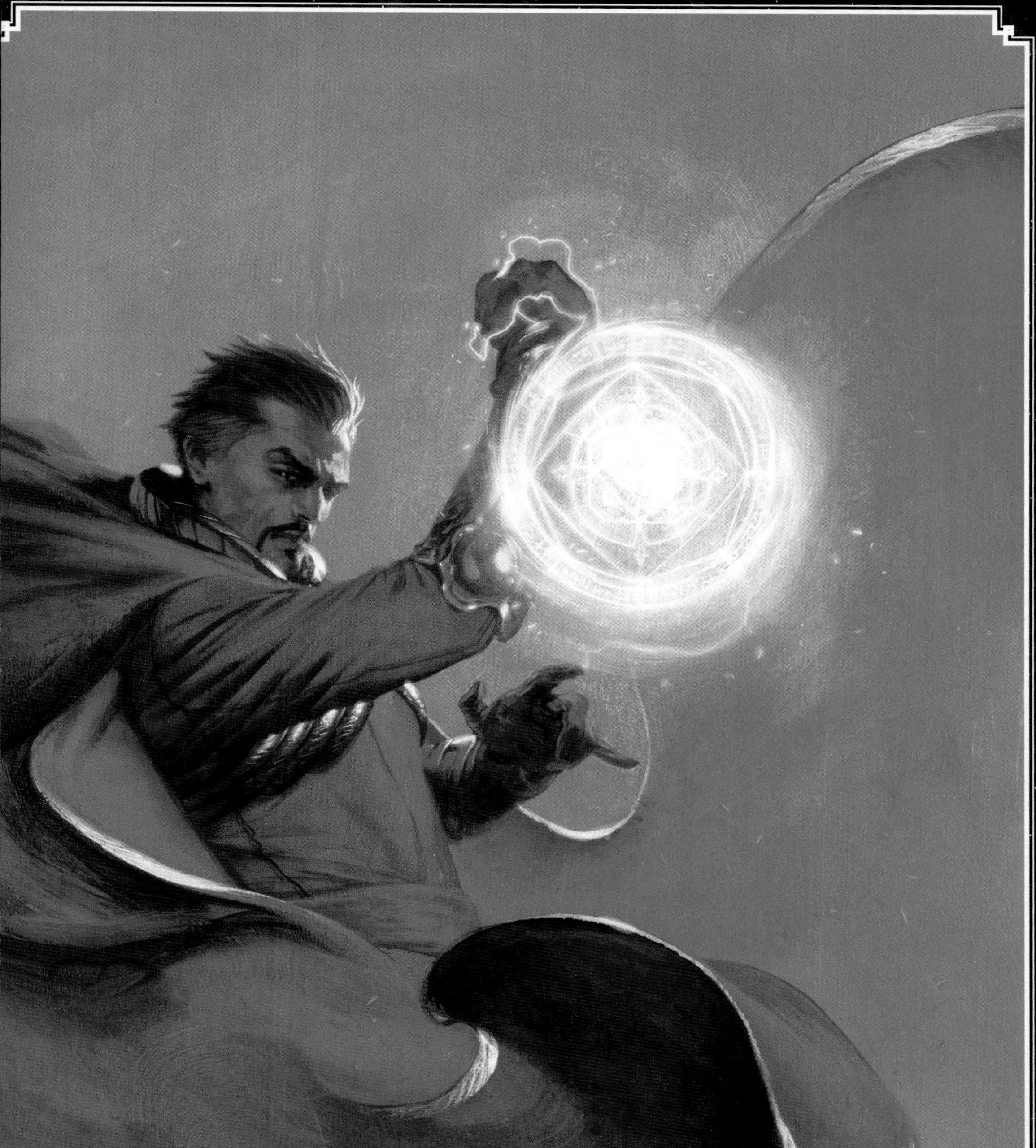

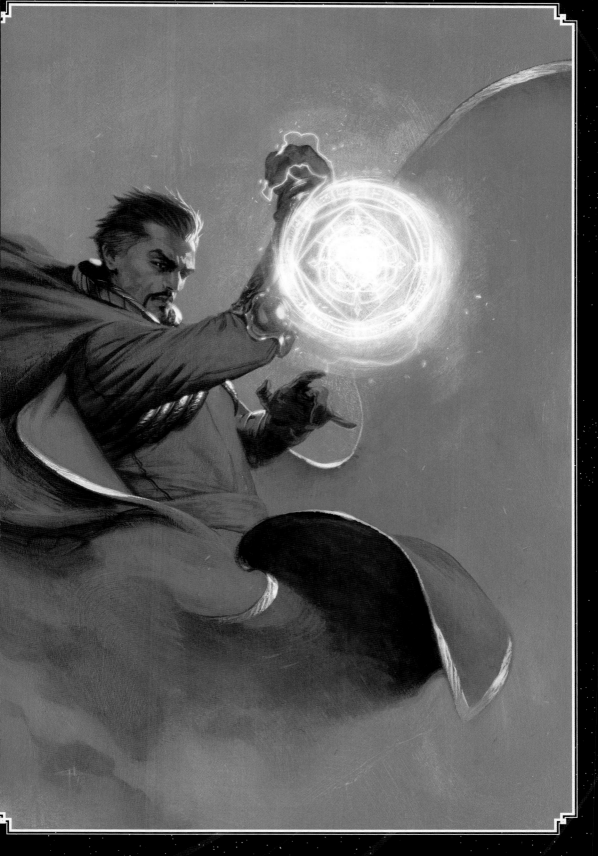

Gabriele Dell'Otto

1 VARIANT

4

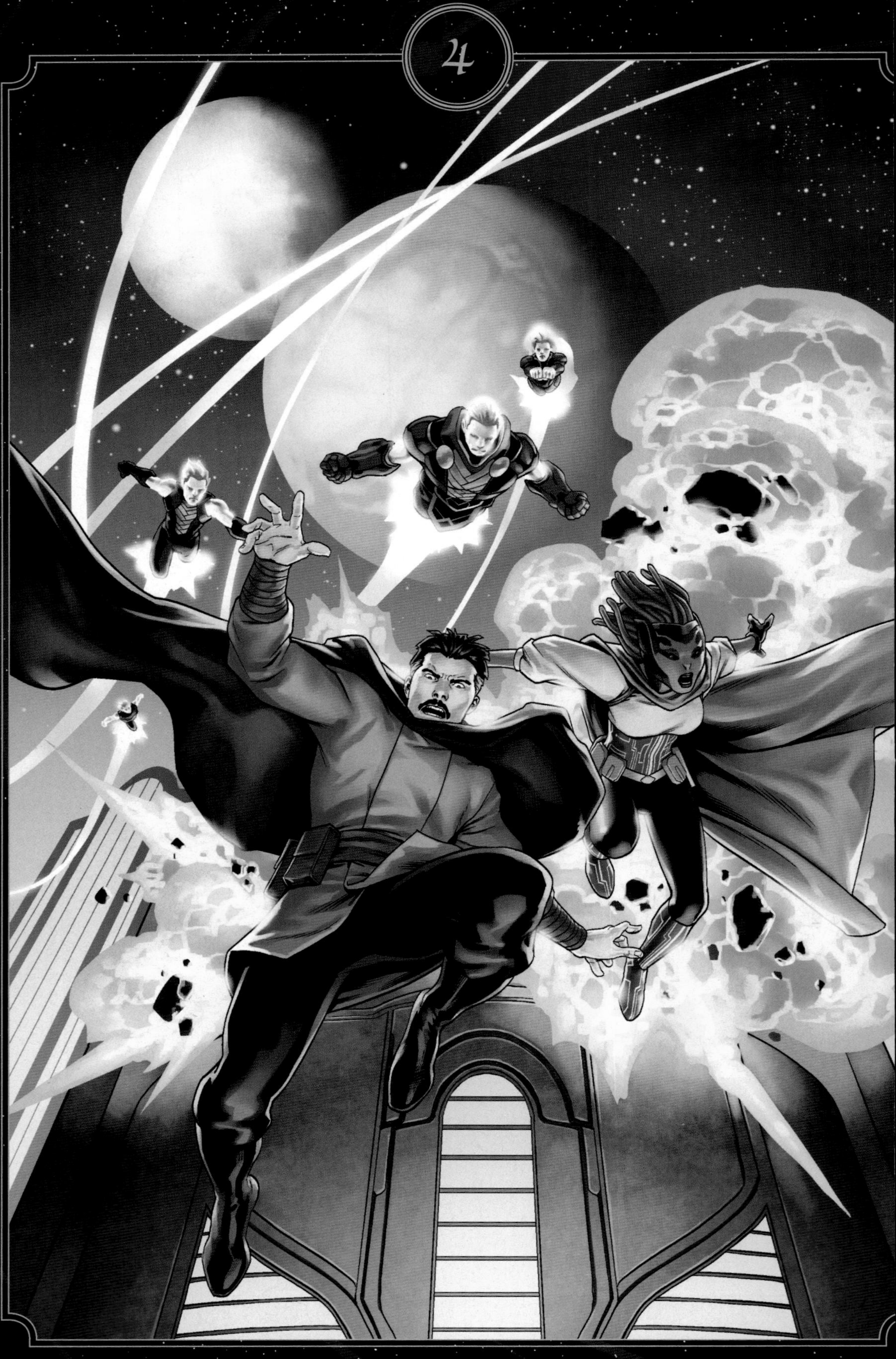

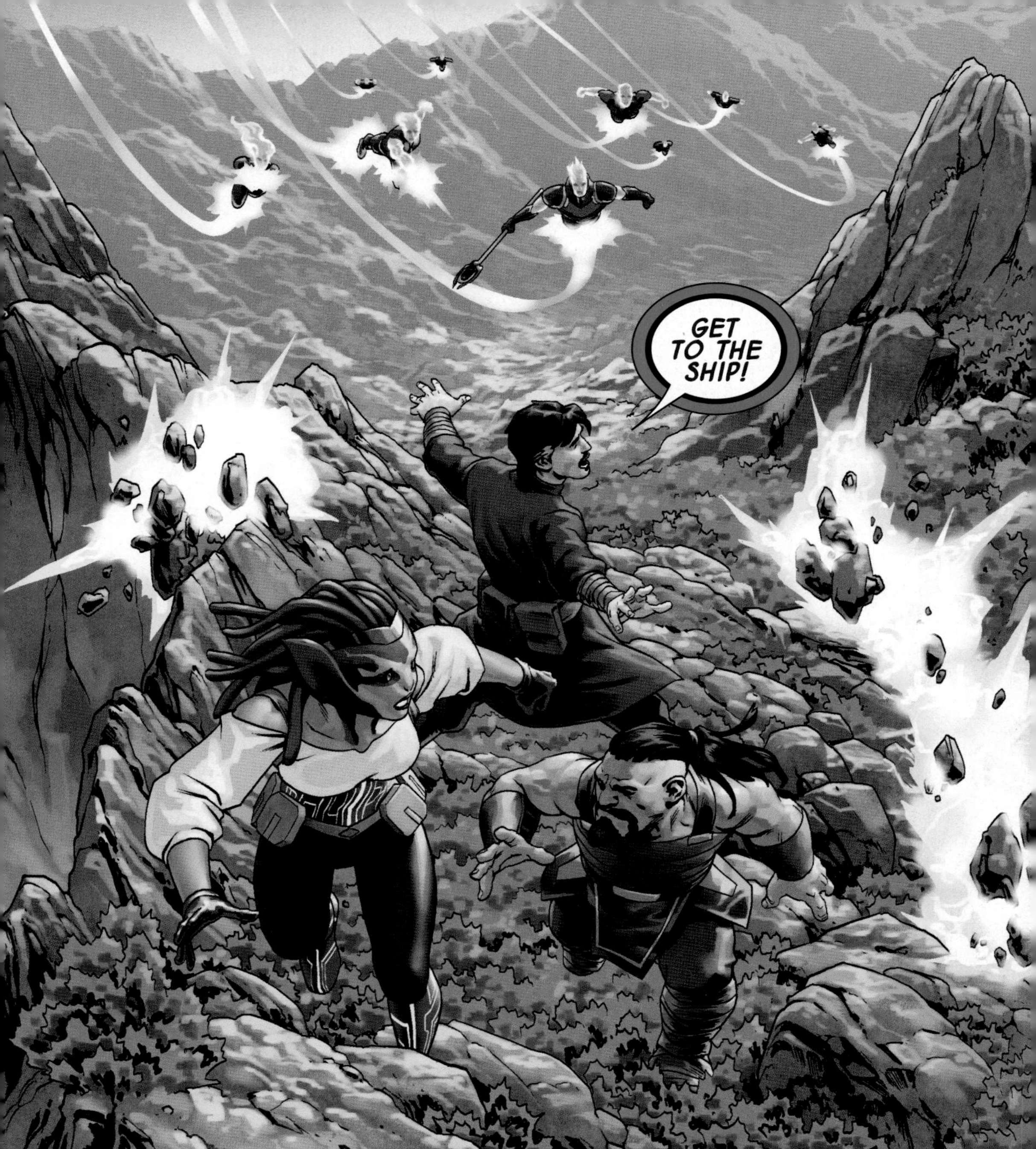
GET TO THE SHIP!

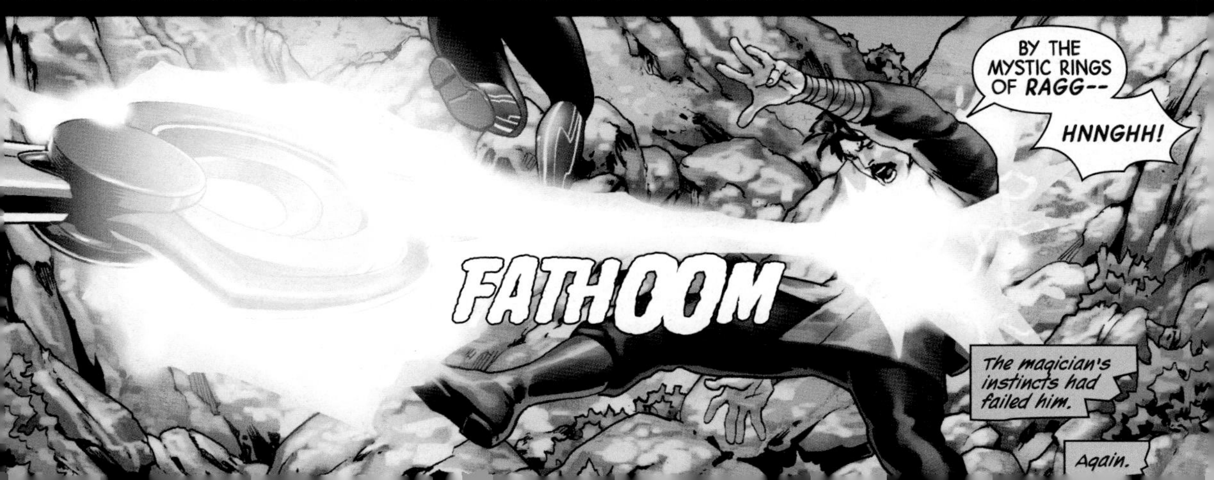
BY THE MYSTIC RINGS OF RAGG--
HNNGHH!
FATHOOM
The magician's instincts had failed him.
Again.

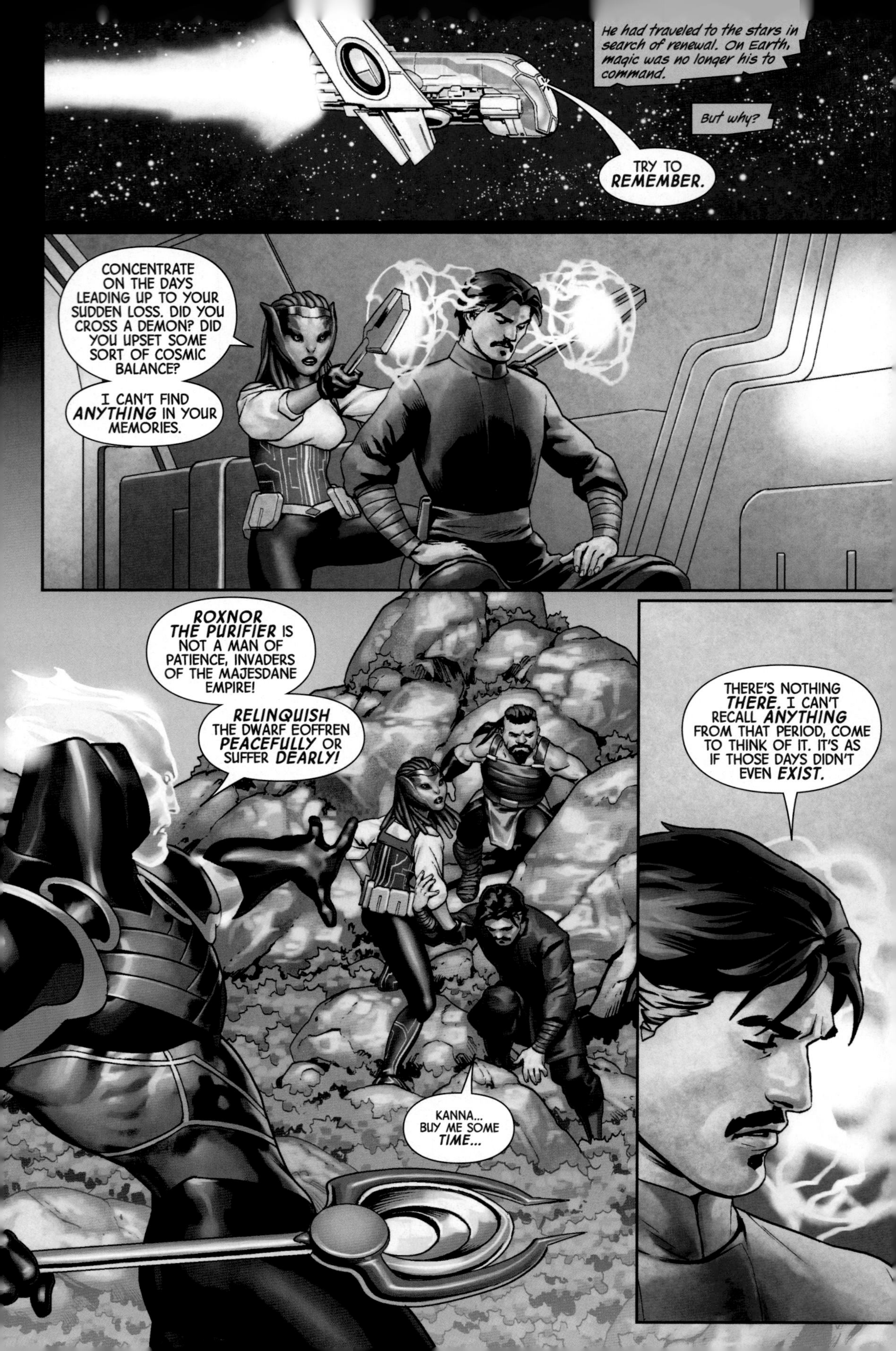
He had traveled to the stars in search of renewal. On Earth, magic was no longer his to command.
But why?
TRY TO REMEMBER.
CONCENTRATE ON THE DAYS LEADING UP TO YOUR SUDDEN LOSS. DID YOU CROSS A DEMON? DID YOU UPSET SOME SORT OF COSMIC BALANCE?
I CAN'T FIND ANYTHING IN YOUR MEMORIES.
ROXNOR THE PURIFIER IS NOT A MAN OF PATIENCE, INVADERS OF THE MAJESDANE EMPIRE!
RELINQUISH THE DWARF EOFFREN PEACEFULLY OR SUFFER DEARLY!
KANNA... BUY ME SOME TIME...
THERE'S NOTHING THERE. I CAN'T RECALL ANYTHING FROM THAT PERIOD, COME TO THINK OF IT. IT'S AS IF THOSE DAYS DIDN'T EVEN EXIST.

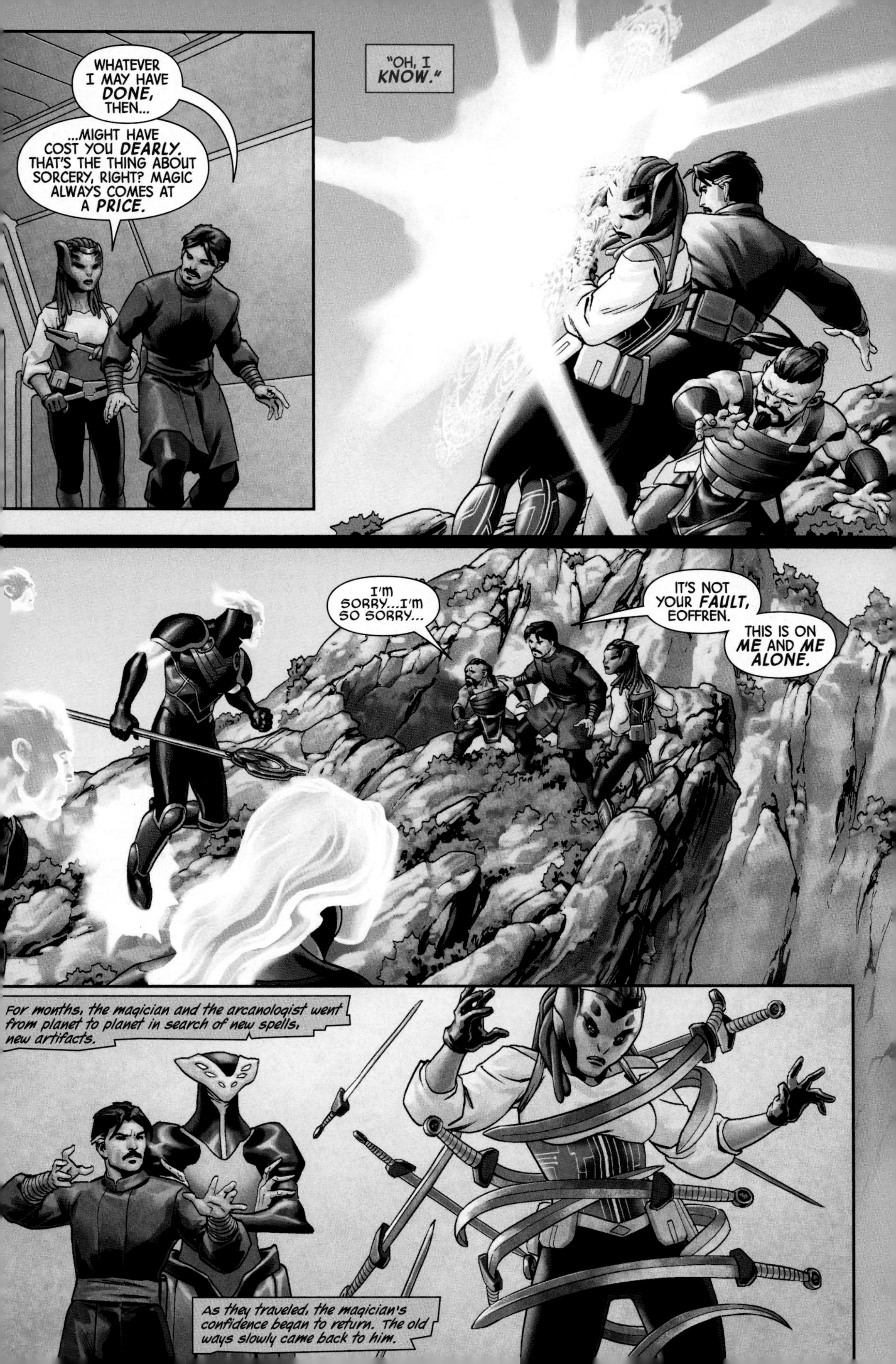
WHATEVER I MAY HAVE DONE, THEN...
...MIGHT HAVE COST YOU DEARLY. THAT'S THE THING ABOUT SORCERY, RIGHT? MAGIC ALWAYS COMES AT A PRICE.
"OH, I KNOW."
I'M SORRY...I'M SO SORRY...
IT'S NOT YOUR FAULT, EOFFREN.
THIS IS ON ME AND ME ALONE.
For months, the magician and the arcanologist went from planet to planet in search of new spells, new artifacts.
As they traveled, the magician's confidence began to return. The old ways slowly came back to him.

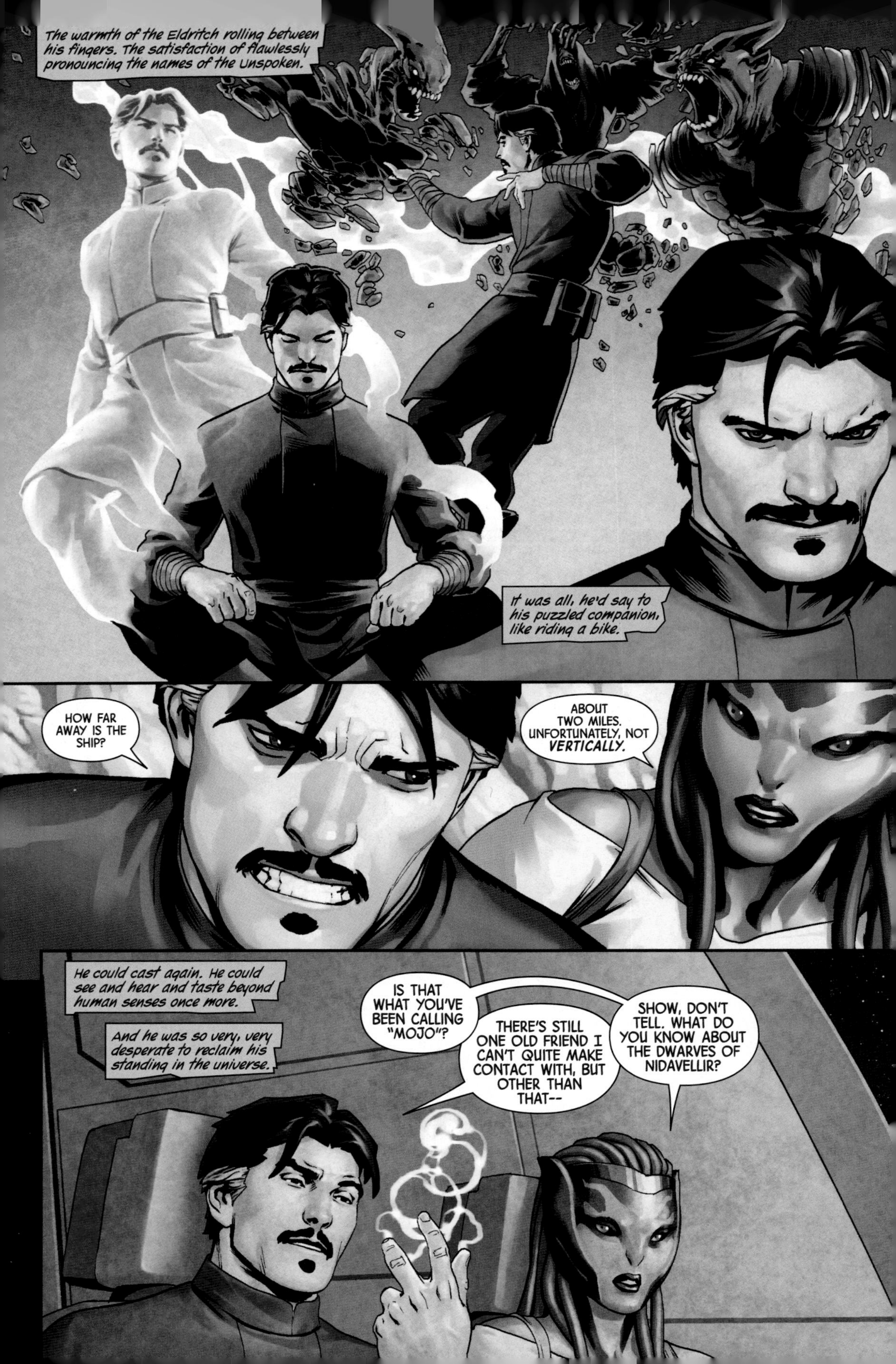
The warmth of the Eldritch rolling between his fingers. The satisfaction of flawlessly pronouncing the names of the Unspoken.
It was all, he'd say to his puzzled companion, like riding a bike.
HOW FAR AWAY IS THE SHIP?
ABOUT TWO MILES. UNFORTUNATELY, NOT VERTICALLY.
He could cast again. He could see and hear and taste beyond human senses once more.
And he was so very, very desperate to reclaim his standing in the universe.
IS THAT WHAT YOU'VE BEEN CALLING "MOJO"?
THERE'S STILL ONE OLD FRIEND I CAN'T QUITE MAKE CONTACT WITH, BUT OTHER THAN THAT--
SHOW, DON'T TELL. WHAT DO YOU KNOW ABOUT THE DWARVES OF NIDAVELLIR?

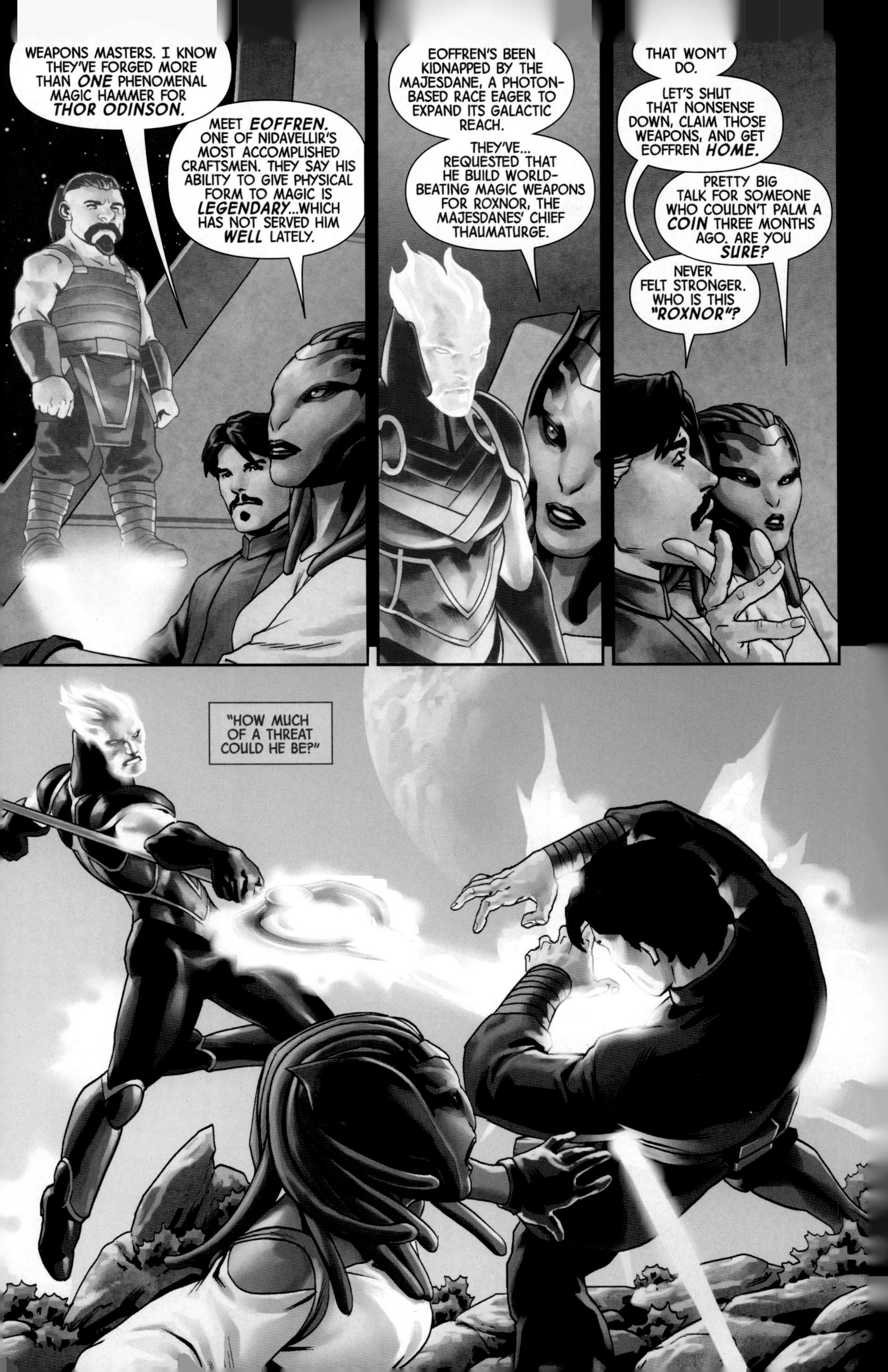
WEAPONS MASTERS. I KNOW THEY'VE FORGED MORE THAN ONE PHENOMENAL MAGIC HAMMER FOR THOR ODINSON.
MEET EOFFREN. ONE OF NIDAVELLIR'S MOST ACCOMPLISHED CRAFTSMEN. THEY SAY HIS ABILITY TO GIVE PHYSICAL FORM TO MAGIC IS LEGENDARY...WHICH HAS NOT SERVED HIM WELL LATELY.
EOFFREN'S BEEN KIDNAPPED BY THE MAJESDANE, A PHOTON-BASED RACE EAGER TO EXPAND ITS GALACTIC REACH.
THEY'VE... REQUESTED THAT HE BUILD WORLD-BEATING MAGIC WEAPONS FOR ROXNOR, THE MAJESDANES' CHIEF THAUMATURGE.
THAT WON'T DO.
LET'S SHUT THAT NONSENSE DOWN, CLAIM THOSE WEAPONS, AND GET EOFFREN HOME.
PRETTY BIG TALK FOR SOMEONE WHO COULDN'T PALM A COIN THREE MONTHS AGO. ARE YOU SURE?
NEVER FELT STRONGER. WHO IS THIS "ROXNOR"?
"HOW MUCH OF A THREAT COULD HE BE?"

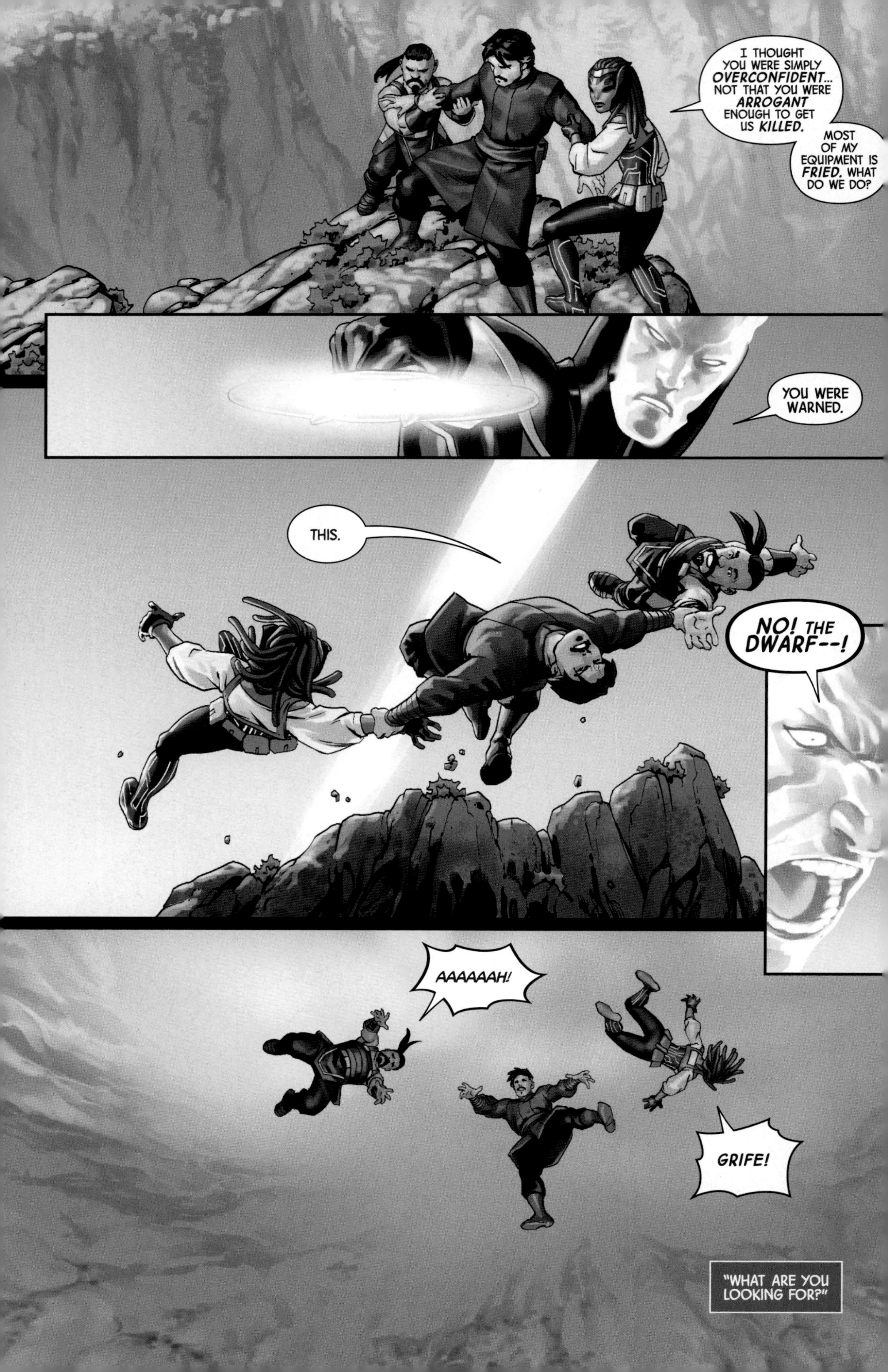

I THOUGHT YOU WERE SIMPLY OVERCONFIDENT... NOT THAT YOU WERE ARROGANT ENOUGH TO GET US KILLED.
MOST OF MY EQUIPMENT IS FRIED. WHAT DO WE DO?
YOU WERE WARNED.
THIS.
NO! THE DWARF--!
AAAAAAH!
GRIFE!
"WHAT ARE YOU LOOKING FOR?"

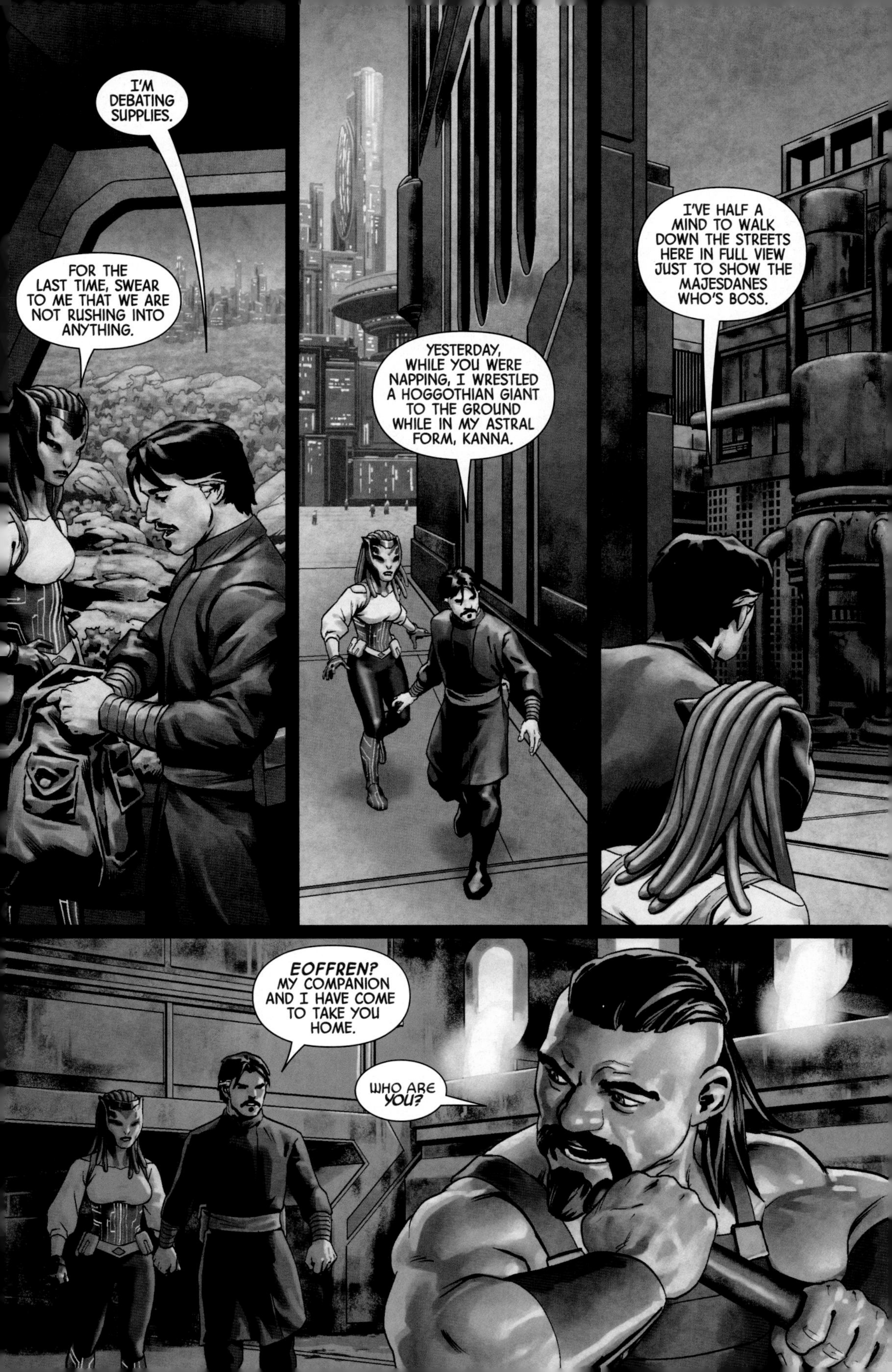

I'M DEBATING SUPPLIES.
FOR THE LAST TIME, SWEAR TO ME THAT WE ARE NOT RUSHING INTO ANYTHING.
YESTERDAY, WHILE YOU WERE NAPPING, I WRESTLED A HOGGOTHIAN GIANT TO THE GROUND WHILE IN MY ASTRAL FORM, KANNA.
I'VE HALF A MIND TO WALK DOWN THE STREETS HERE IN FULL VIEW JUST TO SHOW THE MAJESDANES WHO'S BOSS.
EOFFREN? MY COMPANION AND I HAVE COME TO TAKE YOU HOME.
WHO ARE YOU?

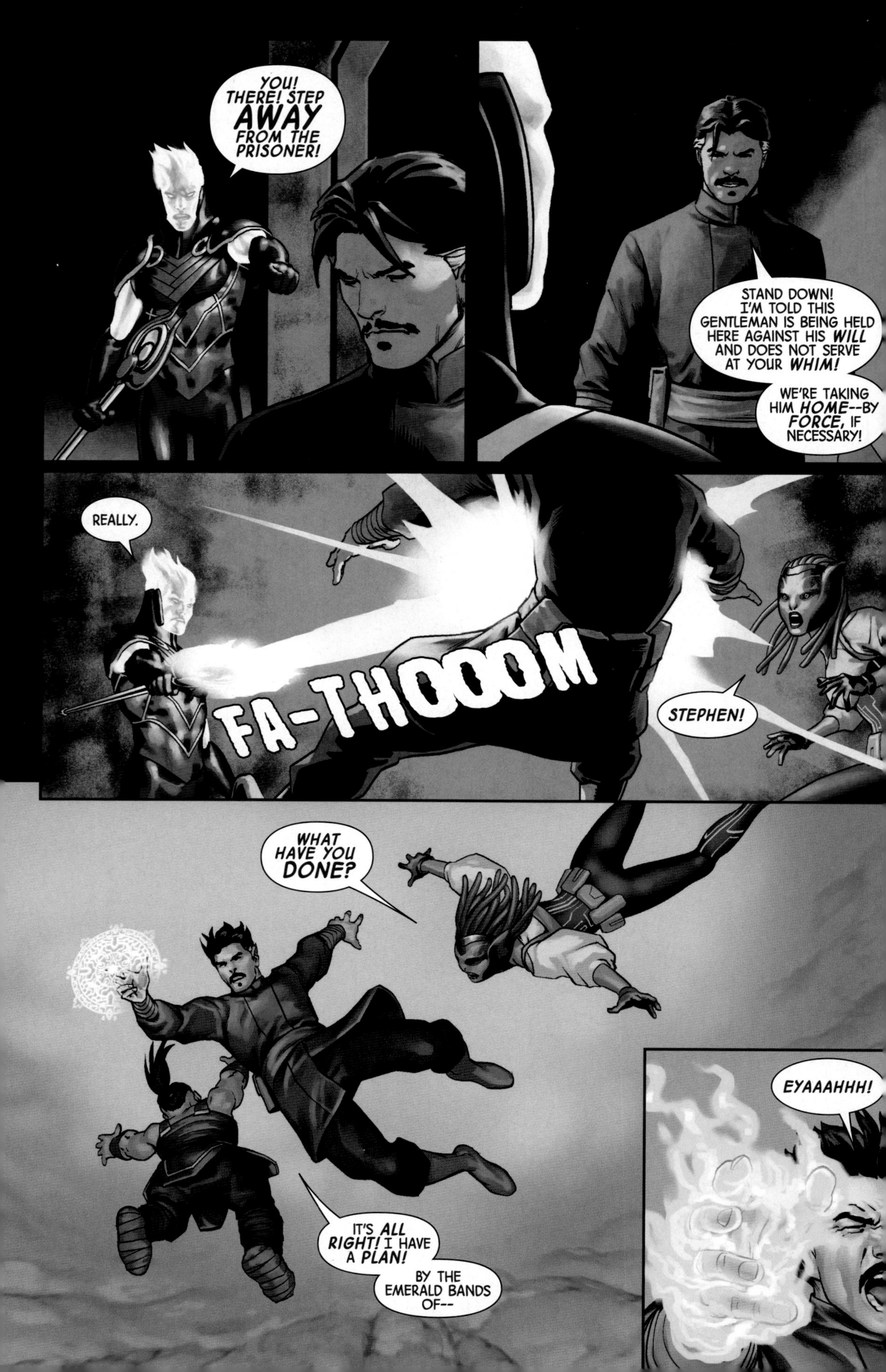
YOU! THERE! STEP AWAY FROM THE PRISONER!
STAND DOWN! I'M TOLD THIS GENTLEMAN IS BEING HELD HERE AGAINST HIS WILL AND DOES NOT SERVE AT YOUR WHIM!
WE'RE TAKING HIM HOME--BY FORCE, IF NECESSARY!
REALLY.
FA-THOOOM
STEPHEN!
WHAT HAVE YOU DONE?
IT'S ALL RIGHT! I HAVE A PLAN!
BY THE EMERALD BANDS OF--
EYAAAHHH!

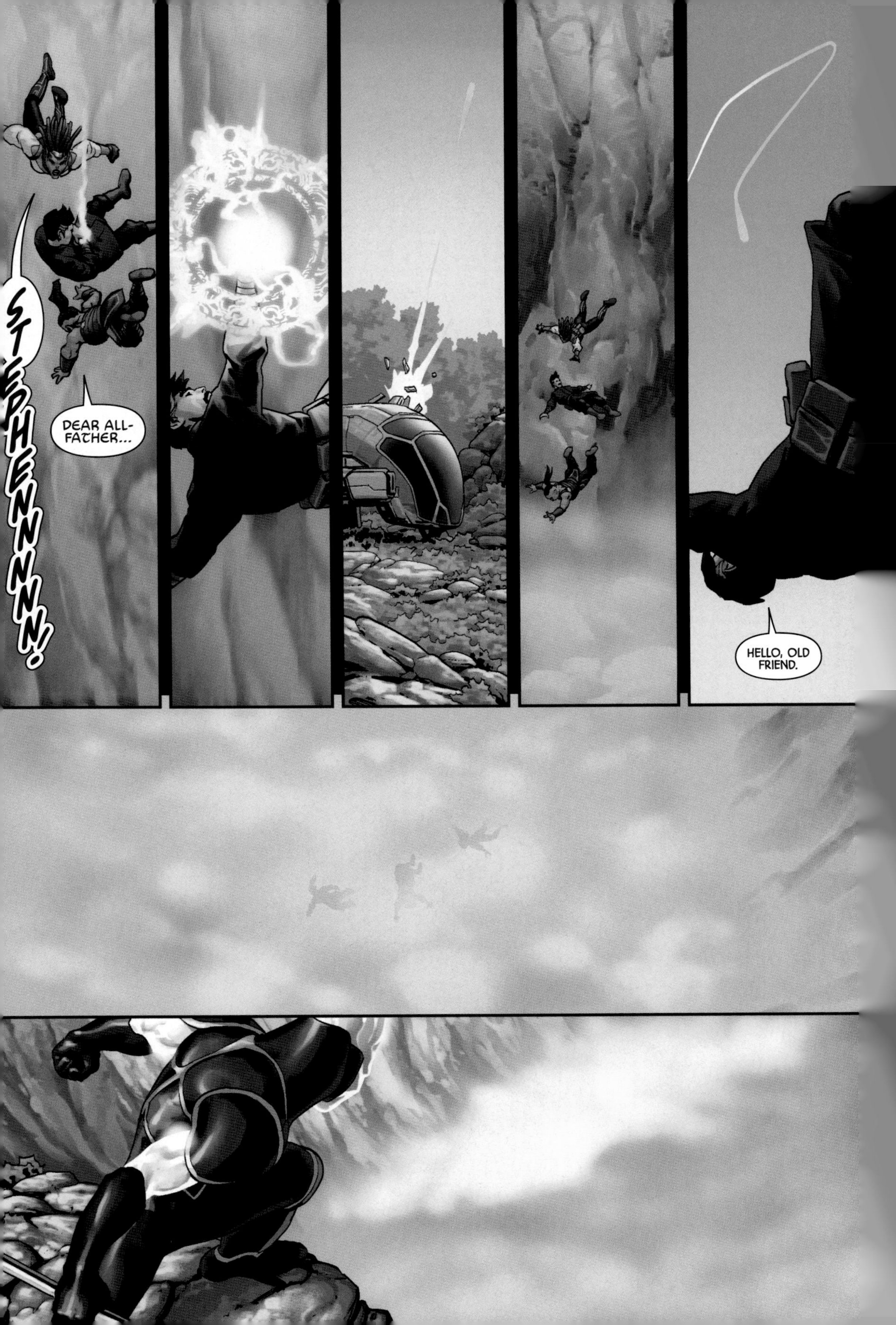
STEPHENNNN!
DEAR ALL-FATHER...
HELLO, OLD FRIEND.

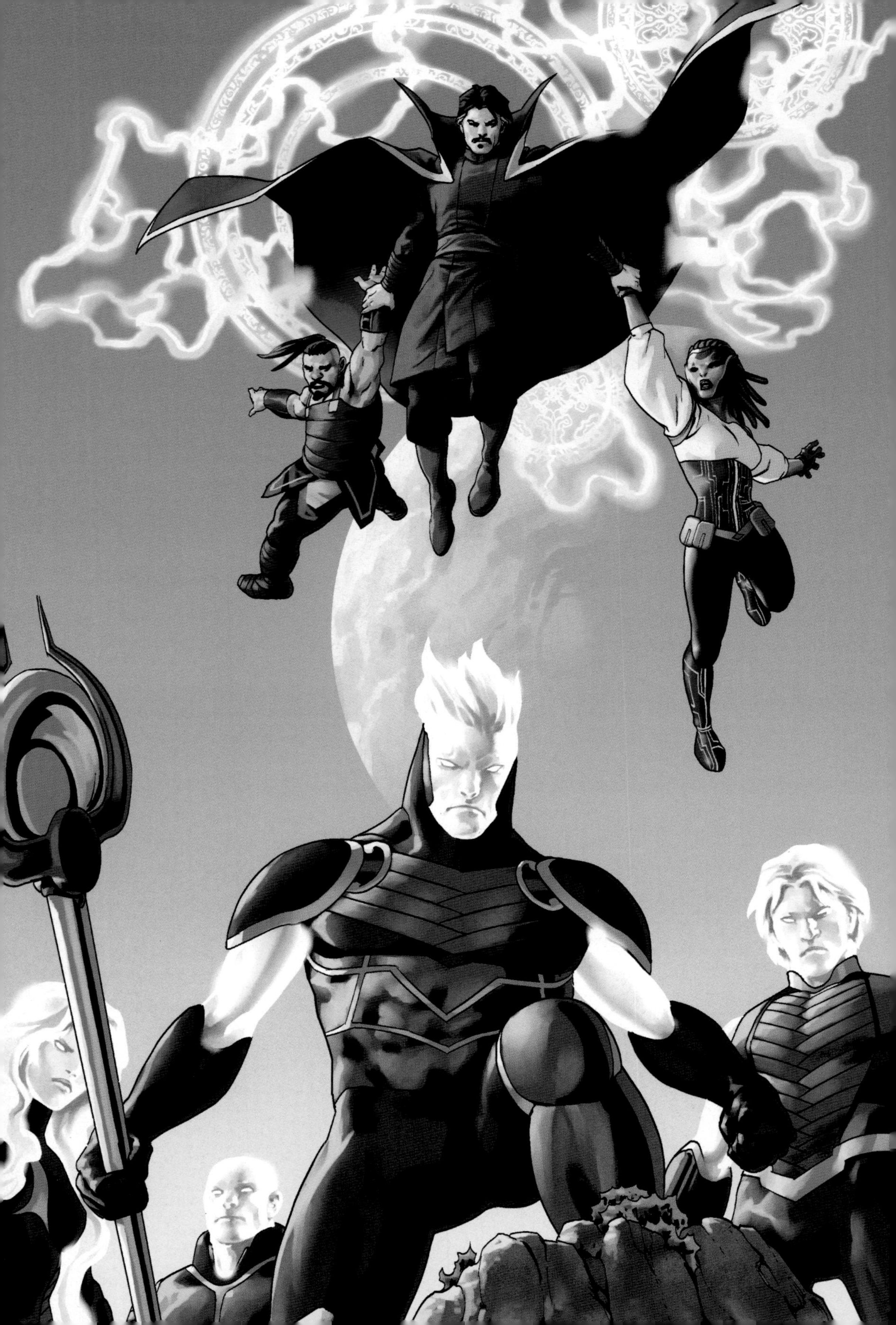

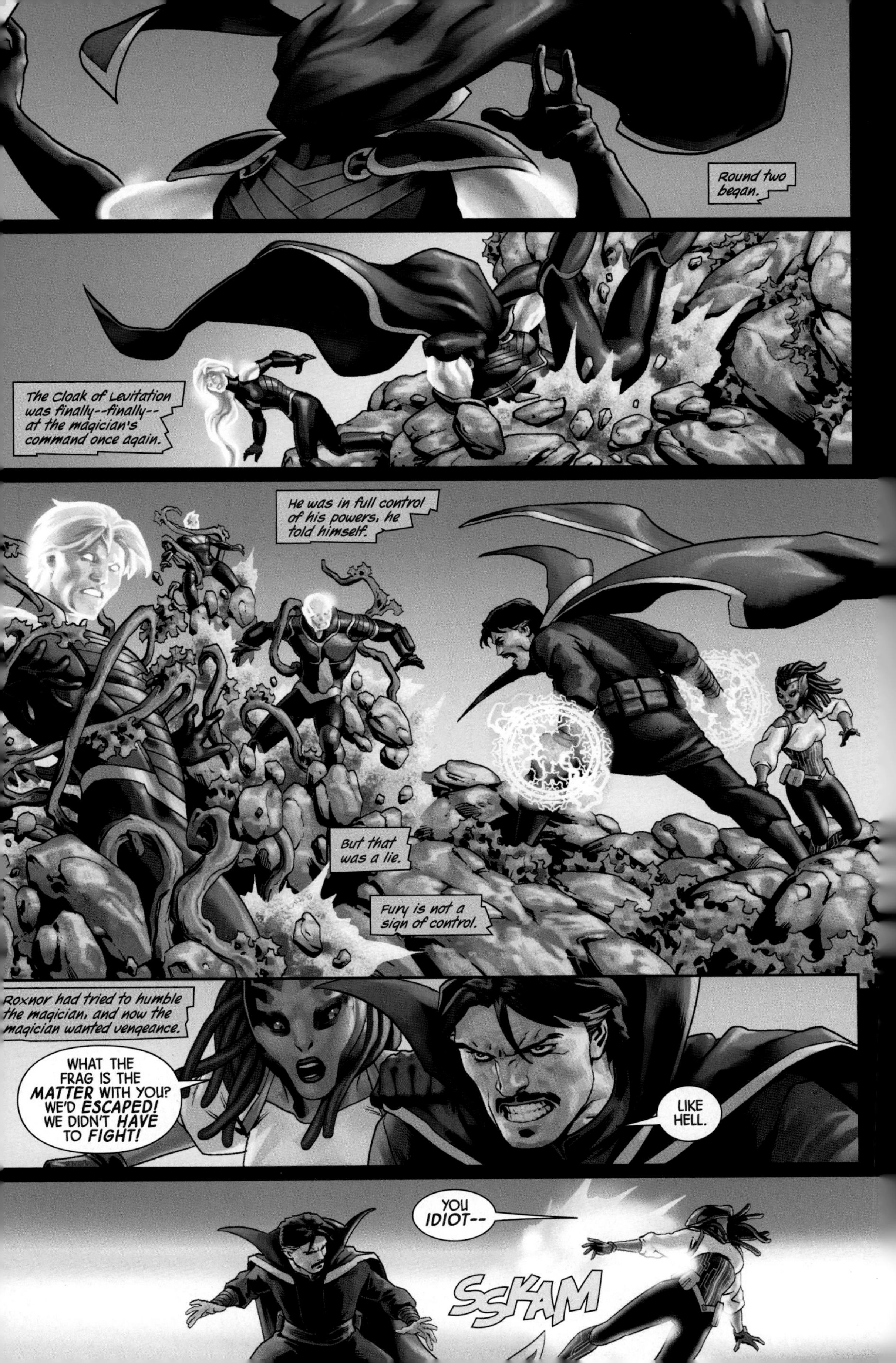
Round two began.
The Cloak of Levitation was finally--finally--at the magician's command once again.
He was in full control of his powers, he told himself.
But that was a lie.
Fury is not a sign of control.
Roxnor had tried to humble the magician, and now the magician wanted vengeance.
WHAT THE FRAG IS THE MATTER WITH YOU? WE'D ESCAPED! WE DIDN'T HAVE TO FIGHT!
LIKE HELL.
YOU IDIOT--
SSKAM

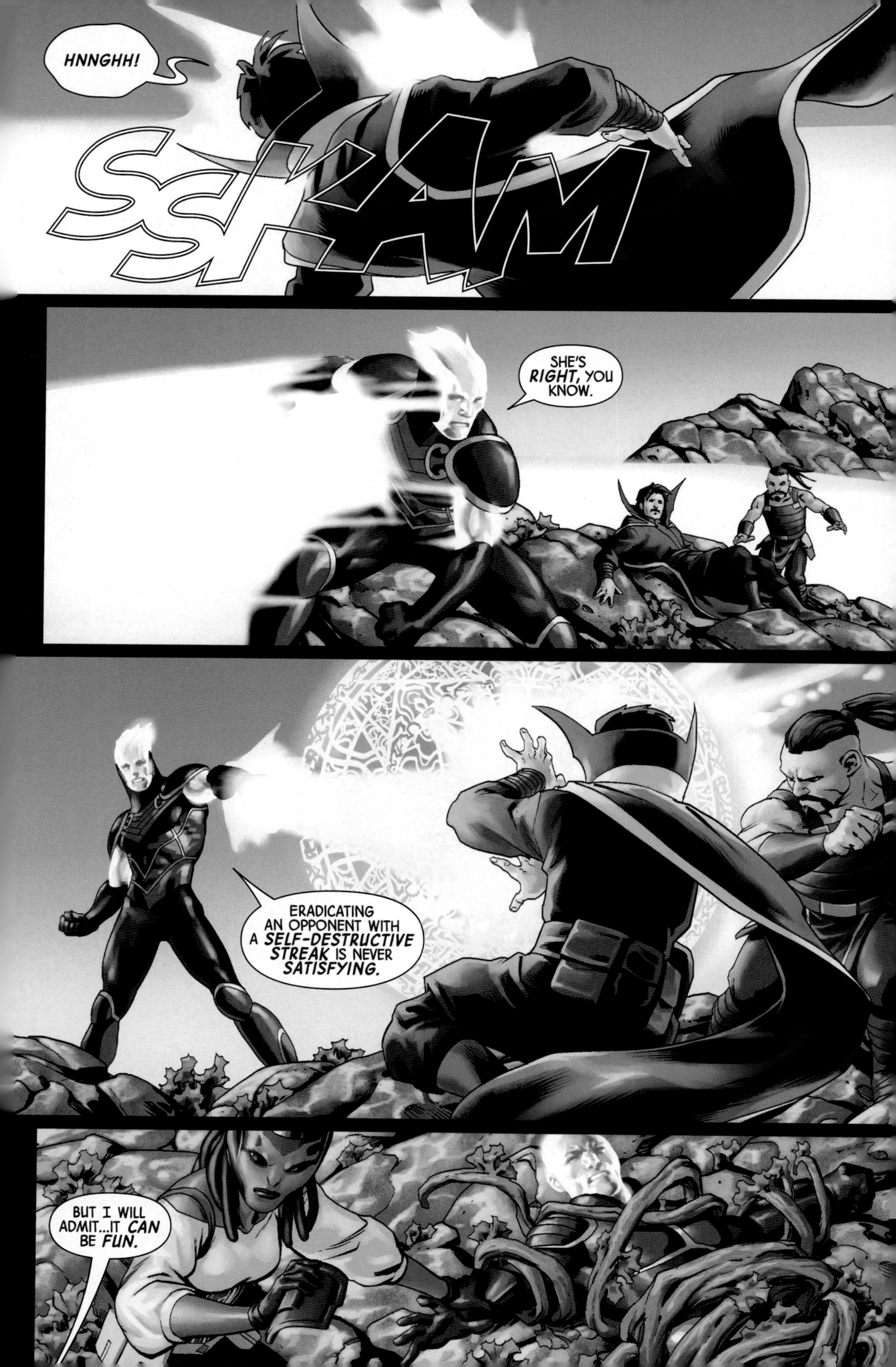
HNNGHH!
SSHKAM
SHE'S RIGHT, YOU KNOW.
ERADICATING AN OPPONENT WITH A SELF-DESTRUCTIVE STREAK IS NEVER SATISFYING.
BUT I WILL ADMIT...IT CAN BE FUN.

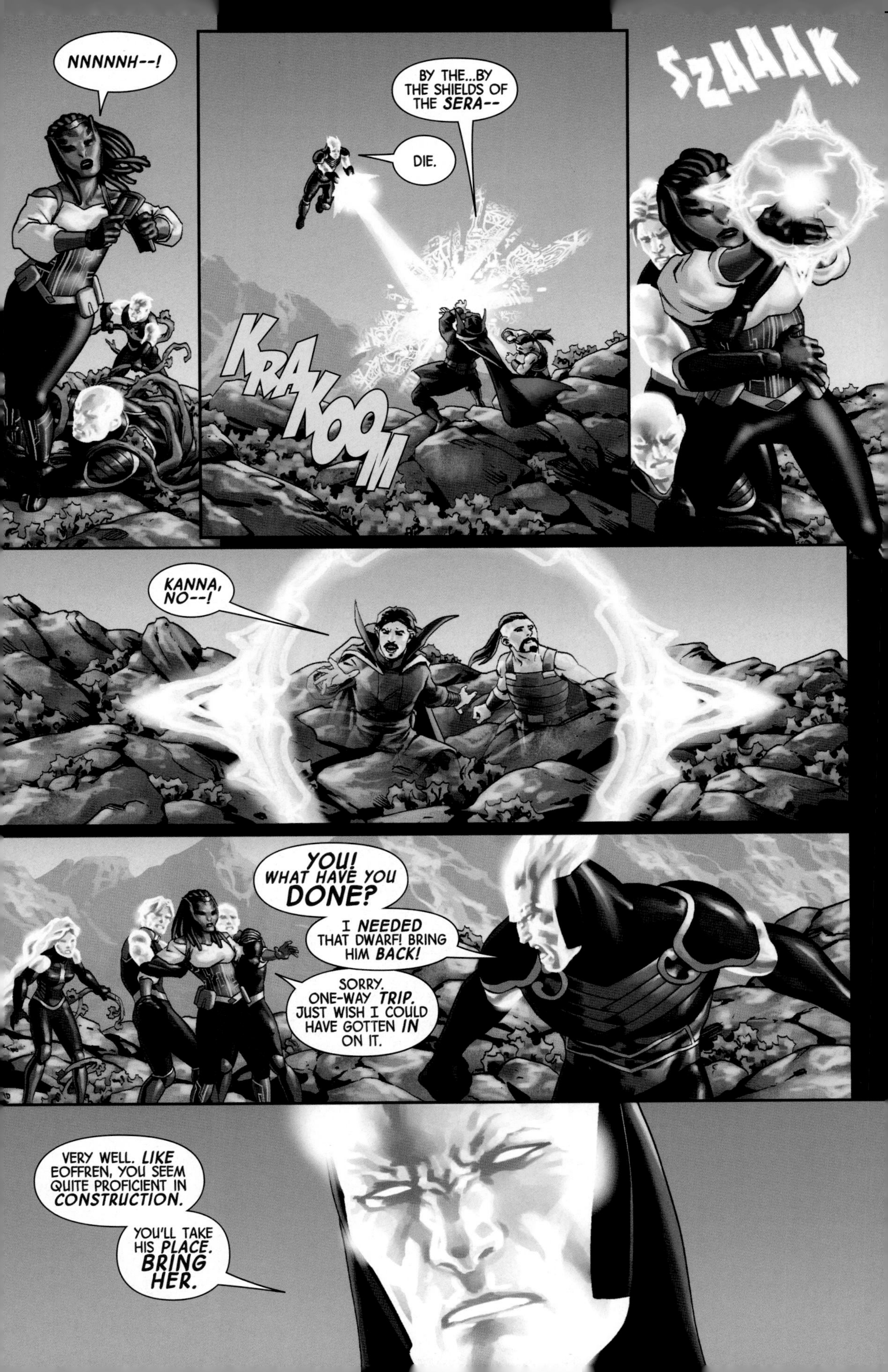
NNNNNH--!
BY THE...BY THE SHIELDS OF THE SERA--
DIE.
KRAKOOM
SZAAAK
KANNA, NO--!
YOU! WHAT HAVE YOU DONE?
I NEEDED THAT DWARF! BRING HIM BACK!
SORRY. ONE-WAY TRIP. JUST WISH I COULD HAVE GOTTEN IN ON IT.
VERY WELL. LIKE EOFFREN, YOU SEEM QUITE PROFICIENT IN CONSTRUCTION.
YOU'LL TAKE HIS PLACE. BRING HER.

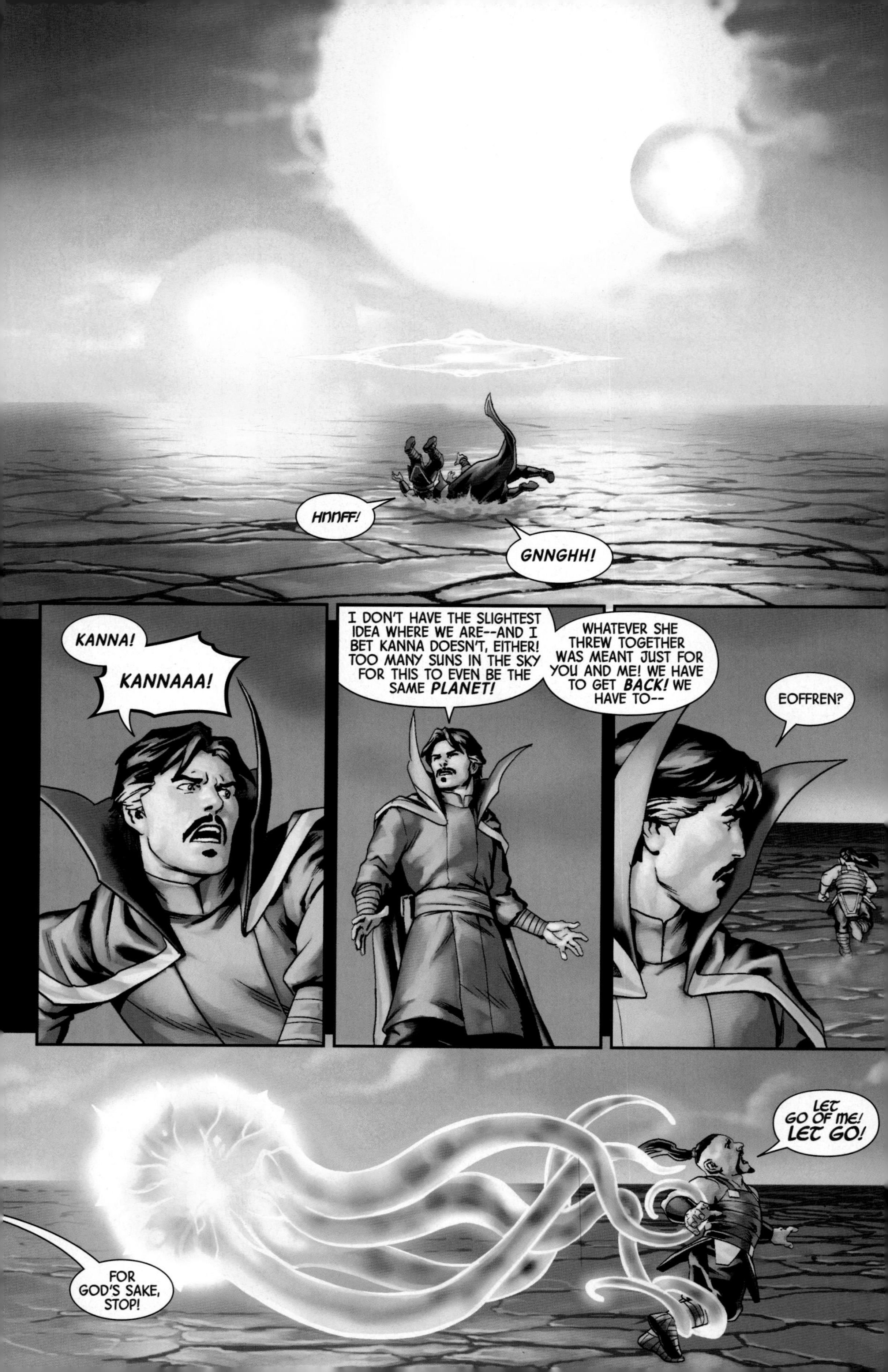

HNNFF!
GNNGHH!
KANNA!
KANNAAA!
I DON'T HAVE THE SLIGHTEST IDEA WHERE WE ARE--AND I BET KANNA DOESN'T, EITHER! TOO MANY SUNS IN THE SKY FOR THIS TO EVEN BE THE SAME PLANET!
WHATEVER SHE THREW TOGETHER WAS MEANT JUST FOR YOU AND ME! WE HAVE TO GET BACK! WE HAVE TO--
EOFFREN?
LET GO OF ME! LET GO!
FOR GOD'S SAKE, STOP!

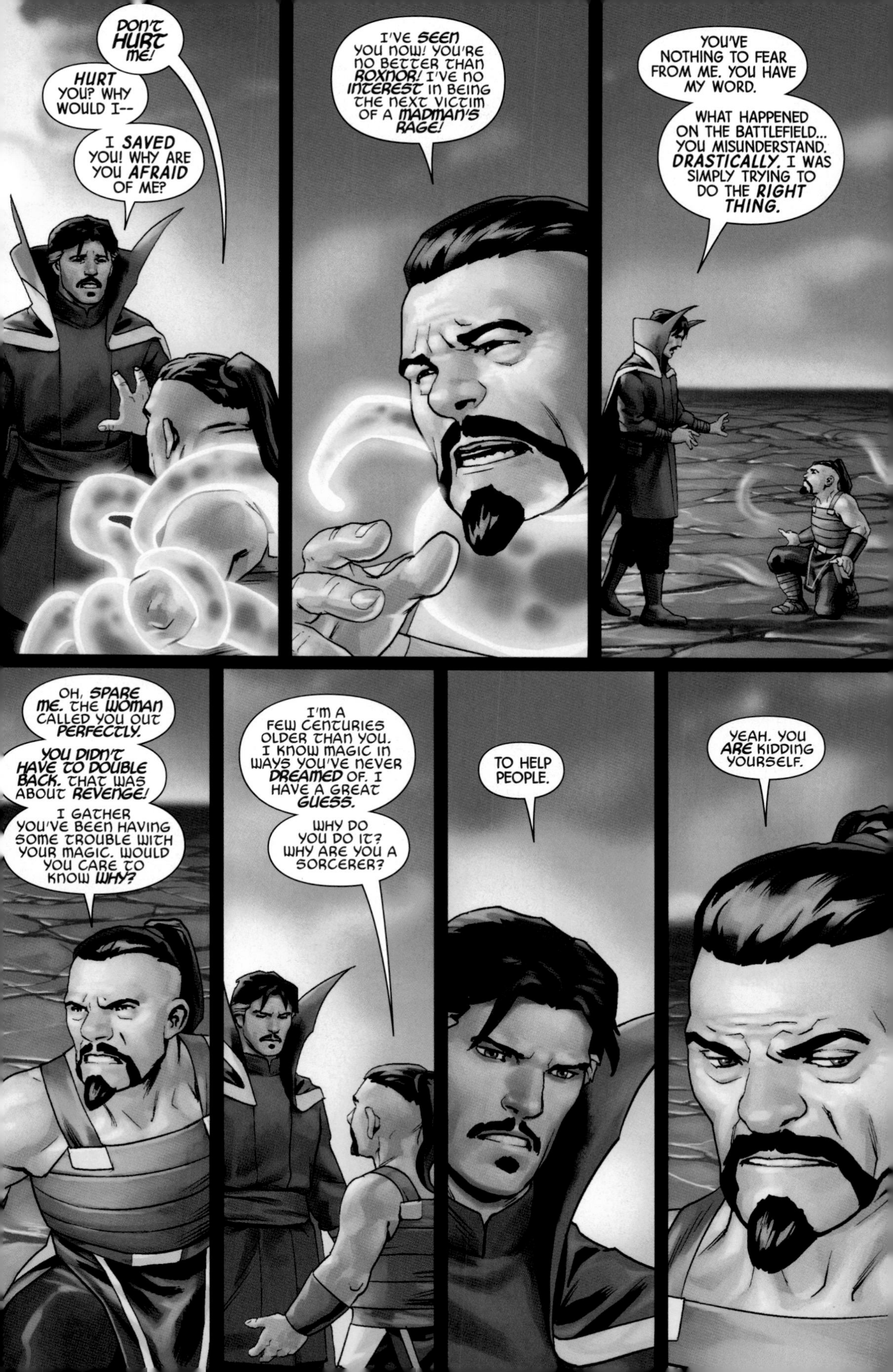
DON'T HURT ME!
HURT YOU? WHY WOULD I--
I SAVED YOU! WHY ARE YOU AFRAID OF ME?
I'VE SEEN YOU NOW! YOU'RE NO BETTER THAN ROXNOR! I'VE NO INTEREST IN BEING THE NEXT VICTIM OF A MADMAN'S RAGE!
YOU'VE NOTHING TO FEAR FROM ME. YOU HAVE MY WORD.
WHAT HAPPENED ON THE BATTLEFIELD... YOU MISUNDERSTAND. DRASTICALLY. I WAS SIMPLY TRYING TO DO THE RIGHT THING.
OH, SPARE ME. THE WOMAN CALLED YOU OUT PERFECTLY.
YOU DIDN'T HAVE TO DOUBLE BACK. THAT WAS ABOUT REVENGE!
I GATHER YOU'VE BEEN HAVING SOME TROUBLE WITH YOUR MAGIC. WOULD YOU CARE TO KNOW WHY?
I'M A FEW CENTURIES OLDER THAN YOU. I KNOW MAGIC IN WAYS YOU'VE NEVER DREAMED OF. I HAVE A GREAT GUESS.
WHY DO YOU DO IT? WHY ARE YOU A SORCERER?
TO HELP PEOPLE.
YEAH. YOU ARE KIDDING YOURSELF.

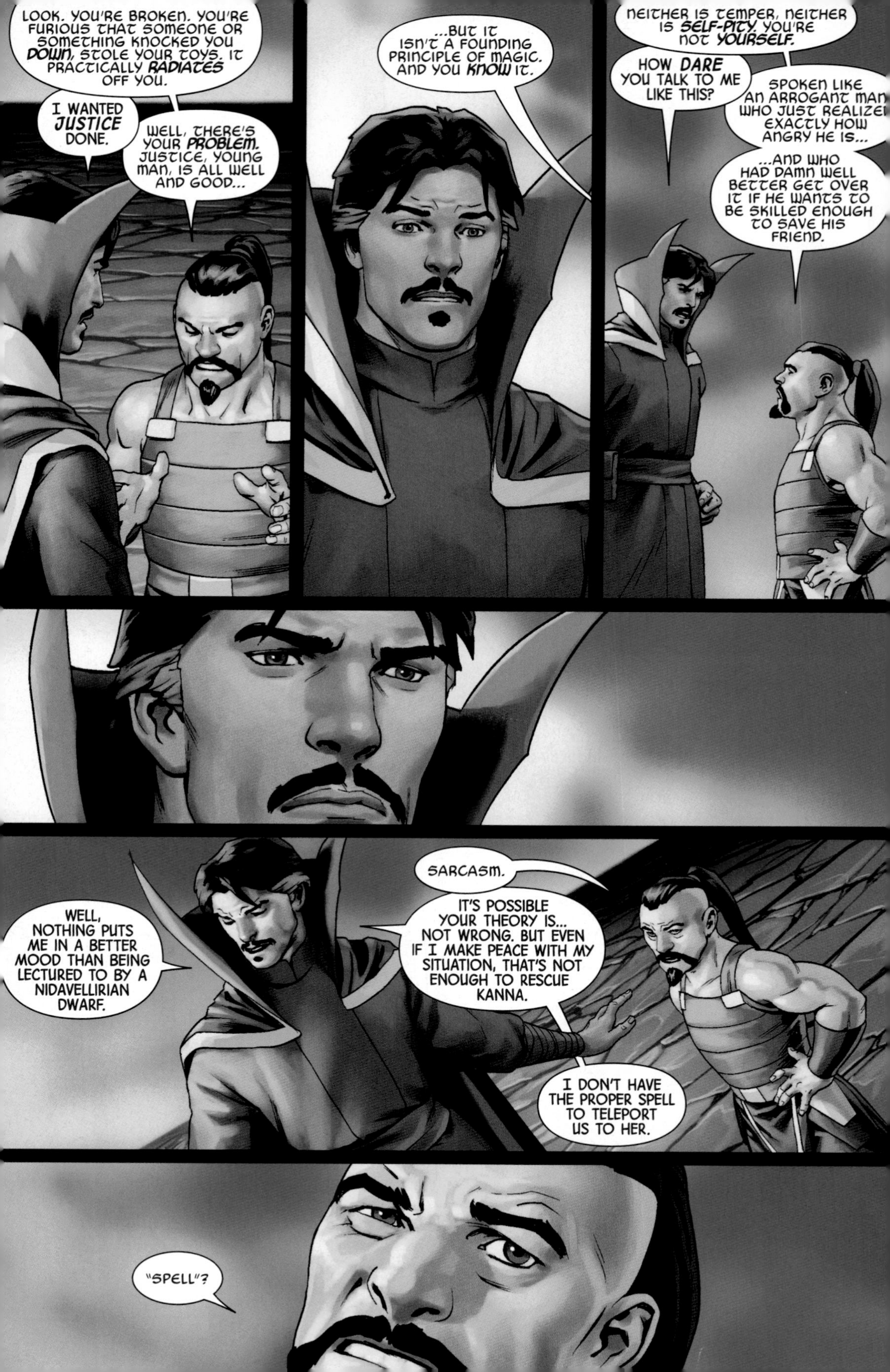
LOOK. YOU'RE BROKEN. YOU'RE FURIOUS THAT SOMEONE OR SOMETHING KNOCKED YOU DOWN, STOLE YOUR TOYS. IT PRACTICALLY RADIATES OFF YOU.
I WANTED JUSTICE DONE.
WELL, THERE'S YOUR PROBLEM. JUSTICE, YOUNG MAN, IS ALL WELL AND GOOD...
...BUT IT ISN'T A FOUNDING PRINCIPLE OF MAGIC. AND YOU KNOW IT.
NEITHER IS TEMPER, NEITHER IS SELF-PITY. YOU'RE NOT YOURSELF.
HOW DARE YOU TALK TO ME LIKE THIS?
SPOKEN LIKE AN ARROGANT MAN WHO JUST REALIZED EXACTLY HOW ANGRY HE IS...
...AND WHO HAD DAMN WELL BETTER GET OVER IT IF HE WANTS TO BE SKILLED ENOUGH TO SAVE HIS FRIEND.
WELL, NOTHING PUTS ME IN A BETTER MOOD THAN BEING LECTURED TO BY A NIDAVELLIRIAN DWARF.
SARCASM.
IT'S POSSIBLE YOUR THEORY IS... NOT WRONG. BUT EVEN IF I MAKE PEACE WITH MY SITUATION, THAT'S NOT ENOUGH TO RESCUE KANNA.
I DON'T HAVE THE PROPER SPELL TO TELEPORT US TO HER.
"SPELL"?

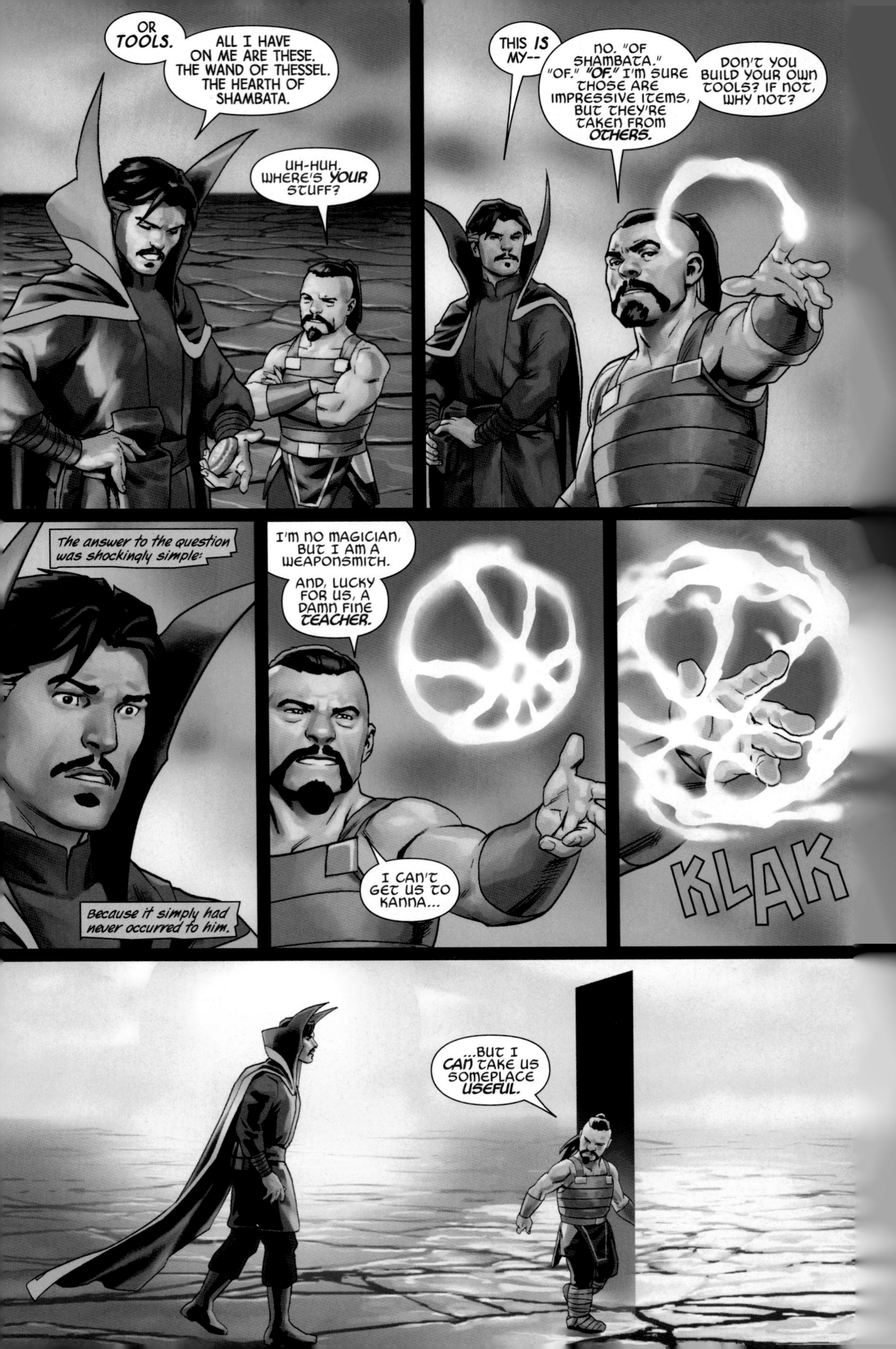
OR TOOLS.
ALL I HAVE ON ME ARE THESE. THE WAND OF THESSEL. THE HEARTH OF SHAMBATA.
UH-HUH. WHERE'S YOUR STUFF?
THIS IS MY--
NO. "OF SHAMBATA." "OF." "OF." I'M SURE THOSE ARE IMPRESSIVE ITEMS, BUT THEY'RE TAKEN FROM OTHERS.
DON'T YOU BUILD YOUR OWN TOOLS? IF NOT, WHY NOT?
The answer to the question was shockingly simple:
Because it simply had never occurred to him.
I'M NO MAGICIAN, BUT I AM A WEAPONSMITH.
AND, LUCKY FOR US, A DAMN FINE TEACHER.
I CAN'T GET US TO KANNA...
KLAK
...BUT I CAN TAKE US SOMEPLACE USEFUL.

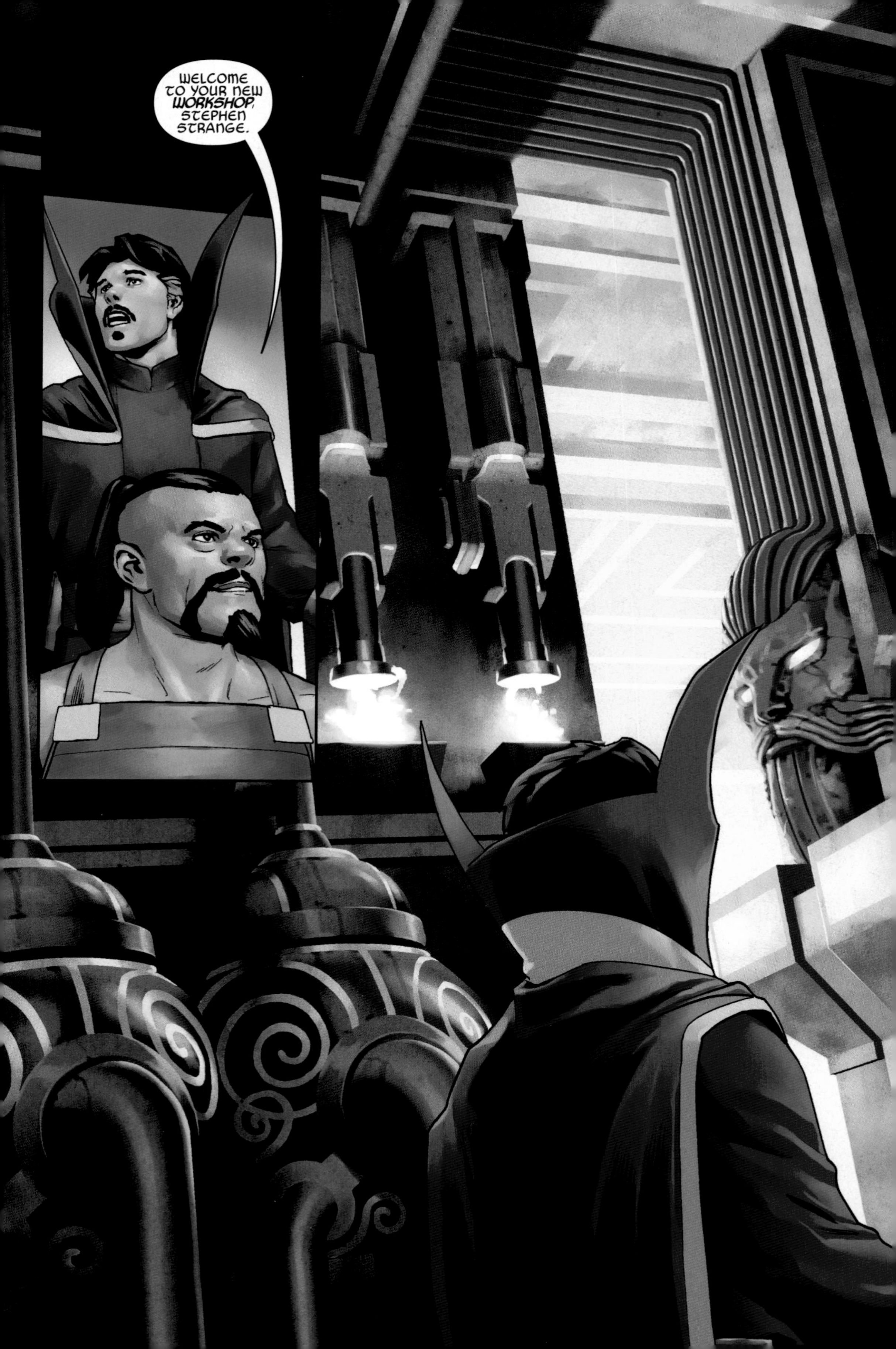
WELCOME TO YOUR NEW WORKSHOP, STEPHEN STRANGE.

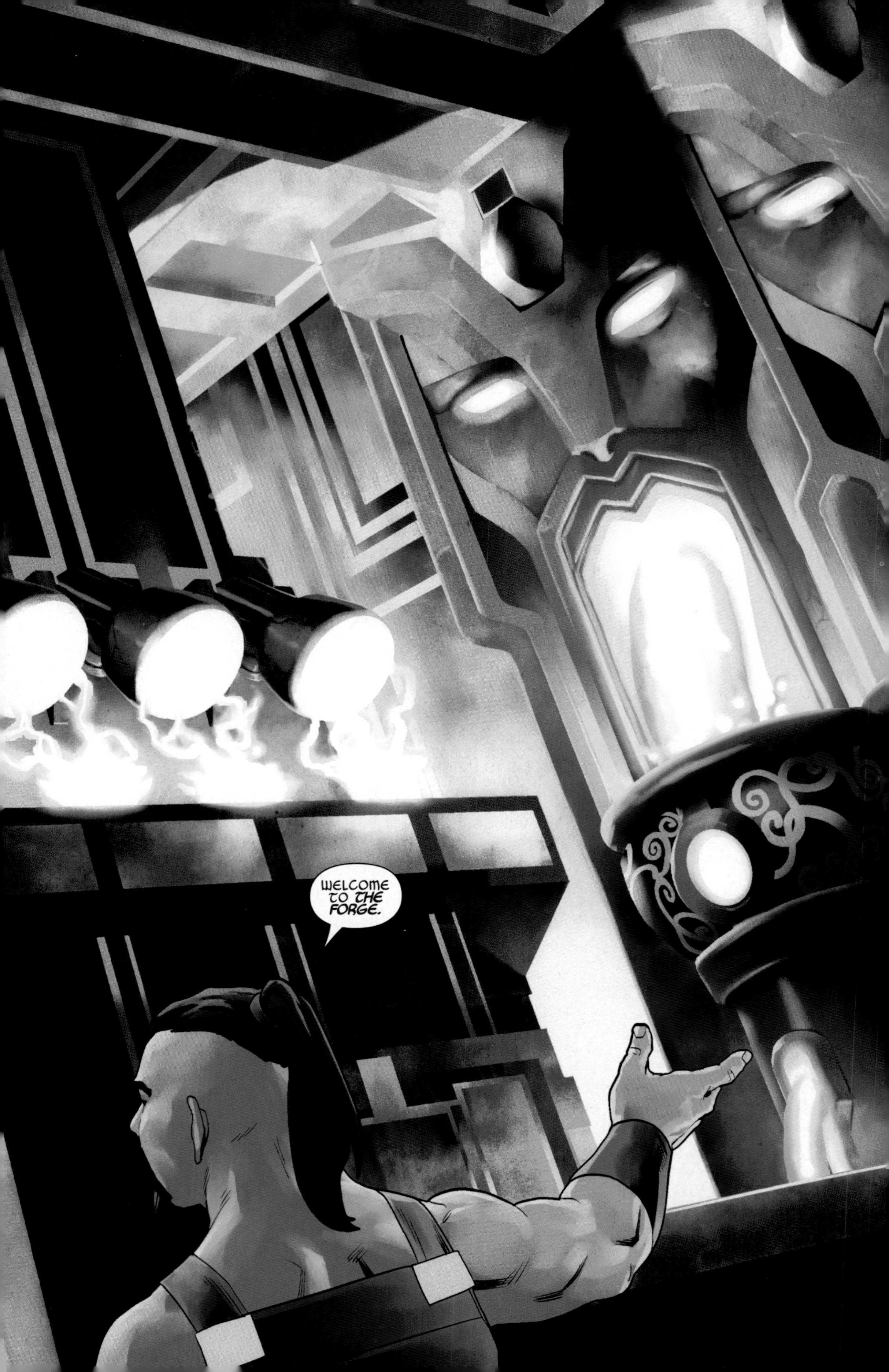
WELCOME TO THE FORGE.

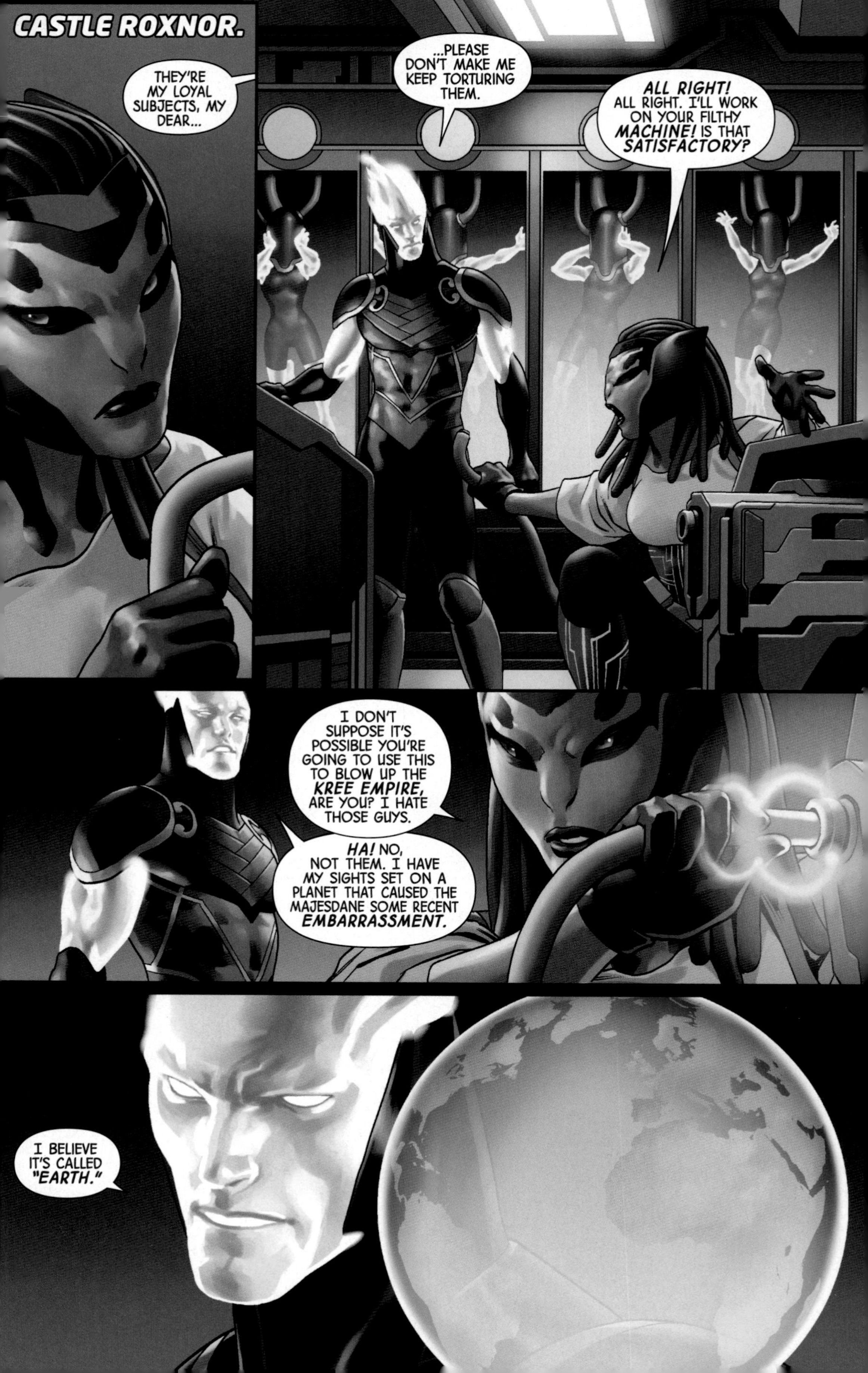
CASTLE ROXNOR.
THEY'RE MY LOYAL SUBJECTS, MY DEAR...
...PLEASE DON'T MAKE ME KEEP TORTURING THEM.
ALL RIGHT! ALL RIGHT. I'LL WORK ON YOUR FILTHY MACHINE! IS THAT SATISFACTORY?
I DON'T SUPPOSE IT'S POSSIBLE YOU'RE GOING TO USE THIS TO BLOW UP THE KREE EMPIRE, ARE YOU? I HATE THOSE GUYS.
HA! NO, NOT THEM. I HAVE MY SIGHTS SET ON A PLANET THAT CAUSED THE MAJESDANE SOME RECENT EMBARRASSMENT.
I BELIEVE IT'S CALLED "EARTH."

5

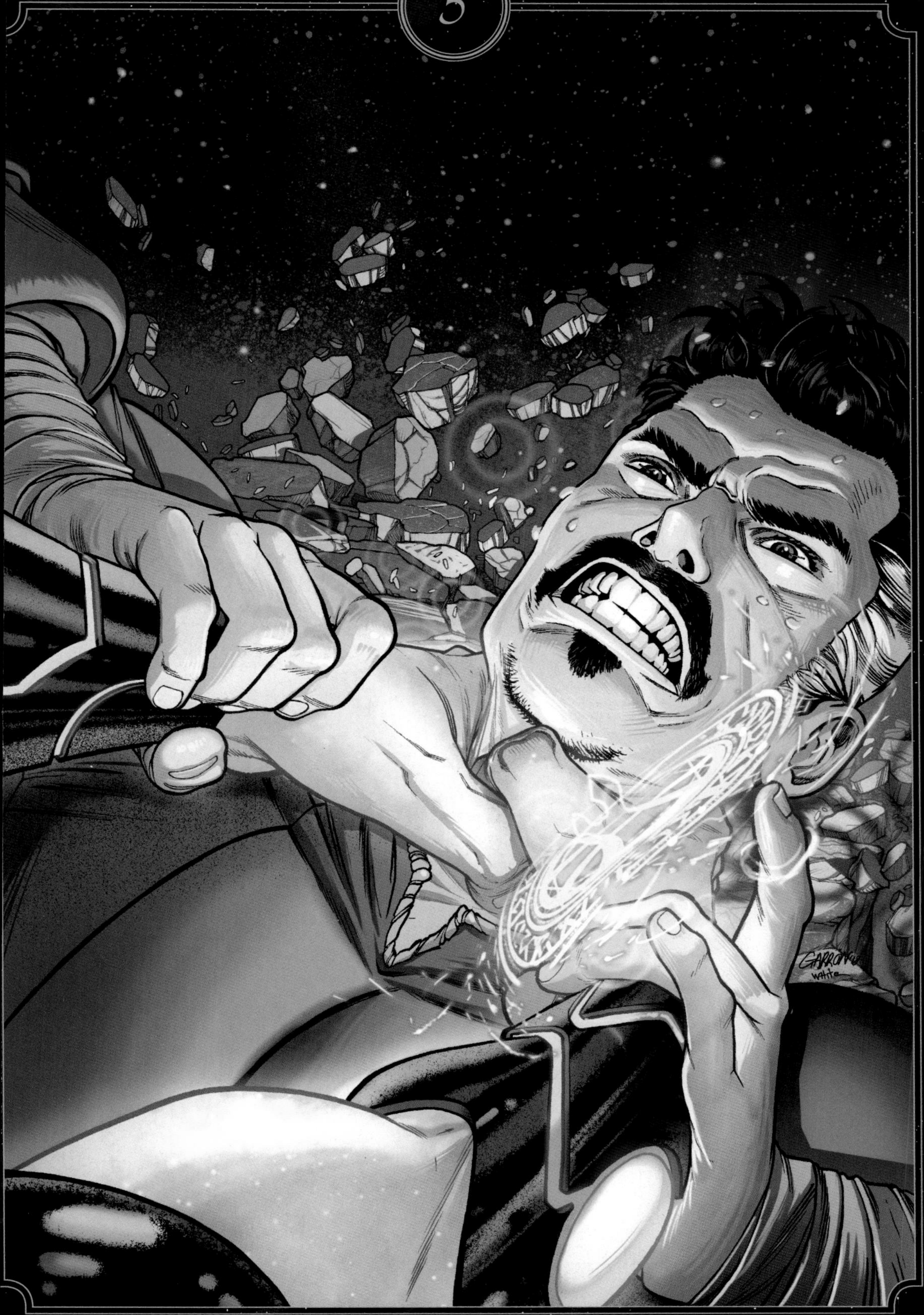

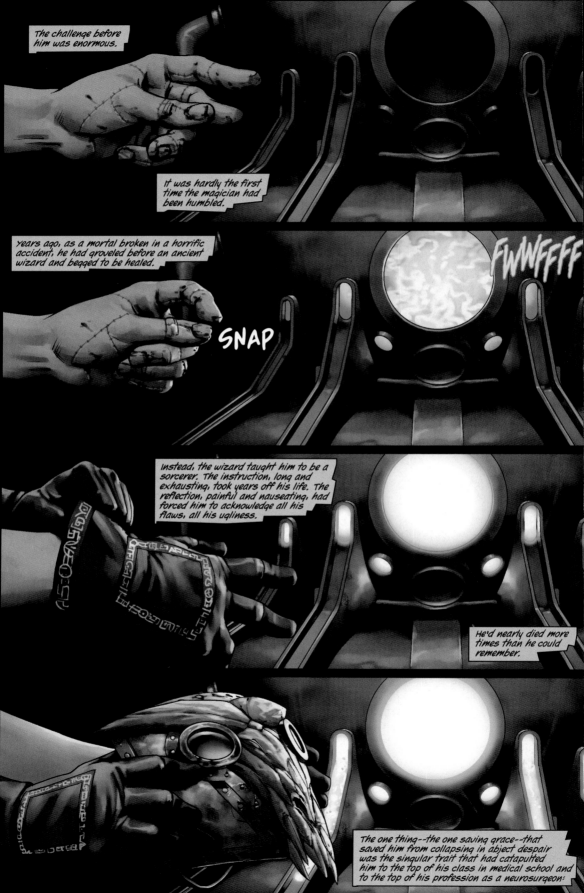

The challenge before him was enormous.

It was hardly the first time the magician had been humbled.

Years ago, as a mortal broken in a horrific accident, he had groveled before an ancient wizard and begged to be healed.

FWWFFFF

SNAP

Instead, the wizard taught him to be a sorcerer. The instruction, long and exhausting, took years off his life. The reflection, painful and nauseating, had forced him to acknowledge all his flaws, all his ugliness.

He'd nearly died more times than he could remember.

The one thing--the one saving grace--that saved him from collapsing in abject despair was the singular trait that had catapulted him to the top of his class in medical school and to the top of his profession as a neurosurgeon:

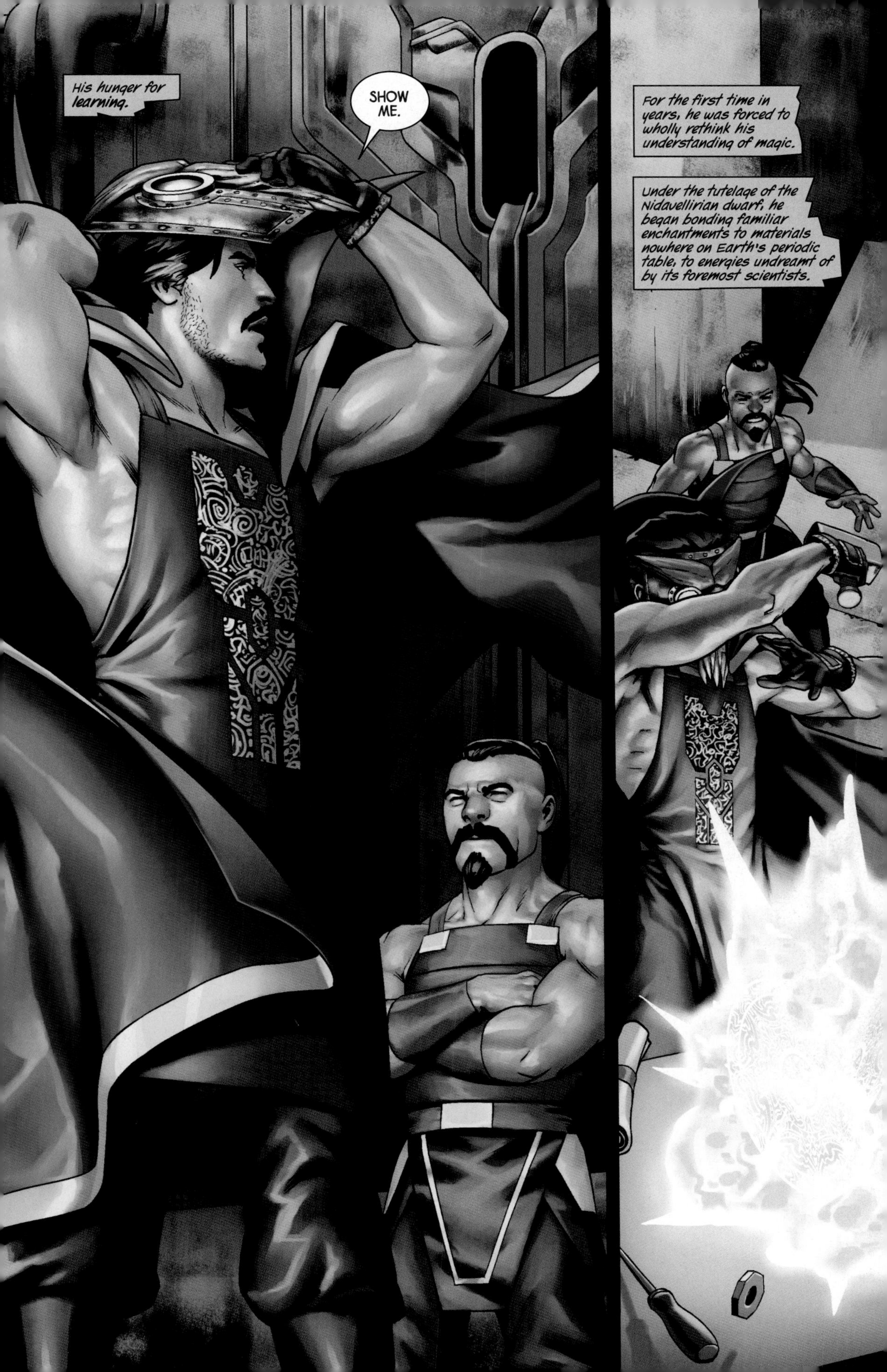
His hunger for learning.
SHOW ME.
For the first time in years, he was forced to wholly rethink his understanding of magic.
Under the tutelage of the Nidavellirian dwarf, he began bonding familiar enchantments to materials nowhere on Earth's periodic table, to energies undreamt of by its foremost scientists.

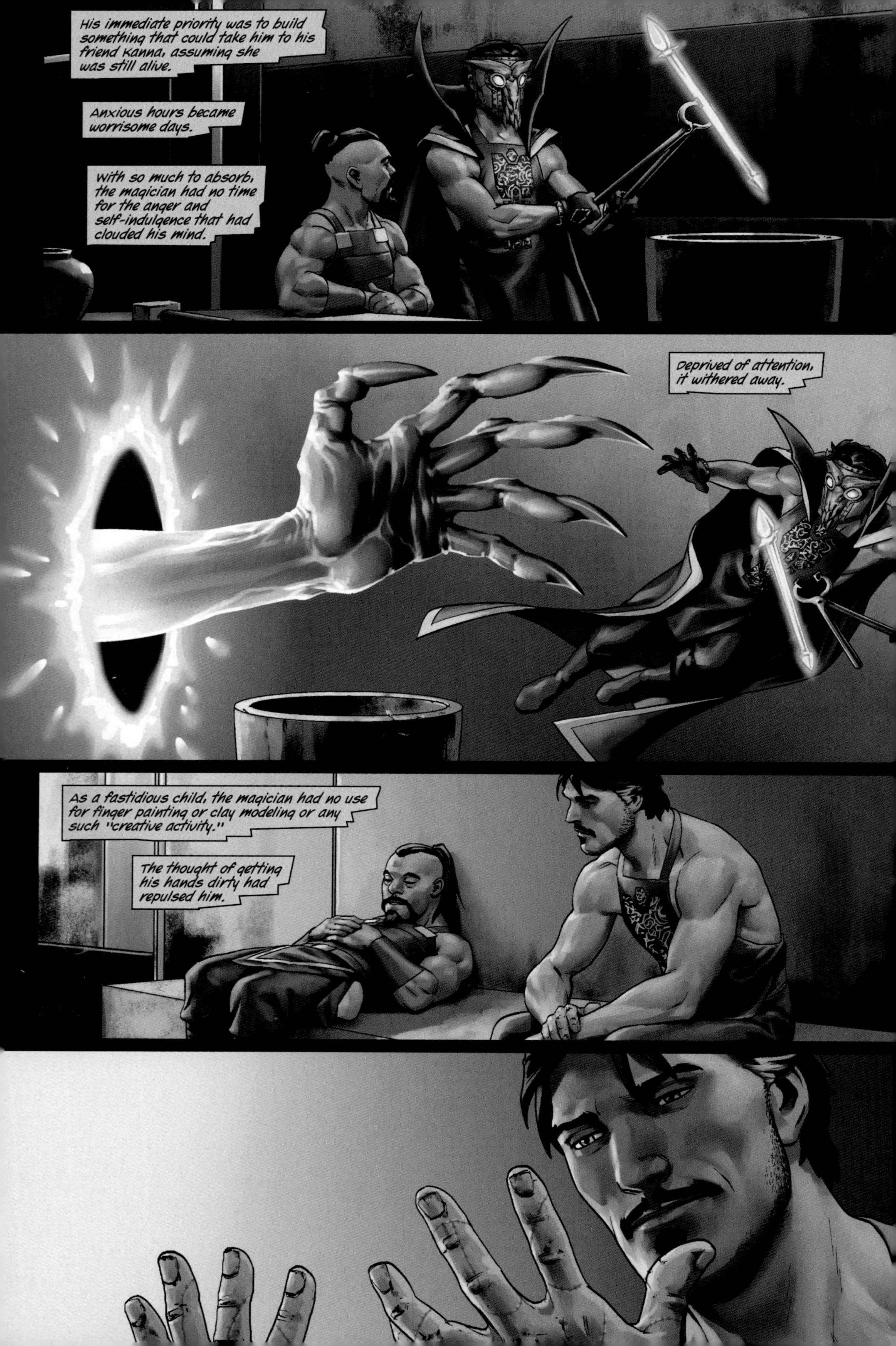
His immediate priority was to build something that could take him to his friend Kanna, assuming she was still alive.
Anxious hours became worrisome days.
With so much to absorb, the magician had no time for the anger and self-indulgence that had clouded his mind.
Deprived of attention, it withered away.
As a fastidious child, the magician had no use for finger painting or clay modeling or any such "creative activity."
The thought of getting his hands dirty had repulsed him.

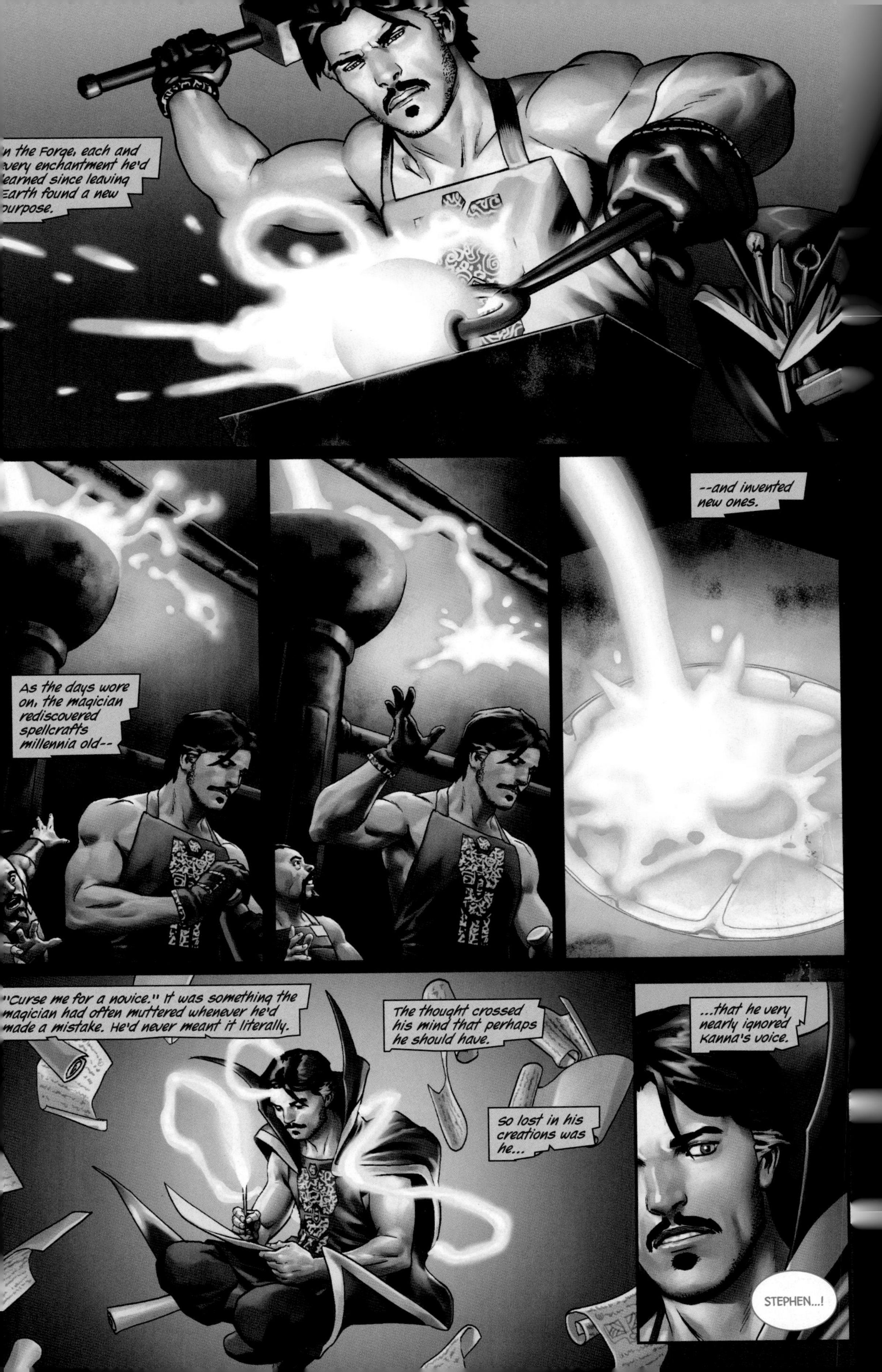
In the Forge, each and every enchantment he'd learned since leaving Earth found a new purpose.
As the days wore on, the magician rediscovered spellcrafts millennia old--
--and invented new ones.
"Curse me for a novice." It was something the magician had often muttered whenever he'd made a mistake. He'd never meant it literally.
The thought crossed his mind that perhaps he should have.
So lost in his creations was he...
...that he very nearly ignored Kanna's voice.
STEPHEN...!

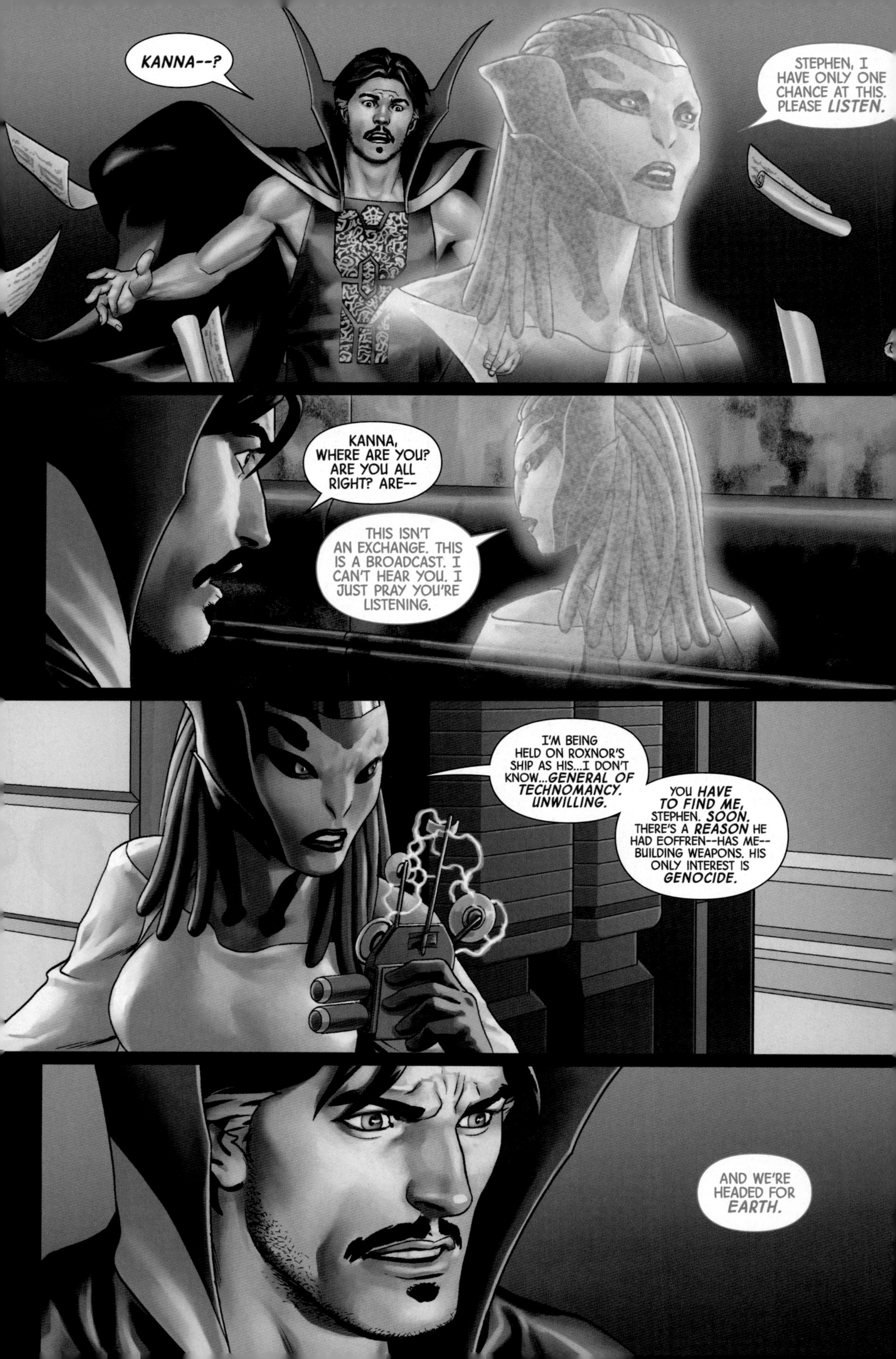
KANNA--?
STEPHEN, I HAVE ONLY ONE CHANCE AT THIS. PLEASE LISTEN.
KANNA, WHERE ARE YOU? ARE YOU ALL RIGHT? ARE--
THIS ISN'T AN EXCHANGE. THIS IS A BROADCAST. I CAN'T HEAR YOU. I JUST PRAY YOU'RE LISTENING.
I'M BEING HELD ON ROXNOR'S SHIP AS HIS...I DON'T KNOW...GENERAL OF TECHNOMANCY. UNWILLING.
YOU HAVE TO FIND ME, STEPHEN. SOON. THERE'S A REASON HE HAD EOFFREN--HAS ME--BUILDING WEAPONS. HIS ONLY INTEREST IS GENOCIDE.
AND WE'RE HEADED FOR EARTH.

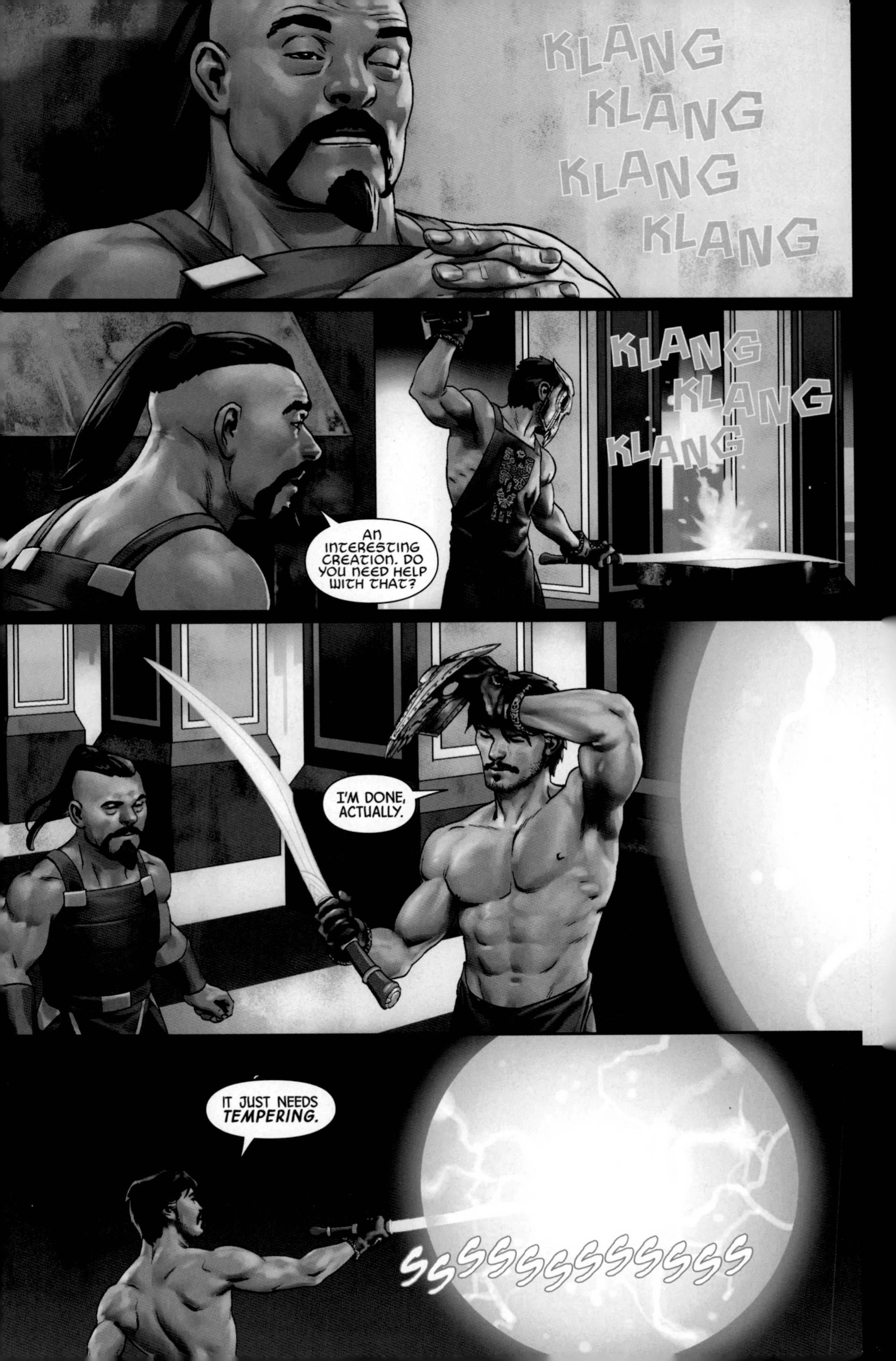
KLANG
KLANG
KLANG
KLANG
KLANG
KLANG
KLANG
AN INTERESTING CREATION. DO YOU NEED HELP WITH THAT?
I'M DONE, ACTUALLY.
IT JUST NEEDS TEMPERING.
SSSSSSSSSSSSSS

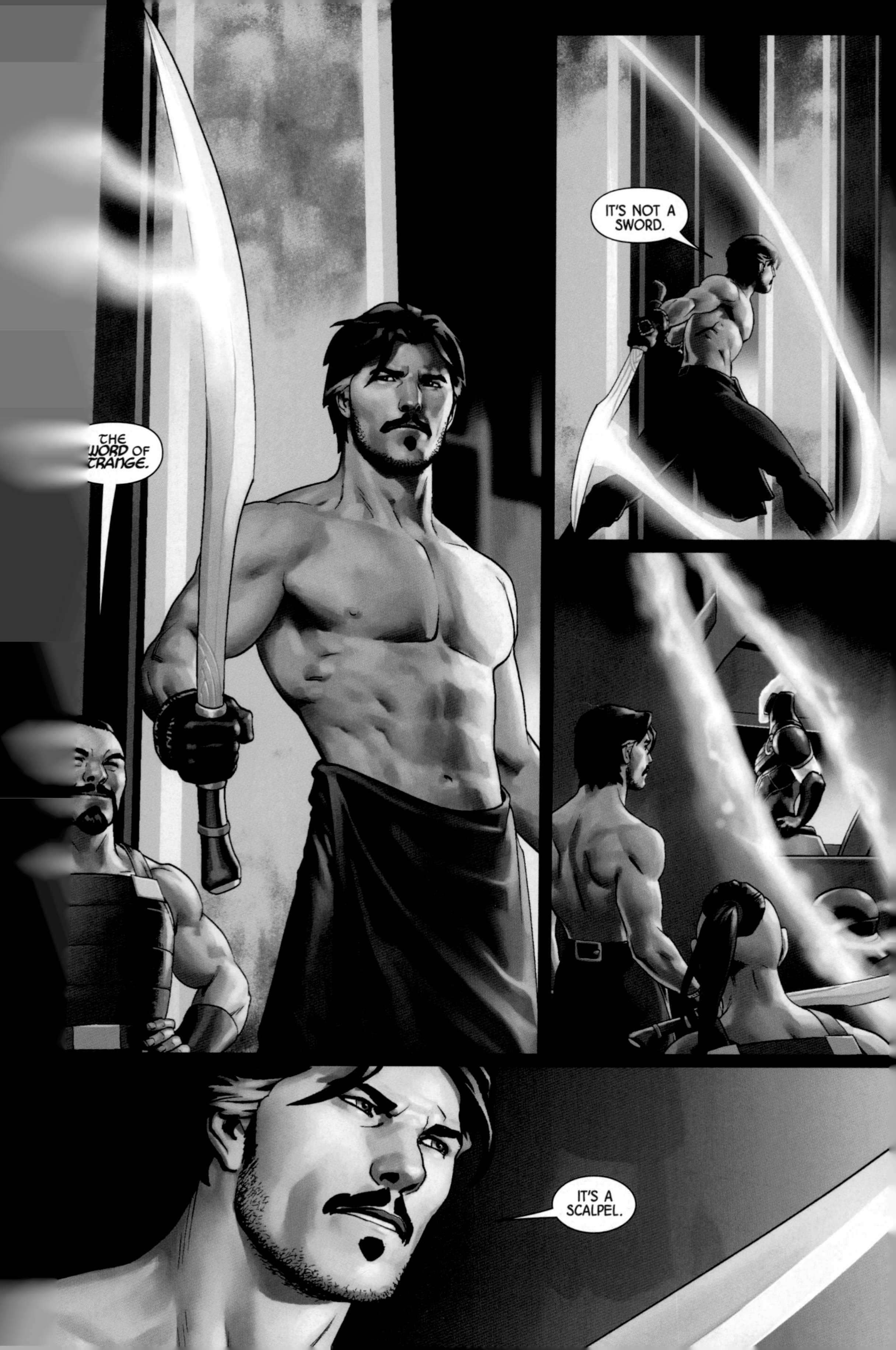
THE WORD OF TRANGE.
IT'S NOT A SWORD.
IT'S A SCALPEL.

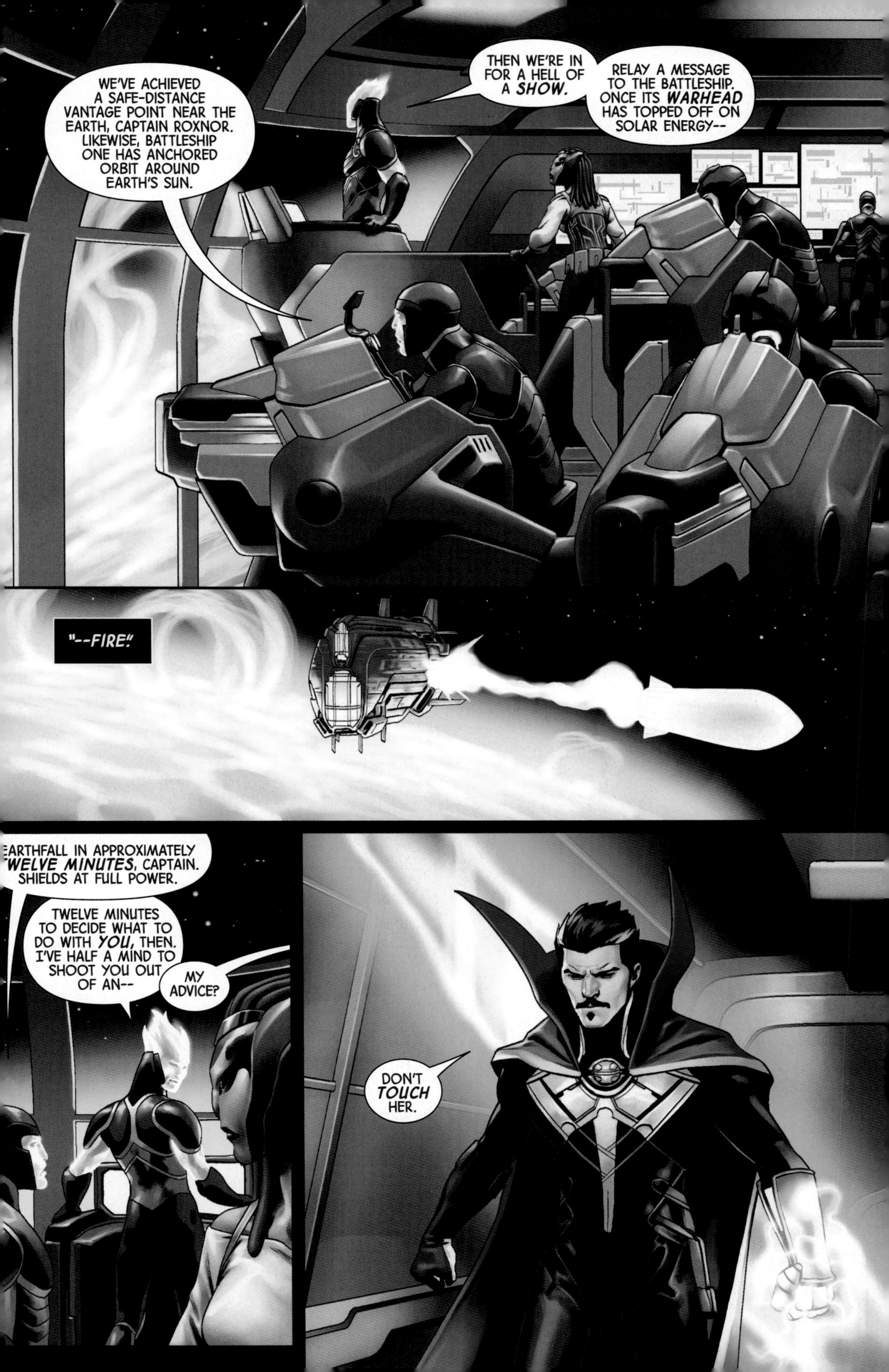
WE'VE ACHIEVED A SAFE-DISTANCE VANTAGE POINT NEAR THE EARTH, CAPTAIN ROXNOR. LIKEWISE, BATTLESHIP ONE HAS ANCHORED ORBIT AROUND EARTH'S SUN.
THEN WE'RE IN FOR A HELL OF A SHOW.
RELAY A MESSAGE TO THE BATTLESHIP. ONCE ITS WARHEAD HAS TOPPED OFF ON SOLAR ENERGY--
"--FIRE!"
EARTHFALL IN APPROXIMATELY TWELVE MINUTES, CAPTAIN. SHIELDS AT FULL POWER.
TWELVE MINUTES TO DECIDE WHAT TO DO WITH YOU, THEN. I'VE HALF A MIND TO SHOOT YOU OUT OF AN--
MY ADVICE?
DON'T TOUCH HER.

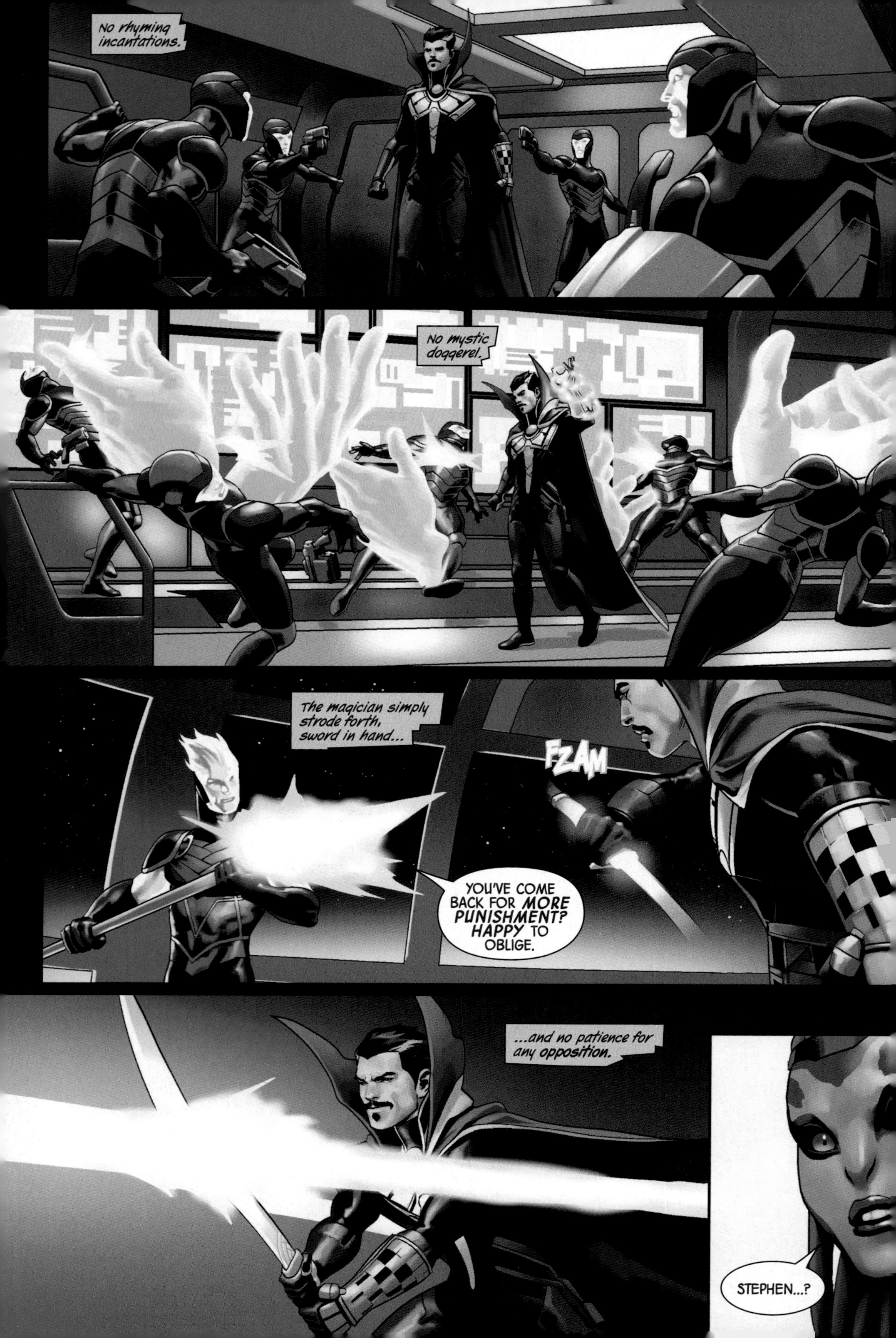
No rhyming incantations.
No mystic doggerel.
The magician simply strode forth, sword in hand...
FZAM
YOU'VE COME BACK FOR MORE PUNISHMENT? HAPPY TO OBLIGE.
...and no patience for any opposition.
STEPHEN...?

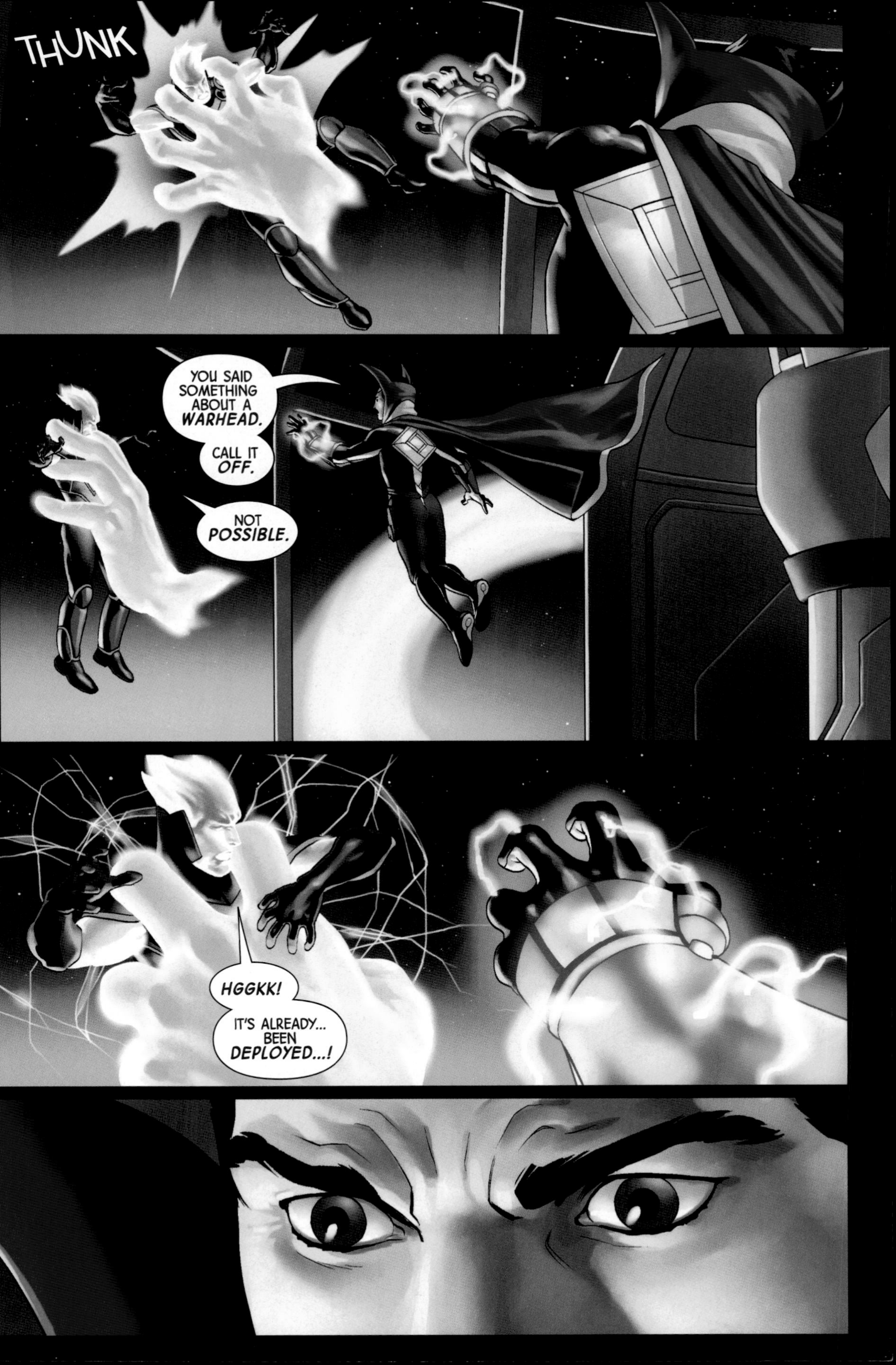
THUNK
YOU SAID SOMETHING ABOUT A WARHEAD.
CALL IT OFF.
NOT POSSIBLE.
HGGKK!
IT'S ALREADY... BEEN DEPLOYED...!

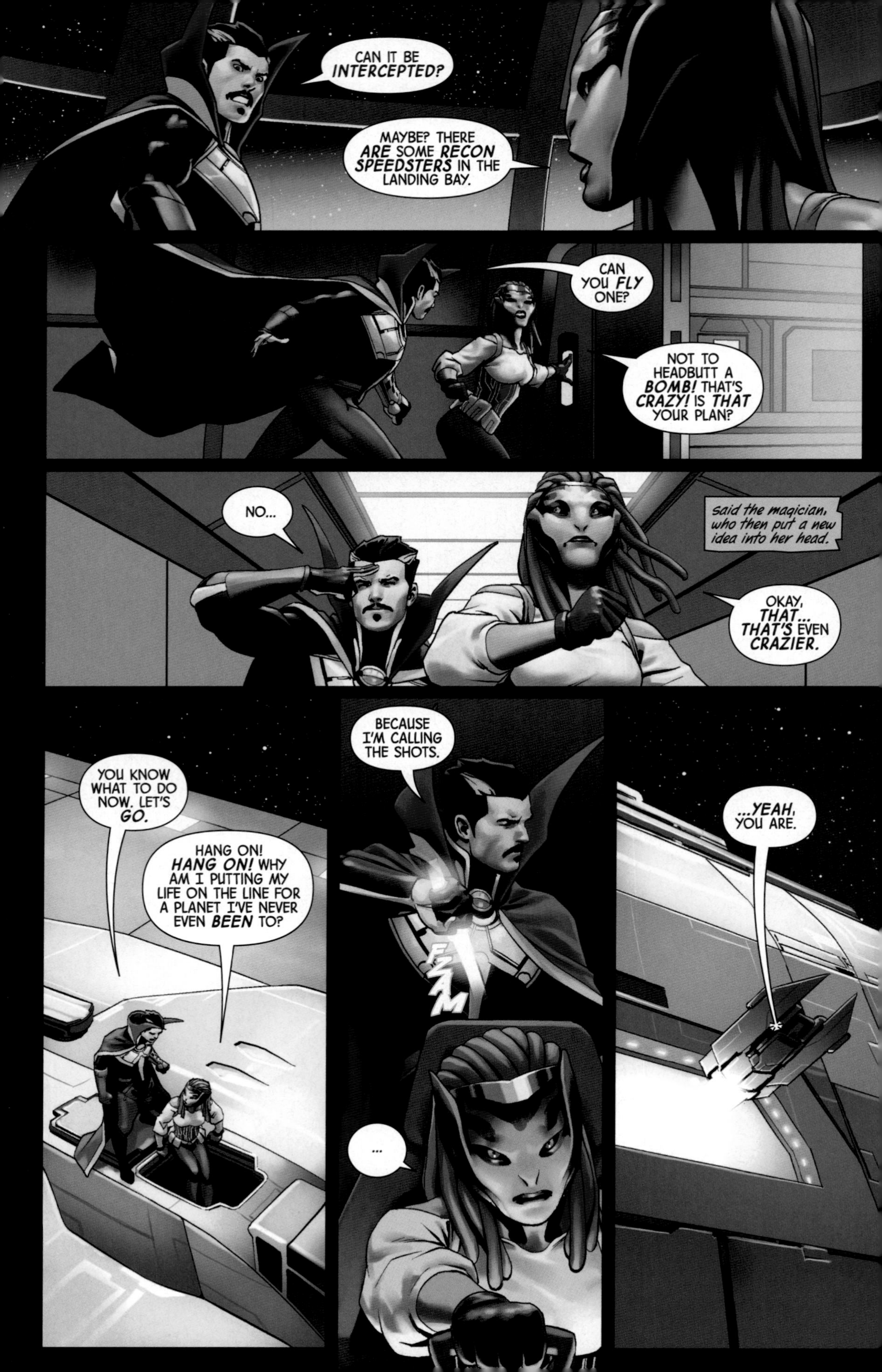
CAN IT BE INTERCEPTED?
MAYBE? THERE ARE SOME RECON SPEEDSTERS IN THE LANDING BAY.
CAN YOU FLY ONE?
NOT TO HEADBUTT A BOMB! THAT'S CRAZY! IS THAT YOUR PLAN?
NO...
said the magician, who then put a new idea into her head.
OKAY, THAT... THAT'S EVEN CRAZIER.
YOU KNOW WHAT TO DO NOW. LET'S GO.
HANG ON! HANG ON! WHY AM I PUTTING MY LIFE ON THE LINE FOR A PLANET I'VE NEVER EVEN BEEN TO?
BECAUSE I'M CALLING THE SHOTS.
FZZAM
...
...YEAH, YOU ARE.

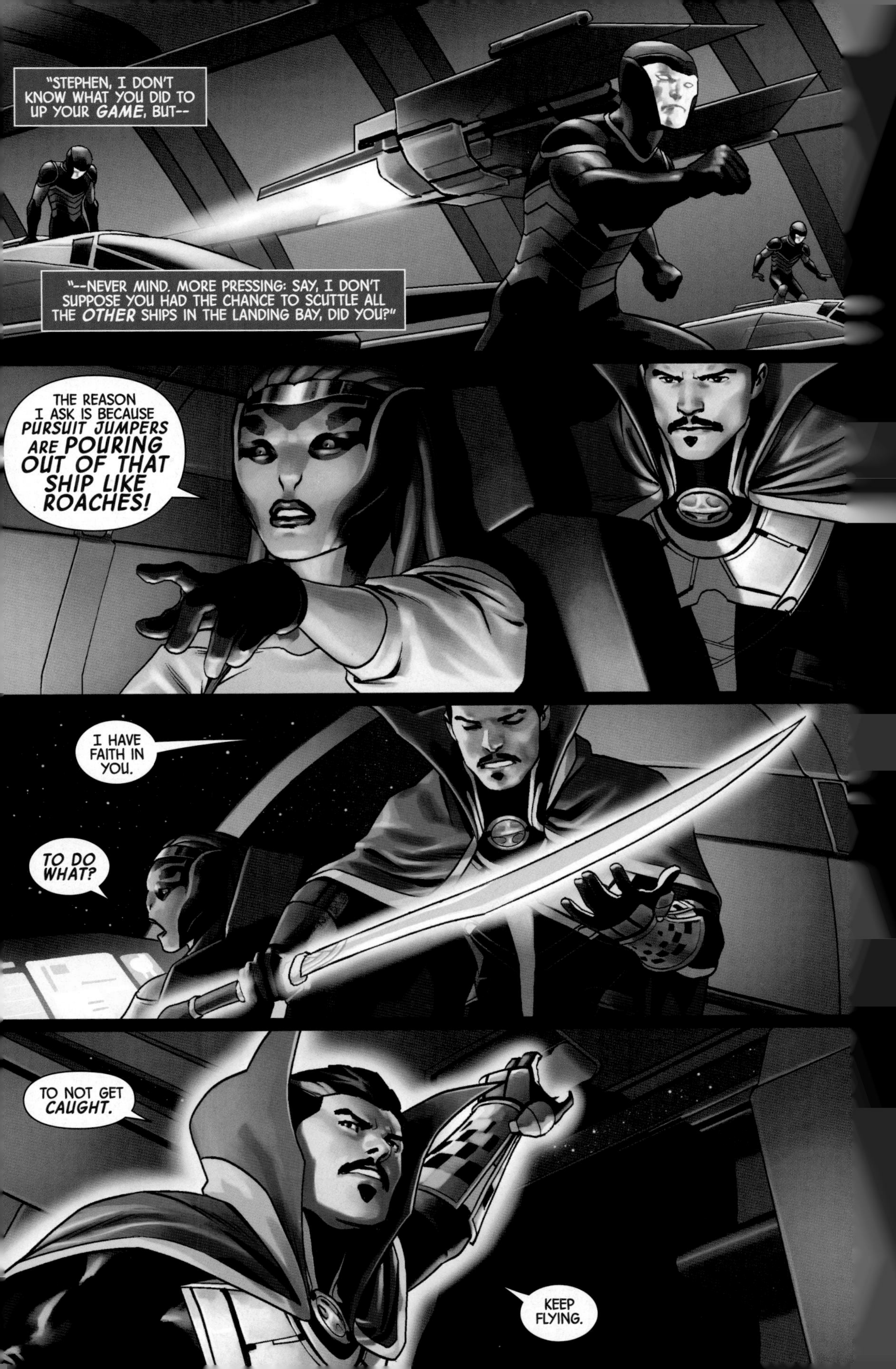
"STEPHEN, I DON'T KNOW WHAT YOU DID TO UP YOUR GAME, BUT--
"--NEVER MIND. MORE PRESSING: SAY, I DON'T SUPPOSE YOU HAD THE CHANCE TO SCUTTLE ALL THE OTHER SHIPS IN THE LANDING BAY, DID YOU?"
THE REASON I ASK IS BECAUSE PURSUIT JUMPERS ARE POURING OUT OF THAT SHIP LIKE ROACHES!
I HAVE FAITH IN YOU.
TO DO WHAT?
TO NOT GET CAUGHT.
KEEP FLYING.

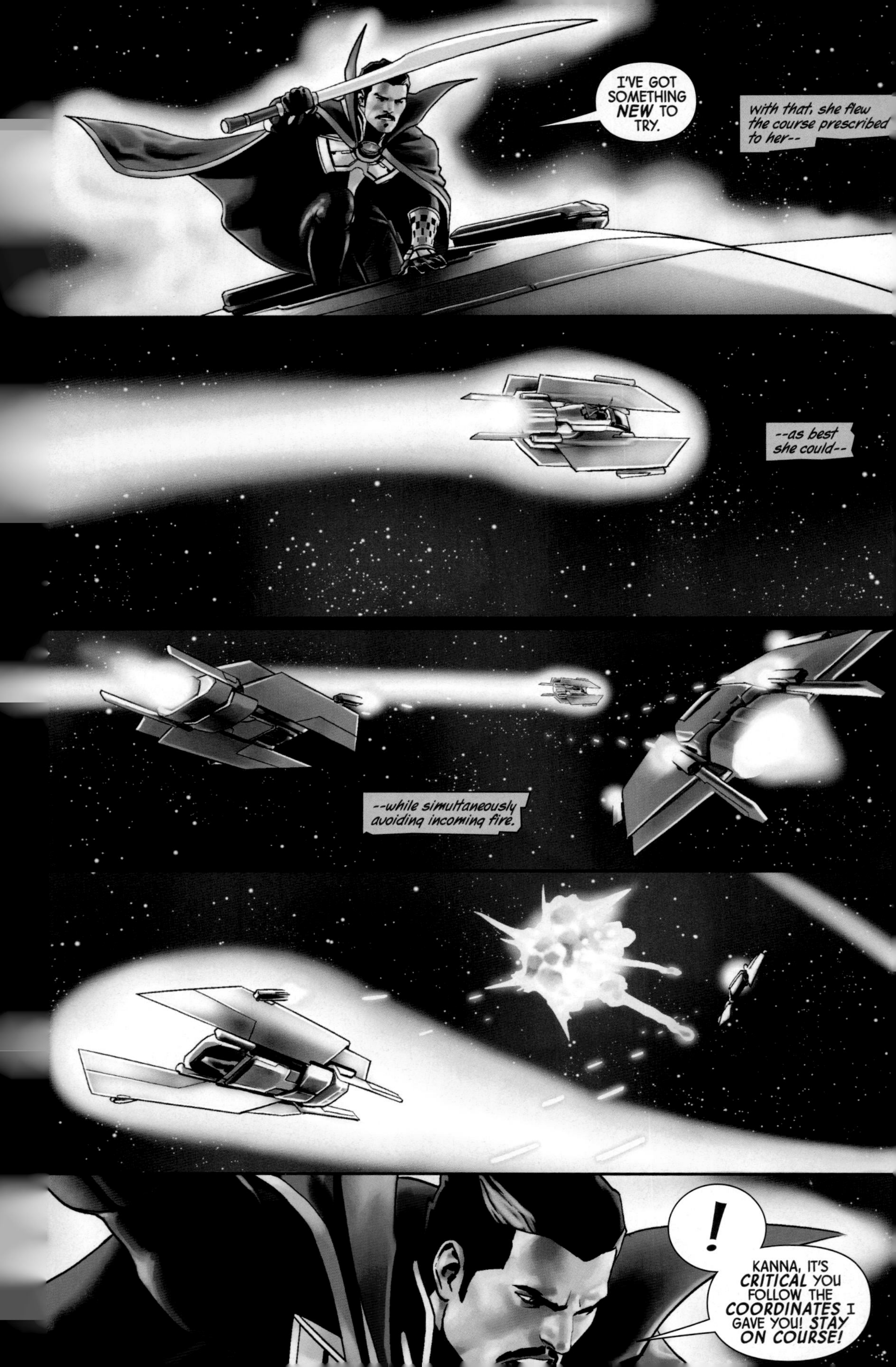

I'VE GOT SOMETHING NEW TO TRY.
with that, she flew the course prescribed to her--
--as best she could--
--while simultaneously avoiding incoming fire.
!
KANNA, IT'S CRITICAL YOU FOLLOW THE COORDINATES I GAVE YOU! STAY ON COURSE!

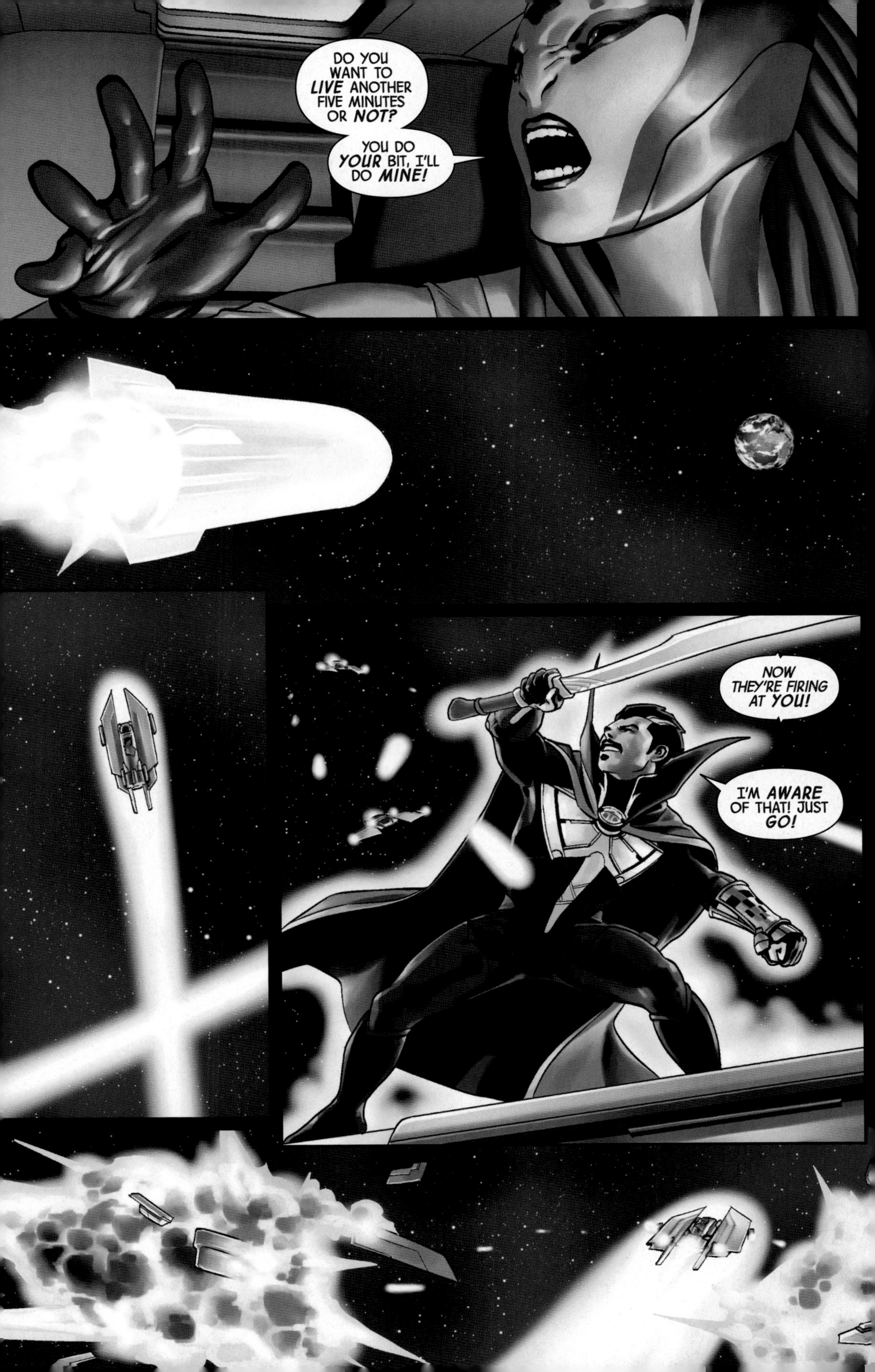
DO YOU WANT TO LIVE ANOTHER FIVE MINUTES OR NOT?
YOU DO YOUR BIT, I'LL DO MINE!
NOW THEY'RE FIRING AT YOU!
I'M AWARE OF THAT! JUST GO!

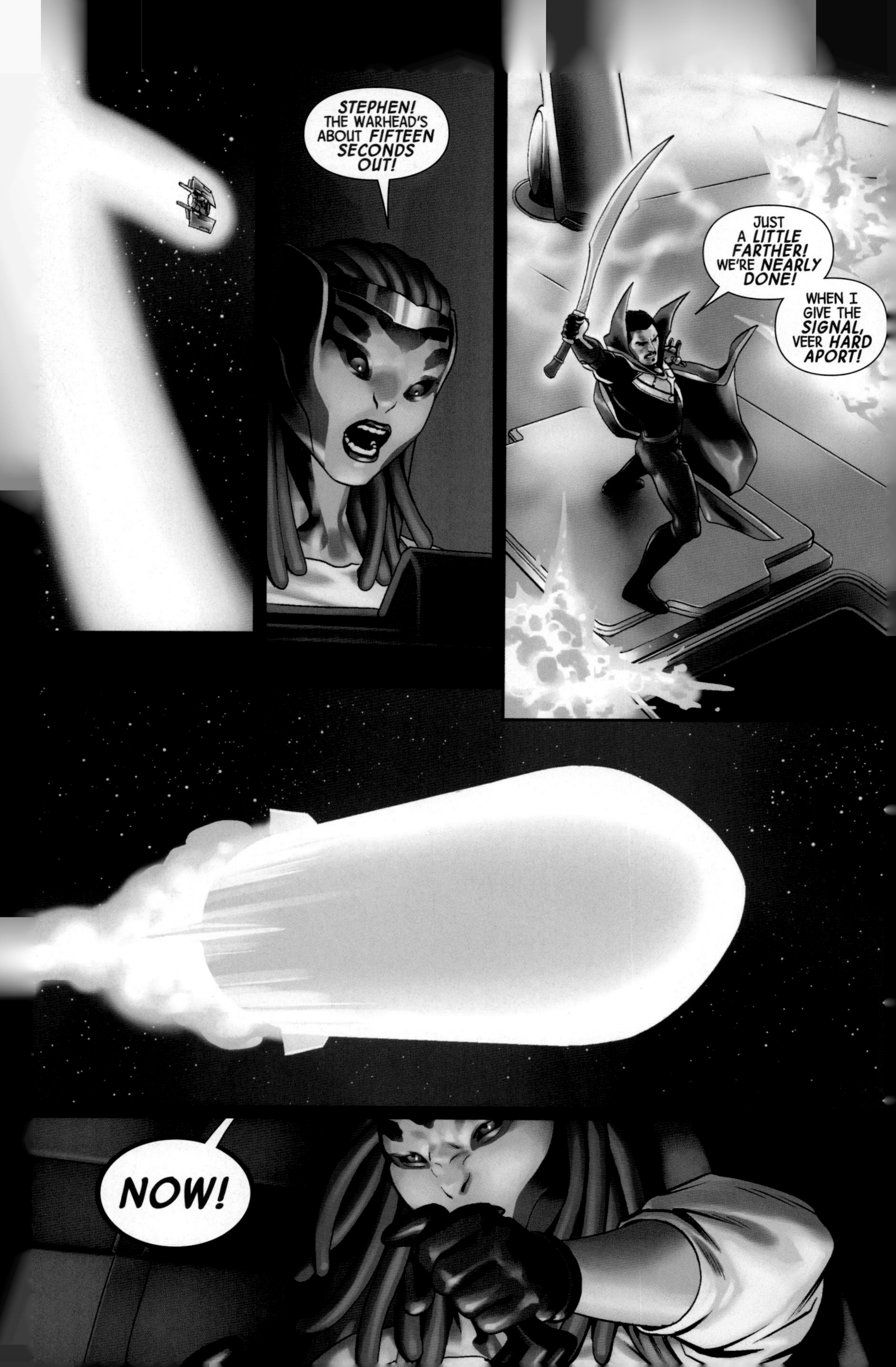
STEPHEN! THE WARHEAD'S ABOUT FIFTEEN SECONDS OUT!
JUST A LITTLE FARTHER! WE'RE NEARLY DONE!
WHEN I GIVE THE SIGNAL, VEER HARD APORT!
NOW!

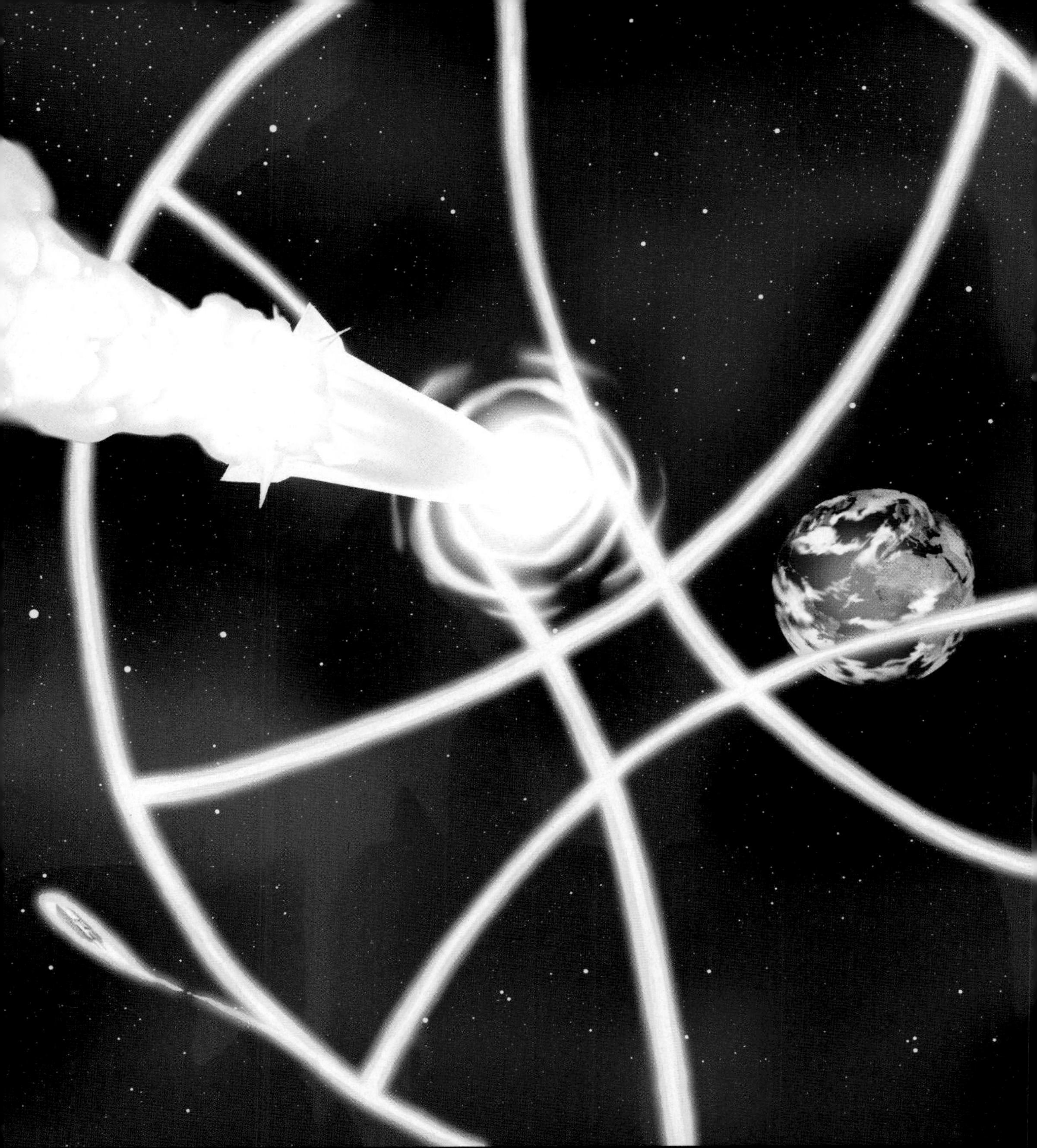
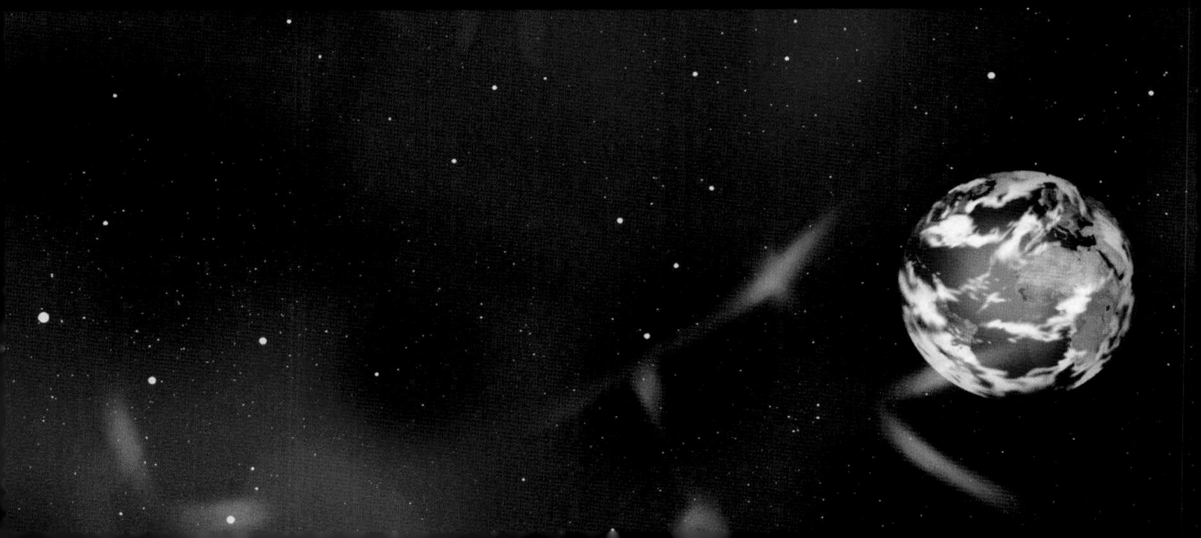

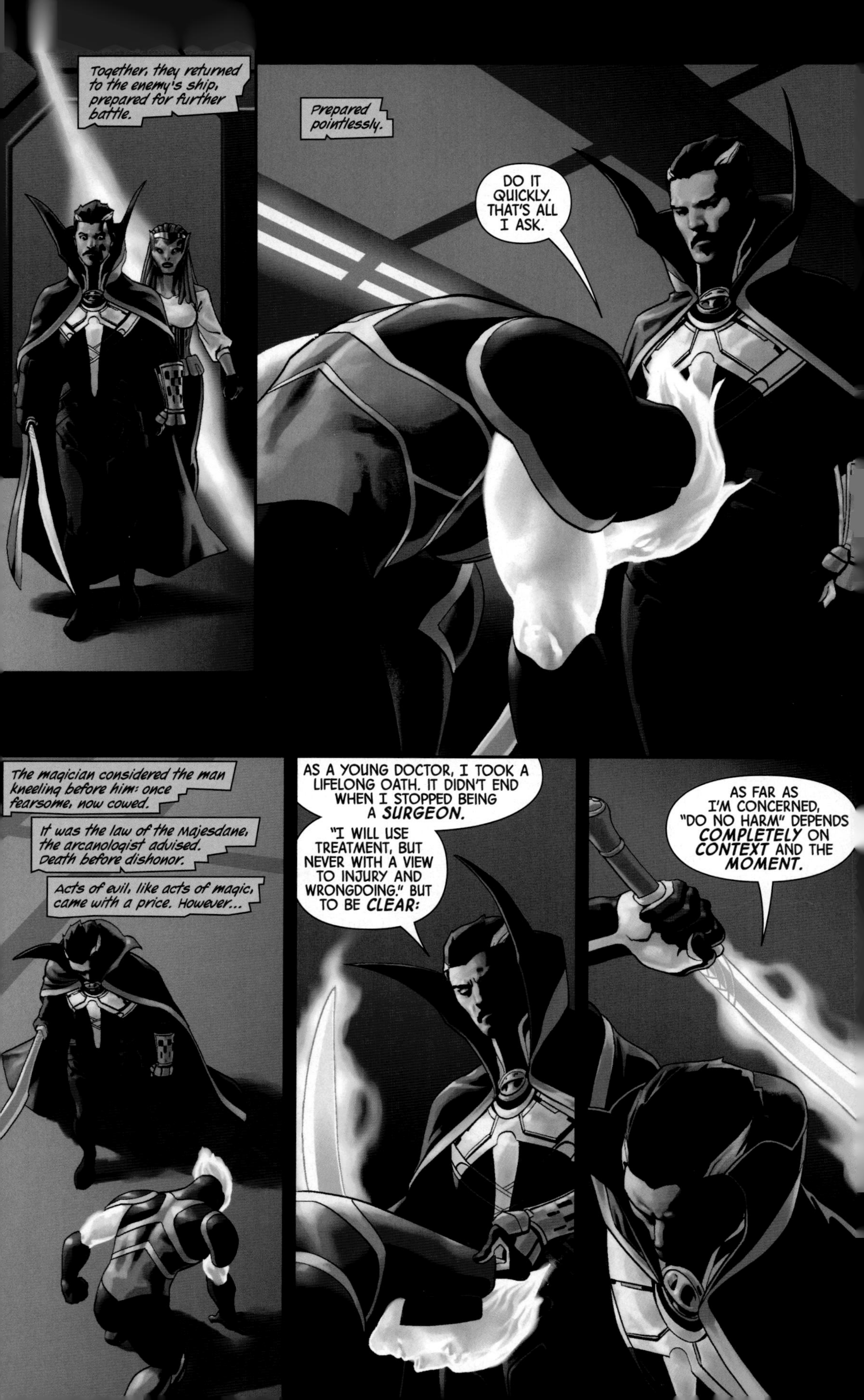

Together, they returned to the enemy's ship, prepared for further battle.
Prepared pointlessly.
DO IT QUICKLY. THAT'S ALL I ASK.
The magician considered the man kneeling before him: once fearsome, now cowed.
It was the law of the Majesdane, the arcanologist advised. Death before dishonor.
Acts of evil, like acts of magic, came with a price. However...
AS A YOUNG DOCTOR, I TOOK A LIFELONG OATH. IT DIDN'T END WHEN I STOPPED BEING A SURGEON.
"I WILL USE TREATMENT, BUT NEVER WITH A VIEW TO INJURY AND WRONGDOING." BUT TO BE CLEAR:
AS FAR AS I'M CONCERNED, "DO NO HARM" DEPENDS COMPLETELY ON CONTEXT AND THE MOMENT.

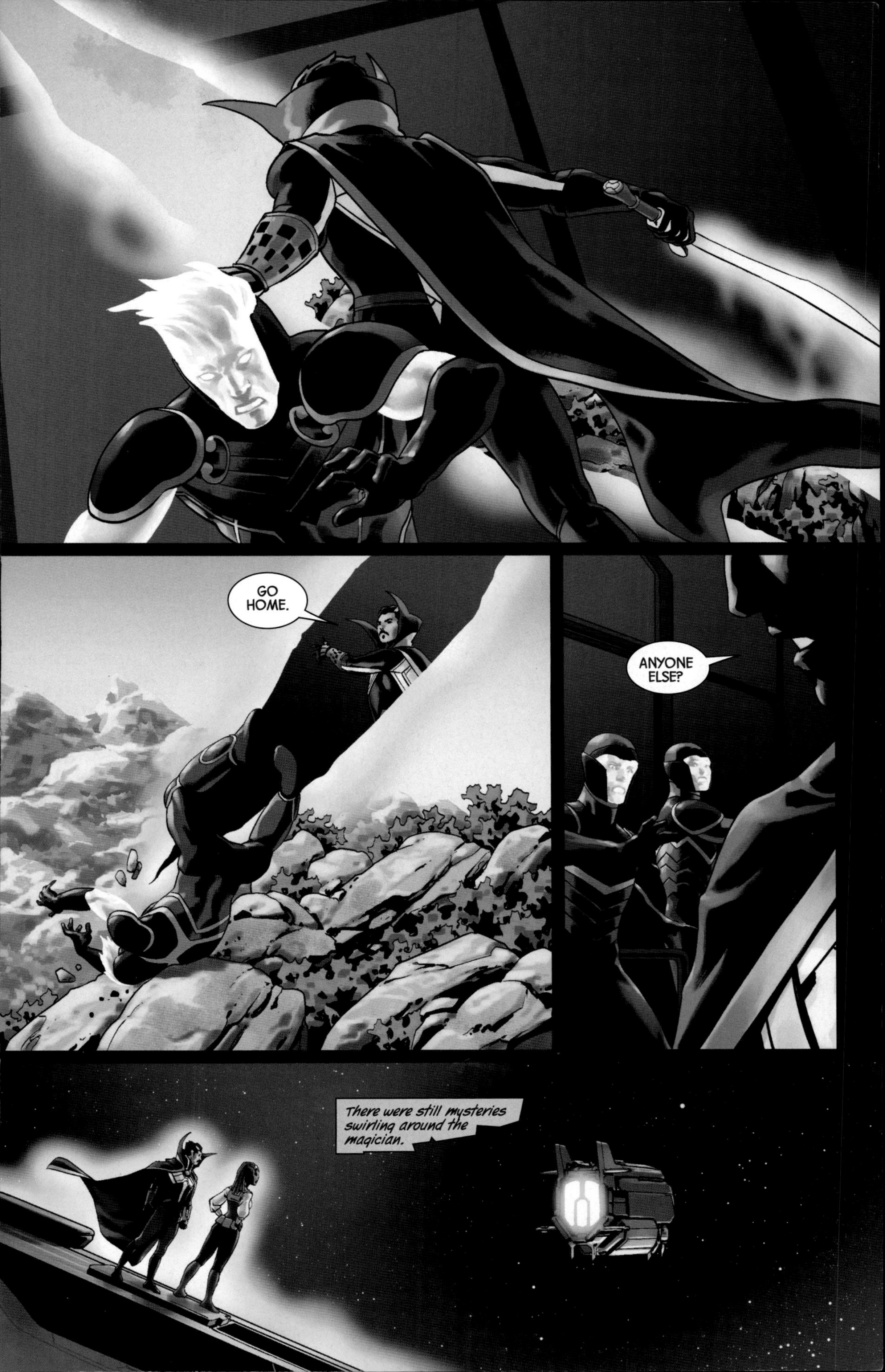
GO HOME.
ANYONE ELSE?
There were still mysteries swirling around the magician.

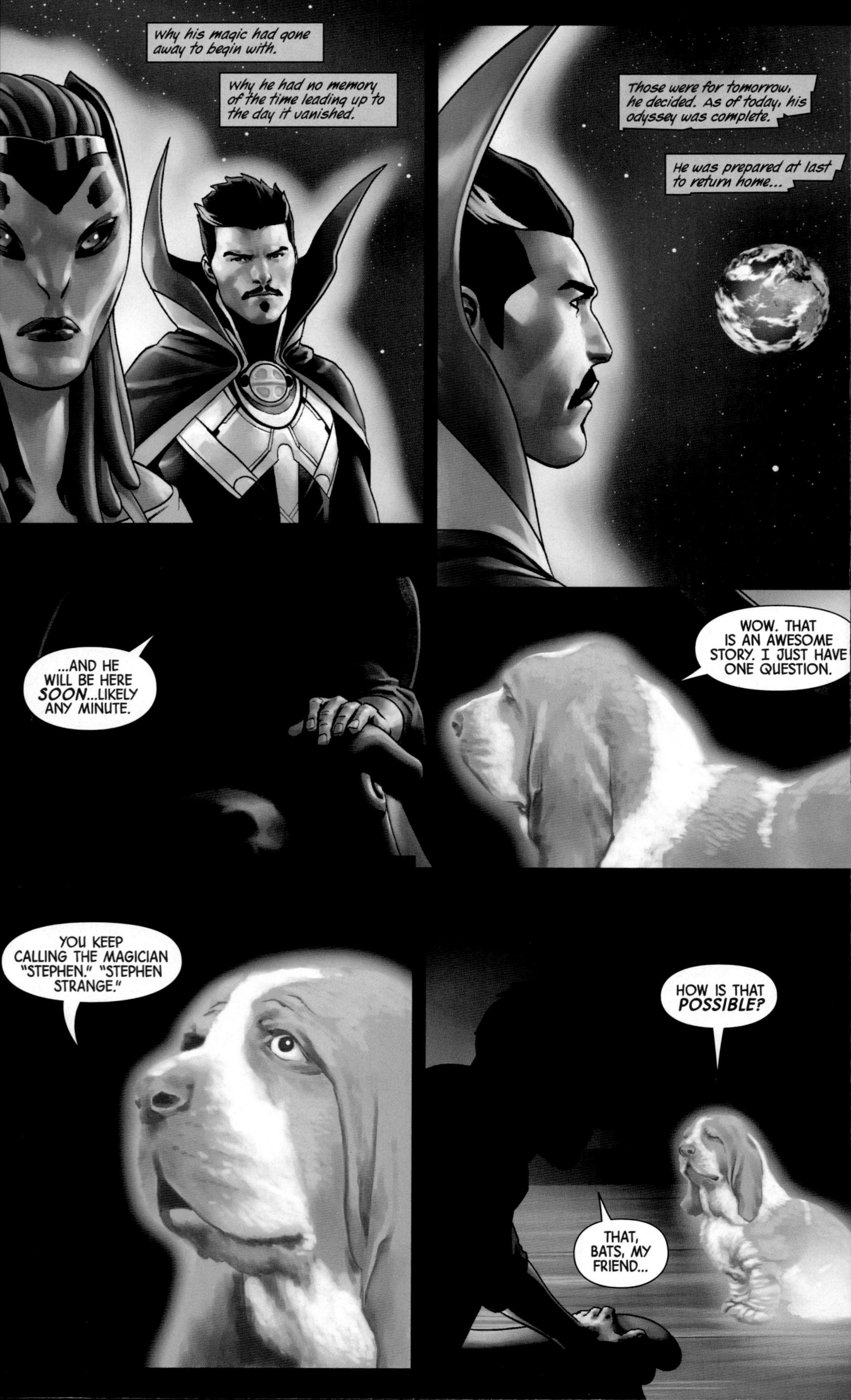
Why his magic had gone away to begin with.
Why he had no memory of the time leading up to the day it vanished.
Those were for tomorrow, he decided. As of today, his odyssey was complete.
He was prepared at last to return home...
...AND HE WILL BE HERE SOON...LIKELY ANY MINUTE.
WOW. THAT IS AN AWESOME STORY. I JUST HAVE ONE QUESTION.
YOU KEEP CALLING THE MAGICIAN "STEPHEN." "STEPHEN STRANGE."
HOW IS THAT POSSIBLE?
THAT, BATS, MY FRIEND...

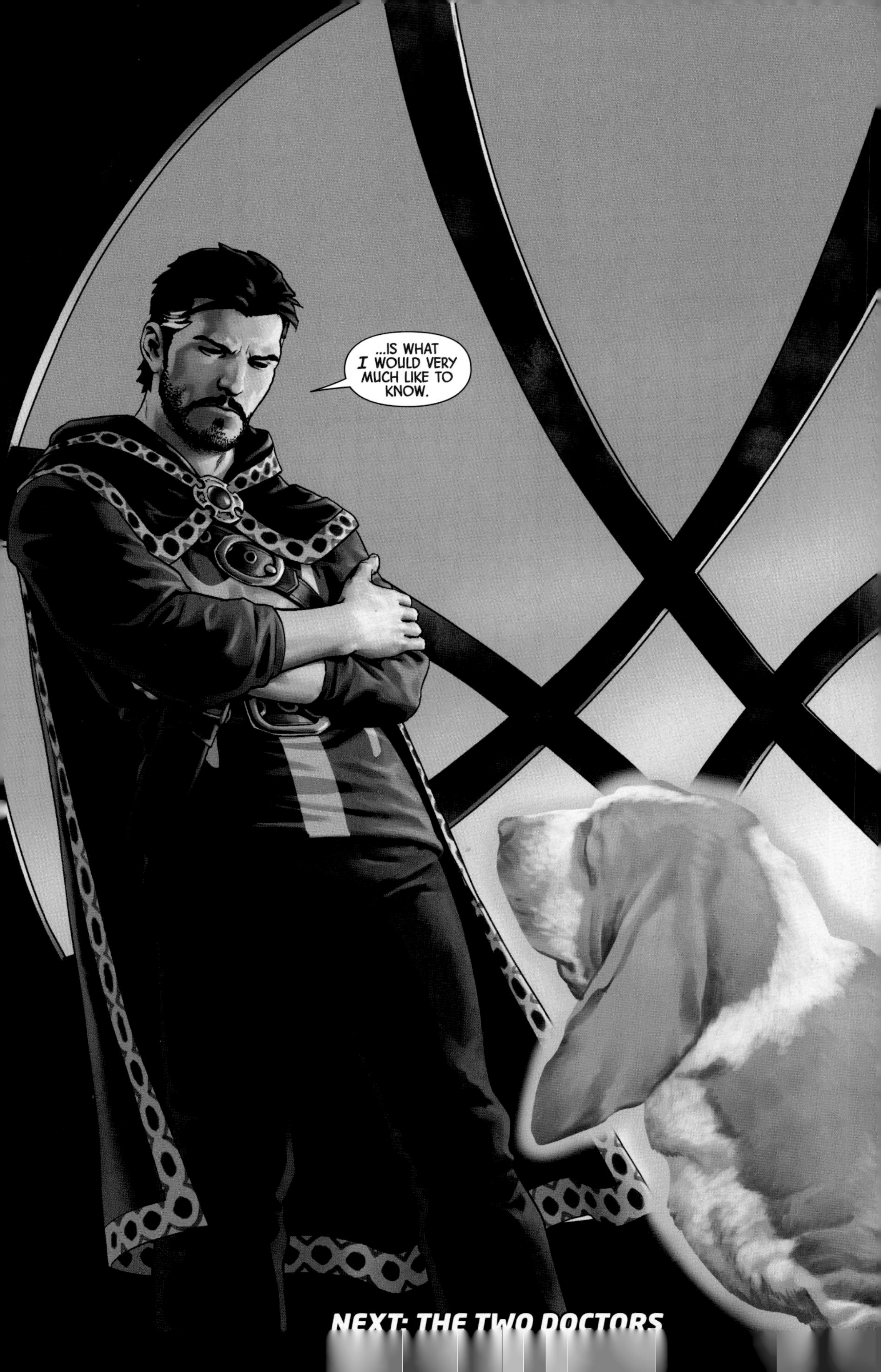
...IS WHAT I WOULD VERY MUCH LIKE TO KNOW.
NEXT: THE TWO DOCTORS

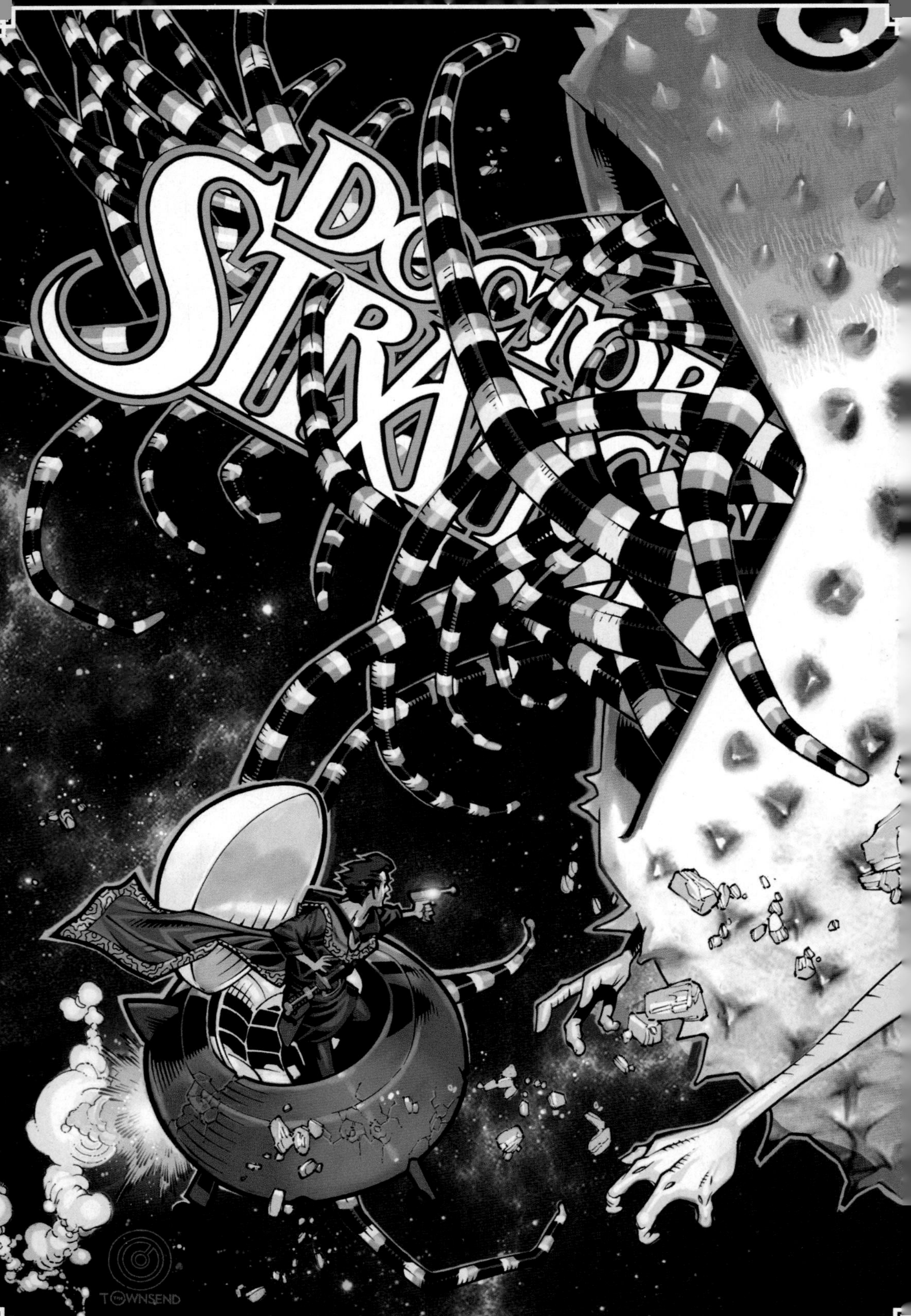

TOWNSEND

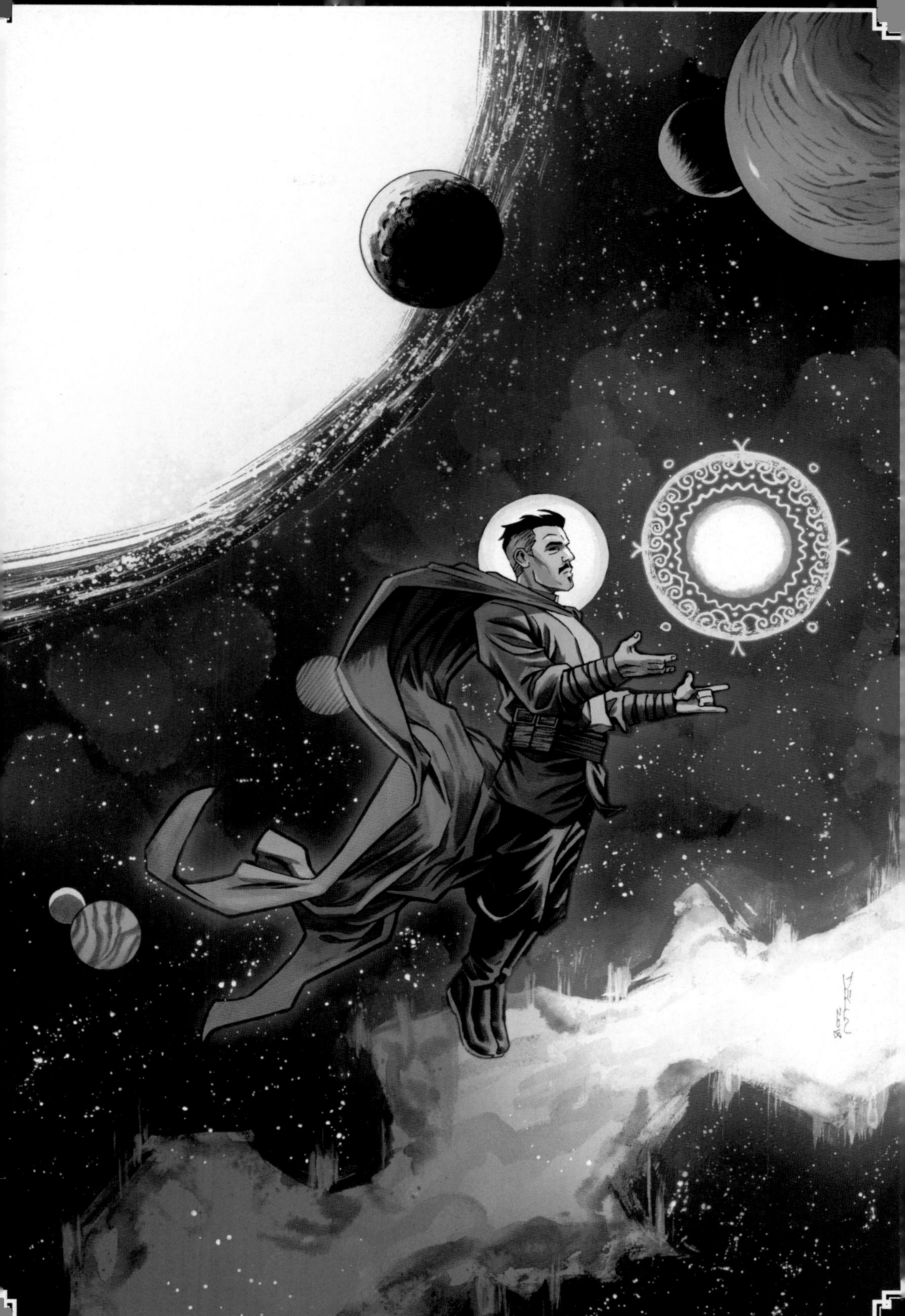

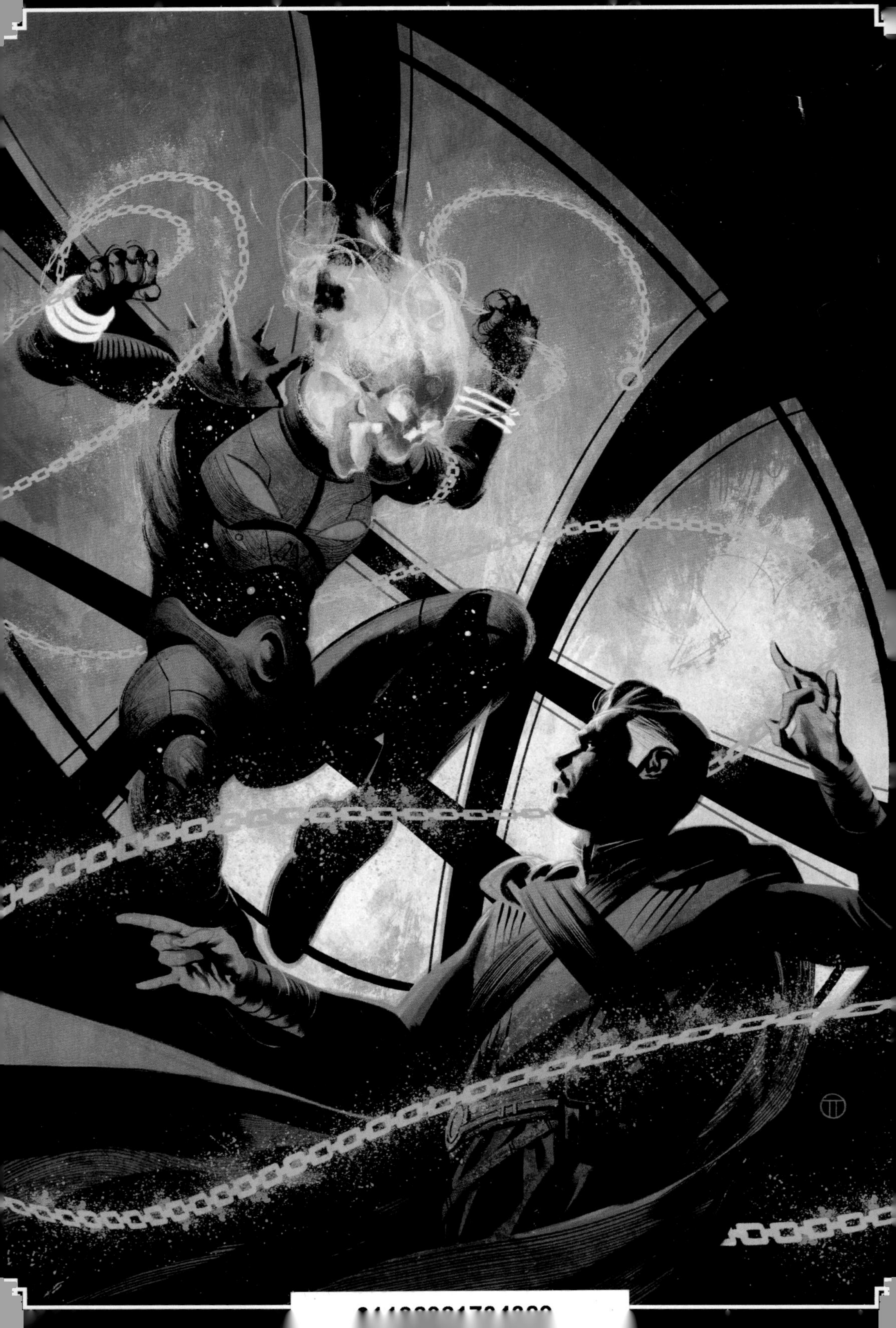